play like

Audio

Joe Pass

The Ultimate Guitar Lesson

by Paul Silbergleit

PLAYBACK+
Speed • Pitch • Balance • Loop

To access audio visit:
www.halleonard.com/mylibrary

"Enter Code"
5513-8122-7109-2979

ISBN 978-1-4950-1079-8

HAL•LEONARD®

Visit Hal Leonard Online at
www.halleonard.com

Contact us:
Hal Leonard
7777 West Bluemound Road
Milwaukee, WI 53213
Email: info@halleonard.com

In Europe, contact:
Hal Leonard Europe Limited
42 Wigmore Street
Marylebone, London, W1U 2RN
Email: info@halleonardeurope.com

In Australia, contact:
Hal Leonard Australia Pty. Ltd.
4 Lentara Court
Cheltenham, Victoria, 3192 Australia
Email: info@halleonard.com.au

CONTENTS

INTRODUCTION

Joe Pass has a singular place in the realms of both jazz and guitar, having set the standard for playing solo through the Great American Songbook as well as for cookin' with ever-inventive single-note lines, and having led a career that intersected with so many all-time jazz greats. He attained success and notoriety only after overcoming the struggles with addiction that kept him sidelined through the 1950s, but then quickly emerged as a preeminent practitioner of the art, and became a primary influence to generations of guitarists. Though clearly a very literate, sophisticated, and highly skilled musician, his approach was not overly academic, and in his own performance he favored soul and spontaneity over perfectionism (in addition to using a torn-in-half guitar pick because it felt more comfortable!). He was, in a way, the quintessential late 20th-century straight-ahead jazz guitarist, continuing to play with an acoustic or plainly amplified sound, and an insistent swing, even while the jazz-rock fusion movement held sway going into the 1970s.

Through five complete songs and ten more excerpted tracks from his recorded catalog, we examine in detail here a marvelous cross-section of his work, encompassing his capabilities as an improviser, an accompanist, and a solo performer, in ballad, bossa nova, and hard-swingin' settings. Within these pages are also a supply of licks in the virtuoso's style, plentiful information and advice on the technique needed to play his music, a list of instruments and amplifiers used throughout his career, recommendations for listening and viewing, and a close-in look at the nitty-gritty elements (the very DNA) that make Joe sound like Joe.

This book can be studied and perused in the order in which these items appear, but depending on your specific abilities on the guitar, you may also find it beneficial to visit the "Integral Techniques" section before tackling the transcribed pieces, whether to brush up on your alternate picking, consider a variety of chord fingerings and scale positions, or get a primer on basic fingerstyle technique (including an explanation of the helpful *pima* symbols for the uninitiated). The "Essential Licks" and "Stylistic DNA" sections may also serve as a good warmup for the lengthier material. In any case, *Play Like Joe Pass* presents an opportunity to explore the rich variety of jazz guitar playing that is the legacy of this unique master!

Special thanks to Dave Braun and Daniel Ivan Ford
for their great insight and support.

ABOUT THE AUDIO

To access the audio examples that accompany this book, simply go to **www.halleonard.com/mylibrary** and enter the code found on page 1. This will grant you instant access to every audio track. The examples that include audio are marked with an audio icon throughout the book.

A finer point regarding the use of the tempo-altering feature of the audio: for those songs or examples that are swung, note that the rhythmic feel will be most natural at the original tempo (the material would likely have been played with a little different swing timing if actually recorded at a faster or slower tempo).

All music on the accompanying audio performed by:

    Guitar: Paul Silbergleit

    Piano: Mark Davis

    Bass: Jeff Hamann

    Drums: David Bayles

    Trumpet: Eric Jacobson

Recorded, mixed, and mastered by Ric Probst/Remote Planet Recording, Milwaukee, WI

GEAR

Though Joe Pass was not the most gear-heavy or gear-conscious guitarist among the greats, we'll take a look here at the specific instruments and amplifiers that helped define his sound.

Guitars

After starting out as a small child on a cheap Harmony steel-string acoustic, Joe graduated to a Martin steel-string (possibly a 00-42) equipped with a DeArmond pickup, and various Gibson hollowbodies, for his early professional years. Our more definitive list of instruments, however, begins with his emergence from rehab and onto the wider jazz scene, and corresponds to the time frame covered by the pieces in this book. Aside from various flat-top acoustics on which he was heard on odd occasion—including a Fender 12-string lent to him in 1963 by close guitar compatriot John Pisano, for use on the appropriately named album *12 String Guitar (Great Motion Picture Themes)*—these are primarily the instruments he played:

Fender Jazzmaster: Joe's recording career really got its start while he still resided at the Synanon rehabilitation center in southern California, at which time he was not in possession of his own guitar. This is believed to be the model first lent to him by the institution. The earliest tracks for which he gained recognition, in the early 1960s, were recorded with Fender solidbody instruments rather than the hollowbody jazz axes usually associated with him and his style.

Fender Jaguar: This close cousin of the Jazzmaster was used as well on some of Joe's first recordings, and can be seen in early footage of the virtuoso at work (such as is referenced in the "Must See" section of this book).

Fender Bass VI: For one track each on two different early sessions for Pacific Jazz, Joe made use of this unusual solidbody instrument, with six strings tuned a full octave lower than a standard guitar, but distinct from an electric bass. It was likely borrowed from the studio at which he recorded (they were new and relatively popular then, and often a fixture in studios).

Gibson ES-355: Joe can be seen with this thinline archtop model in a photo from his 1963 session with pianist Les McCann.

Gibson ES-175: His standby guitar for decades, this hollowbody model—identified also with other jazz greats such as Wes Montgomery, Jim Hall, and Kenny Burrell—was given to him for his birthday by Mike Peak, a supportive fan (in 1963 according to Joe, but judging by when he began to use it on recordings, one could suspect it was actually 1964).

Jimmy D'Aquisto custom archtop: Joe acquired this fine instrument in the early 1970s and used it on several recordings.

Roger Borys Jazz Classic: Among his nylon-string excursions, Joe used this modified version of a classical guitar (with a radiused fretboard to feel more comfortable to steel-string or electric players) at least on the late *Unforgettable/Song for Ellen* session.

Ibanez JP20 Joe Pass signature model: Introduced in 1981 after contribution to its design from the artist himself, Joe would use one of these full hollowbody archtops often in the years that followed. He can be seen with his endorsed instrument in a few of the YouTube videos mentioned in the "Must See" section, including the 1982 performance of "Tricrotism" with bassist Niels-Henning Ørsted Pedersen.

Custom Gibson ES-175: In 1992, Joe acquired this special version of his longtime main axe, tailored to his particular needs with a thinner body and a single humbucking pickup placed right at the end of the fingerboard. It's the guitar he used on his very last few recordings.

Epiphone Emperor II: A later endorsement deal in the early '90s presumably resulted in some modification to this archtop model, which wouldn't actually bear Joe's name until after his death in 1994. It never really caught on with him, and he continued to favor his custom 175 through his final years.

Amps

Fender Twin Reverb: A standby of the 1960s for many a guitarist, Joe often used it and other Fender tube models throughout this era.

Fender Bandmaster: This was paired well with the Fender Jaguar he played in the early 1960s, on occasions such as his captured-on-video *Frankly Jazz* appearance (listed with the YouTube videos in the "Must See" section as "Joe Pass —Jazz Master").

Ampeg combo: Joe used one of these at least during the 1964 *For Django* session, according to photographic evidence.

Polytone 102: Like numerous notable mainstream jazz guitarists of his time, Joe became a user of solid-state Polytone amplifiers when they were introduced in the early 1970s, initially leaning towards this multi-speaker combo (but seen with a Polytone 104 in his 1975 performance in Hannover, Germany with Ella Fitzgerald, which is found among the YouTube videos described under "Must See").

Polytone Mini-Brute II: In the 1980s, he again followed suit with the trend and began using the compact, easily portable, single 12-inch speaker unit from this jazz-world favorite amp manufacturer.

SONGS

Yours Is My Heart Alone
From *On Time* (Les McCann), 1962

"Yours Is My Heart Alone," from a quartet session led by soul jazz pianist Les McCann, is a unique gem among the early recordings of Joe Pass. The perennial standard is cleverly arranged here such that, during the melody, the A sections of its usual 32-bar AABA form are delivered with a half-time ballad feel (generally resulting in one measure for every two that would be there at a medium tempo). Also, these sections are left largely to just Joe and bassist Leroy Vinnegar for an extra-intimate presentation of the song's main theme, within which we have a pristine example of Joe's chord-melody playing at an easy pace, in mostly smaller voicings or double stops and embellished with pretty, pre-arranged fills.

By the end of the second A section though, they double up the pulse to go into a medium swing groove, with drums creeping in and the piano finally making an entrance to take the melody on the bridge. Wherever McCann has the lead, whether here or in the solos, we get a taste of Joe's *comping* (chordal accompaniment) behind a pianist—a particularly sensitive task, as so much rhythmic and harmonic space is already being filled. For the last A section, they return to the ballad tempo, the guitar-bass duo, and the chord-melody rendering of the tune, only to pick it up again by the end of this section to set up medium swing for all the soloing to follow (which will indeed be on 32-bar choruses made up of the usual four 8-bar sections).

After two choruses of a spirited, swingin' piano solo, Joe busts into a tasty, melodic, and burnin' solo chorus with the crisp sound of the Fender Jaguar solidbody guitar he was using at the time. A shout chorus ensues, involving a stop-time figure with chordal tremolos for the first A section, a drum break for the next one, an additional eight measures of piano improvisation for the bridge, and a return to the stop-time shout figure for the last eight… after which they immediately break it back down to ballad time and the duo of guitar and bass as they return to the *head* (melody). They then play through the tune much like they did at the beginning, but this time they keep the swing feel going after the bridge, wrapping up with some chordal kicks and a big finish in a full-band coda.

An interesting thing to note when listening to the original tracks of this or other songs he recorded for the Pacific Jazz label (as either a leader or a sideman) is that many of them got profusely spliced by the producer before their release—and not always gracefully so. This is especially true on "Yours Is My Heart Alone," where some of the changes of groove, although they were indeed intended, seem conspicuously sudden. Nonetheless, there are so many sides of Joe on display at once in this performance! In preparation to play the whole song, complete with all his chord-melody work, comping, soloing, and everything, we'll take a detailed look here at what's needed for each of these aspects.

Chord-Melody Arrangement of the Head

Let's start with an exercise for dealing with the fret-hand stretches that are needed for the chord-melody passages here, often due to part of a chord being held while other tones are moving melodically. This drill is based on his material in the first A section, with an extra-tough stretch in the Fmaj7 ending part that really comes from measure 154 in the head out (the melody at the end of the performance). Follow the given fingerings to see how these somewhat intricate guitar figures can be managed:

Yours Is My
Heart Alone
Example 1

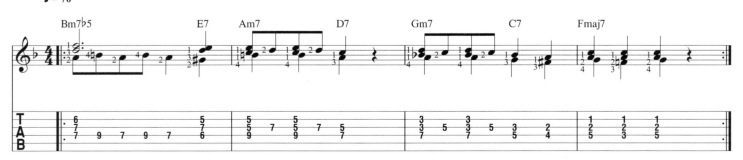

We'll put that study to use by actually playing the beginning section of the piece, from measure 1 through the first half of measure 4. Again, follow the fingerings provided—similarly to what we might encounter in a lot of classical guitar pieces, it's often a case of using whatever finger is left available to you, or whichever one is necessary so that you're in position for the next chord:

Yours Is My
Heart Alone
Example 2

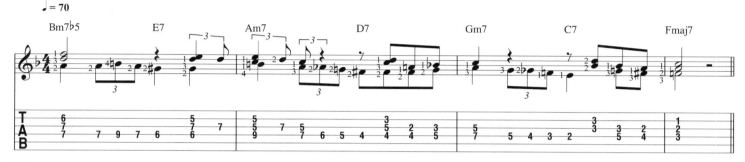

Now we come to a particularly interesting, beautiful, and awe-inspiring feature of this performance, which is the pickup in measure 4 to the second A section at measure 5, a sweeping upward run that begins in a blazing blur of notes and lands prettily on a high tone of the melody, which is now taken up an octave (this is essentially also the pickup to the second A of the head out at measure 155, but it is only paraphrased before the last A of the head in at measure 18). Bear in mind that this is one of the fastest and most difficult lines in this book, and in all the work of the virtuosic Joe Pass. Though it appears early in this volume due to chronological order, don't be discouraged or allow yourself to get stuck here if this is exceedingly tough. The same will apply when we get to the fastest part of his solo!

It can be good to note that part of the impression of speed at this point even comes from a bit of (understandable) messiness in his execution. For one thing, in measure 4 on the original recording, there's an inadvertent hammer-on of the E on string 5, fret 8, just before it is picked, effectively creating yet another note in that initial jumble (this is not notated here—the intended phrase is dense enough as it is!). For another, in both instances here where there are two notes in a row at the same fret (on neighboring strings), he allows them to ring together, inadvertently barred, while at a more normal speed he would likely have made the effort to play them legato but not overlapping.

To successfully play this figure, we will probably need to work out its smaller components, beat by beat, and down from the actual tempo, before putting them back together into a whole. We'll start with just the initial 32nd-note triplet and the note it leads to on the "and" of beat 3. Sweep pick down through the first two notes, making sure not to simply play them completely together as a double stop (even though we'll barre them with the index finger and not worry about the first one sustaining into the next). You can angle the pick upwards a bit from a hand held slightly beneath those two strings, in order to *pull* it down with greater control.

From there, use alternate picking. Also, be aware that the time values of those first three notes, as written here, are really just approximate:

Yours Is My
Heart Alone
Example 3:

Relax the pick hand for quick alternate picking of the 32nd notes in the second half of beat 3. It may be tempting to sweep pick the first three of these, but it's harder to get as crisp a definition of time values in this way. You may want to keep the pick at a slight upwards angle, and here again allow the index to barre, now at fret 7, letting those two notes ring together rather than bothering to roll off of the first one. Mercifully, we get to slide-slur into the first note of beat 4, catching a super-quick breather for the pick hand:

Remember that the 16th notes of beat 4 are not actually that fast at this tempo, but the fret hand—or more specifically, the ring finger—needs to accurately zip higher up the fretboard along string 2, quickly enough to minimize any audible slide between the A and D at frets 10 and 15, respectively. This is the slower part of the line, but the success of executing the whole thing can rely on how ready and confident we are to make that quick upwards move. With this upwards momentum, we might as well use the ring finger all the way until landing on the high F on beat 1 (and then allow just enough of a breath to move the fret hand back down a bit for the next notes). Here's a drill for this part, including the note that slides into beat 4:

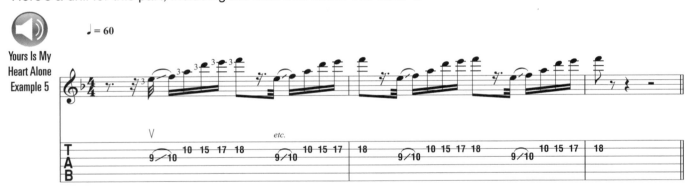

Now we can try to put these parts together for the whole glorious pickup phrase. Note that it is metrically shifted for this exercise, starting within beat 1 and landing on beat 3 (while it runs from beat 3 to beat 1 in the actual song):

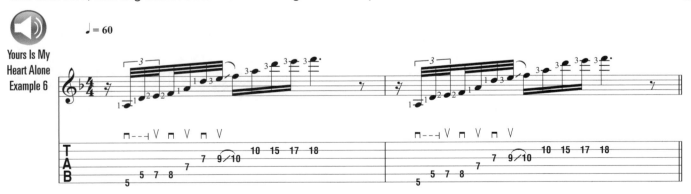

Accompaniment Under Piano Solo

During the piano chord-melody lead on the bridge of the head, the two choruses of piano solo, or the improvised piano bridge in the shout chorus, Joe is chording and percussively picking the stopped strings in a fairly regular rhythm, and mostly with small, double-stop versions of the chords that we could call *chordal shells*. In this way, and also by staying largely in the midrange of the guitar, he manages to stay out of McCann's way even while the pianist naturally comps for himself with the left hand (as he solos melodically with the right).

The basic idea with the shell voicings is that chords are boiled down to their essential defining tones: the root, 3rd, and 7th. These by themselves, without the 5th or any upper extension, can determine whether a 7th chord is basically major, minor, or dominant. These shells also tend to move smoothly from one to another and avoid conflicting with someone else's choice of voicings (in which various other tones could be added or altered). In the case of Joe's approach here, a fairly common one for guitar, they are reduced even further to omit the root, by and large leaving us with 3rd-and-7th units that sit nicely on the middle two strings. Here's how we might find such shells within a couple of common larger chord forms:

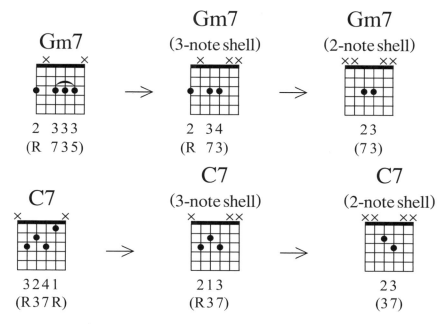

Joe's most typical groove during these sections involves a percussive tick of the strings (usually the top three) on beat 2 and a pair of 8th-note shells on beat 4, between which the chord change is often made… and also a little pickup note to beat 4, usually a chord member itself, like the root or 5th. The whole thing seems to simulate the sort of rhythm that would be played on the conga drums in a swingin' setting! To get the feel of it, we can try this summarized version of the pattern through an A section of the tune, played entirely with downstrokes aside from the single notes on upbeats. The striking of stopped strings is shown on the notation staff according to where the fret hand might naturally mute them on each occasion (as is the case in the full transcription as well)—which, in this exercise, means at fret 8 in the first measure and one fret lower each time after that. Joe himself was also prone to quickly moving the hand higher up the neck to stop the strings and then back down again to the area in which he was fretting notes. Harmonically, notice that at the Gm7 in this progression, he often subs a G7, represented by the F and B♮ double stop that comes in just before the fifth measure here:

Yours Is My
Heart Alone
Example 7

From this starting point, he actually varies the pattern quite a bit along the way, both rhythmically and with the interjection of some three- or four-string chords. Here's a sample of his playing from within the first bridge in the piano solo, measures 42–45, with recommended fingerings and pick strokes. In addition to doubling up on his percussive ticking, we can see him moving down chromatically into a B♭m7 shell at the end of the first measure, and anticipating the Fmaj7 measure with an F6 chord shape, before making a quick F°7 shape resolve to the single note C (the 5th of Fmaj7) to conclude.

Yours Is My
Heart Alone
Example 8

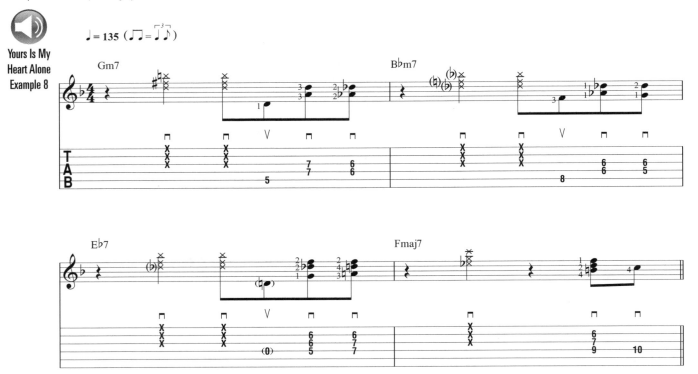

Further variation abounds as the piano solo progresses, and Joe occasionally allows himself to briefly step forward with more noticeable chordal commentary like he does with the higher double stop in measure 51, or the emphatic and high-pitched Dm triad on measure 67, beat 3 (part of a G9 chord).

Guitar Solo

Joe's one-chorus solo statement is a tastefully swingin' trip through the form of this tune, with affirmative, moderately paced 8th-note bop lines that nicely bring out the chord changes, as well as some simple and groovy melodic ideas that leave plenty of space… and one blistering barrage of continuous 16th notes that stretches from measure 97 to measure 101 within the second A section. This, too, is some of the fastest playing on record by this famously cookin' guitarist, and here again, we shouldn't get too caught up in this passage if it seems out of reach.

Of course there is plenty in this solo to observe, admire, and try that is *not* so difficult to play: the couple of isolated rhythmic high E's that start things off in measure 87 (the chordal 11th, in relation to the Bm7♭5 chord), the beautiful outlining of D7♭9 in measure 90 that will resolve neatly to the 3rd of Gm7, the nice phrase endings (and subsequent breaths) in measures 91 or 94, the more rhythm-oriented gestures of measures 103–104 (or within measure 105), or the *enclosure* (circling around) of Fmaj7 chord tones in measures 109–110.

But that long stretch of 16ths is indeed a particular challenge; playing it will likely require breaking the line down into smaller chunks at a slower tempo, in addition to carefully mapping out our fingerings, as we move across the strings or far up and down the fretboard to accommodate its sprawling range. Our technical exercises here will therefore focus on this process.

The beginning of the line in measure 97 lies neatly in 10th position, but by the next measure, we need to be prepared to move. So on the following page is most of measure 98 in repeated-exercise form, with tab, fingerings, and slide-slurs that show where to go and how to get there, as well as suggested pick strokes (we don't necessarily have to sweat the "hammer-on from nowhere" that occurs in the actual recording).

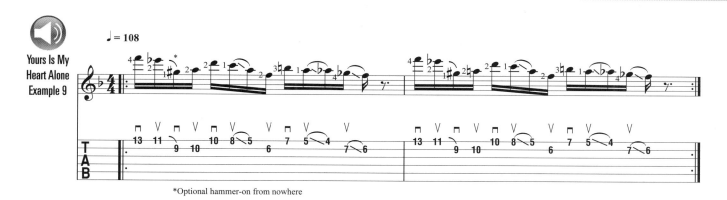

*Optional hammer-on from nowhere

Moving further into the line—with some overlap from the last chunk to make sure we practice these rapid changes of position with a little context—we now look at the last half of measure 98 up to beat 2 of the next measure (the material is metrically displaced for this drill from how it lies in the transcription, starting on beat 1 instead of beat 3). Here the trickiest movements to be aware of are with the fret-hand index finger, which must jump from fret 3 down to fret 1, and then back (after a quick break from the use of the open string 2), before an imminent shift to 5th position:

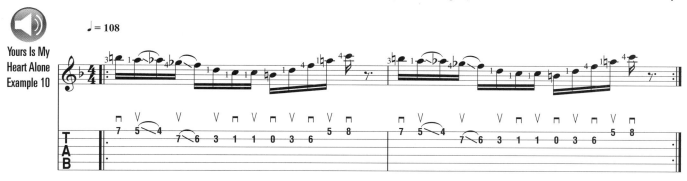

We'll pick up right where we left off to check out the next mid-neck maneuverings (this part appears one beat earlier here than where it actually starts in measure 99):

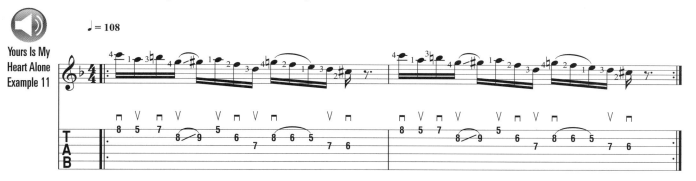

For this next exercise, we'll detail most of measure 100. Keep in mind that this is another spot, with its quick jumps between strings, where it is only with a little bit of sloppiness that Joe himself manages to get through it: the double stop results from an inadvertent barre on fret 5 plus a less-controlled movement of the pick (only the G on string 4 appears to be intended), and where a note is sounded by the fret hand alone on string 6, he simply misses it with the pick in his hurry to move over to string 3. Allowing ourselves the same can actually help us make it through!

Having worked through various difficult corners of this breathless 16th-note run, it's time to try putting the whole thing together in sequence:

Yours Is My
Heart Alone
Example 13   ♩ = 108

Ultimately, it's important to look at this mammoth phrase (or amalgam of phrases) as being something other than merely tough. It itself is filled with brilliant bop linear material that brings out the chord changes in expert fashion, ideas that can be explored and drawn upon at any tempo, like the nice mix of scalar and arpeggio movement in measure 97 (where the tones, more or less, anticipate an altered D7sus4), the amazing use of purely diminished scale tones in the dizzying descent of measure 98 (D half-whole diminished, one could say, relating well to the D13♭9 variation of D7), and the multitude of melodic shapes that stay within a framework of G9 in measures 99–100 (most clearly spelled out on beat 1 of measure 99 and beat 3 of measure 100), followed by a quick landing on the note B♭ in measure 101 to bring out the change to C7 with its chordal 7th.

Shout Chorus and Ending

After the guitar solo comes a *shout chorus*, akin to the climactic part of a big band arrangement where the horn dynamics are all-out. Through the first A section (measures 119–126), the band basically performs chordal figures together for the drummer to play around, the whole section acting as a sendoff for an 8-bar drum break (the chordal figures will return for the last A after the pianist is featured on the bridge). These figures are a combination of sustained chords, with tremolo from piano and guitar, and shorter rhythmic kicks. Twice we need to be ready for a quick switch from a tremolo chord to a different chord played short, so let's first get comfortable with just the movement from one chord shape to the next for measures 119–122, without yet complicating it with the tremolo.

**Yours Is My
Heart Alone
Example 14**

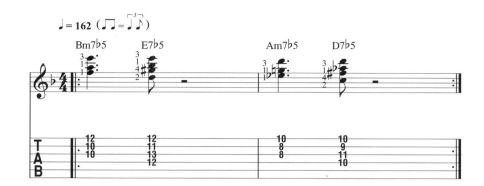

Now let's full-on practice our chordal tremolo picking, with rapidly alternating downstrokes and upstrokes on the strings involved, towards the effect of a tremulously sustained chord. In this exercise, we try the tremolo on the Bm7♭5 and Am7♭5 chords alone at first, and then integrate the quick change to a short, non-tremolo E7♭5 or D7♭5, respectively. And finally, we practice a sustained tremolo on a bigger F6/9♯11 voicing, like Joe plays at the dramatic conclusion to this performance:

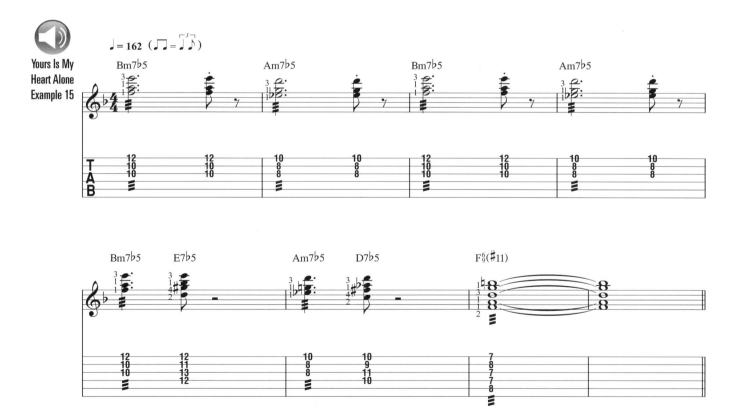

**Yours Is My
Heart Alone
Example 15**

Chord-melody playing on a ballad, subdued comping behind a pianist, both songful and smokin' solo lines on a joyous medium-tempo swing groove, big band–like chordal hits… all these elements of Joe's playing are here for us to explore on this remarkable rendition of a classic tune.

Yours Is My Heart Alone
Full Song

YOURS IS MY HEART ALONE

Music by Franz Lehar
Original German Lyrics by Ludwig Herzer and Fritz Loehner
English Lyrics by Harry Smith

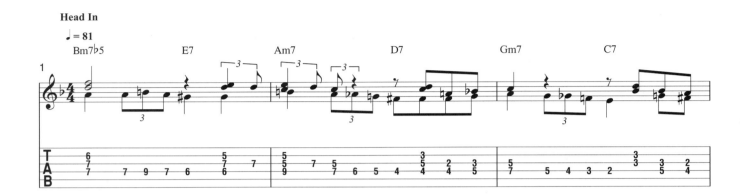

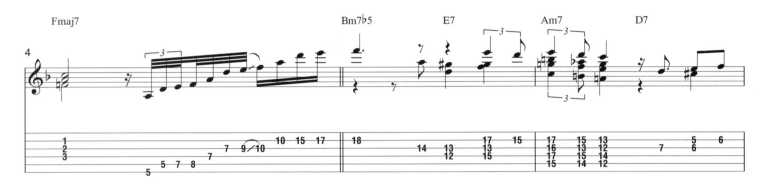

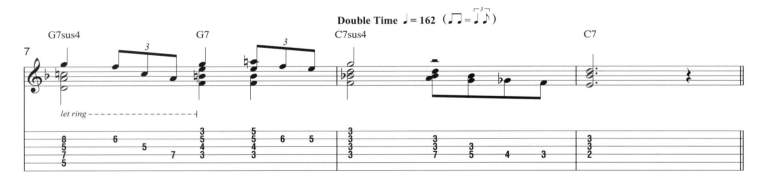

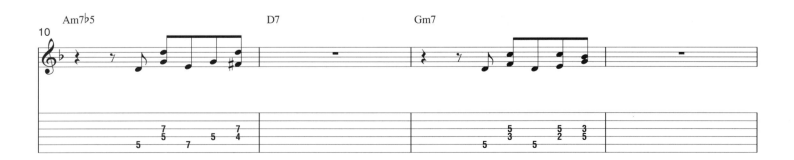

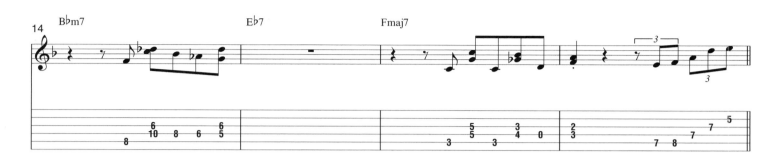

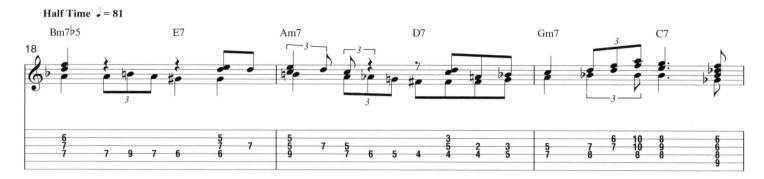

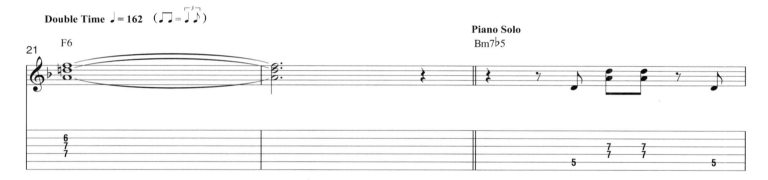

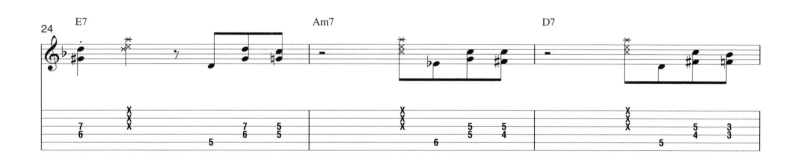

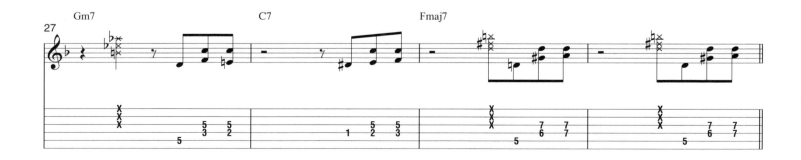

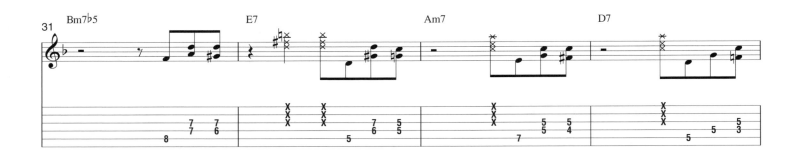

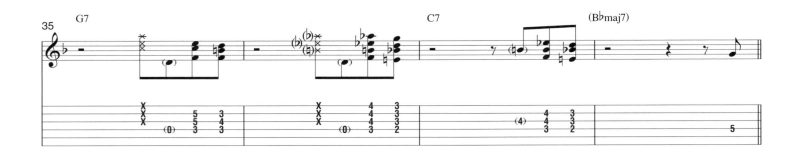

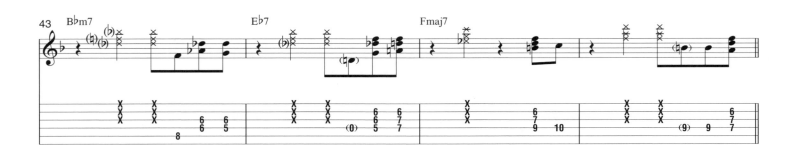

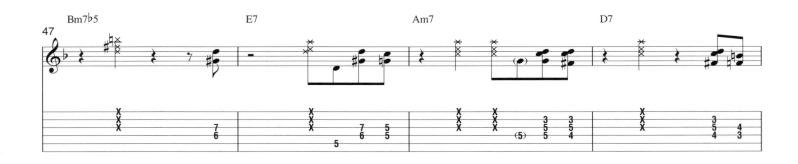

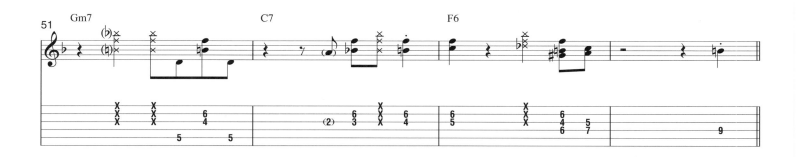

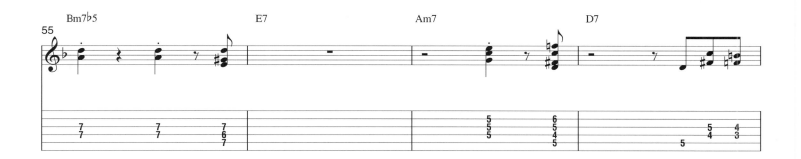

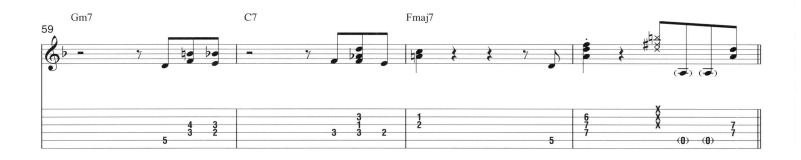

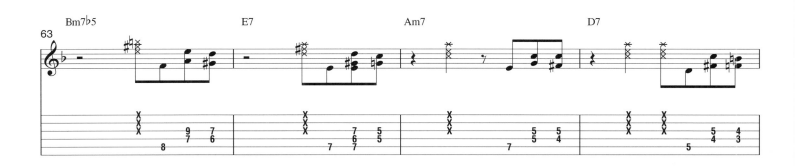

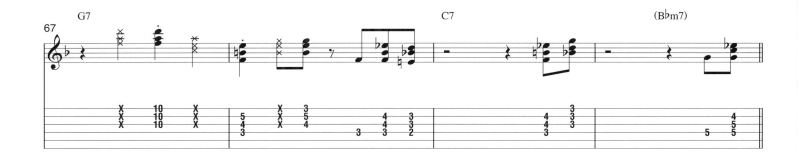

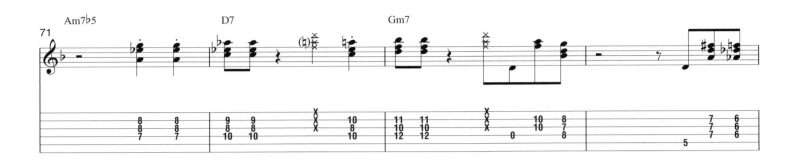

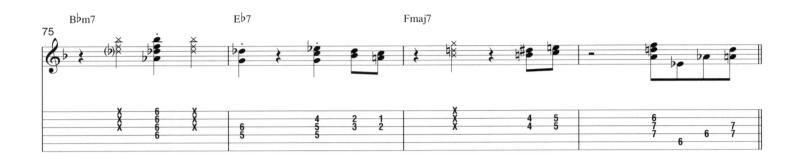

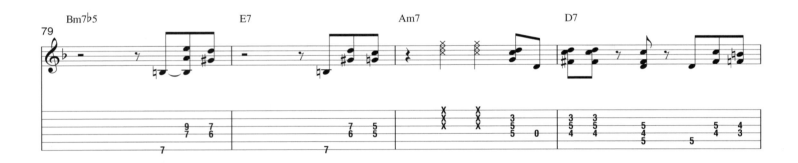

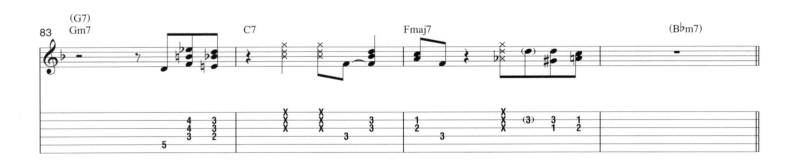

Guitar Solo

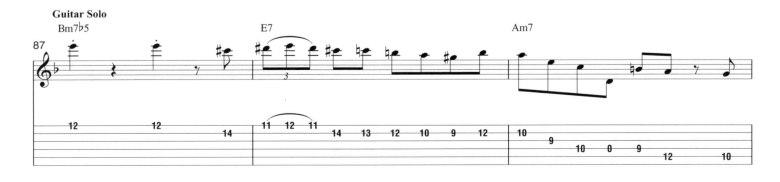

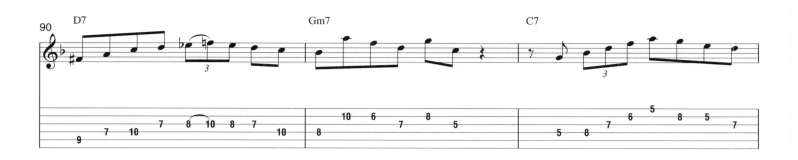

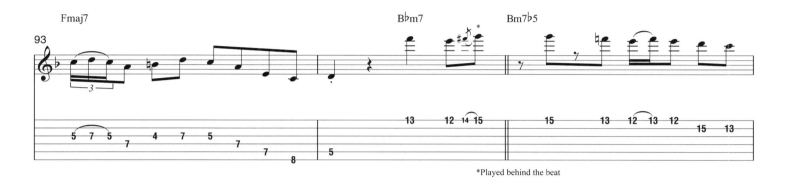

*Played behind the beat

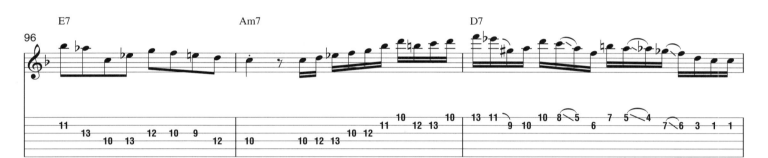

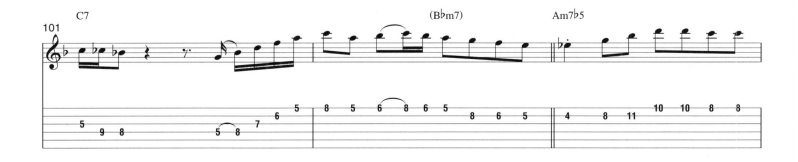

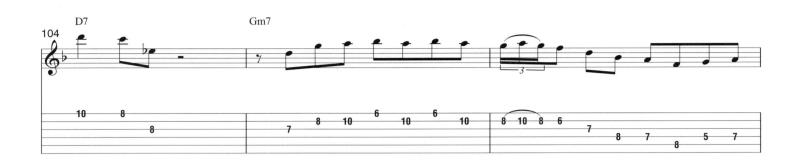

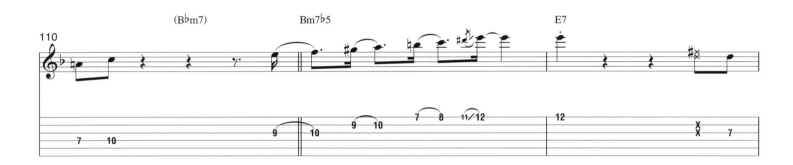

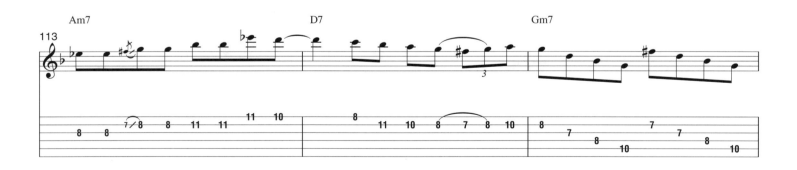

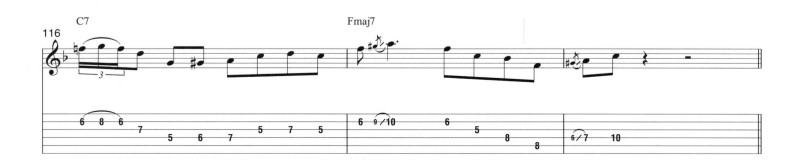

Shout Chorus

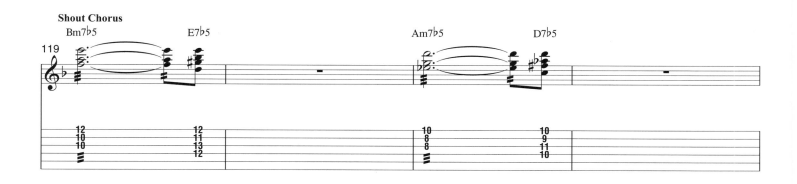

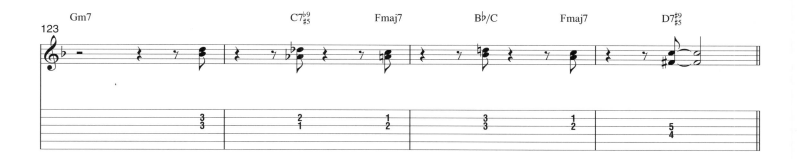

Drum Break, 8 measures

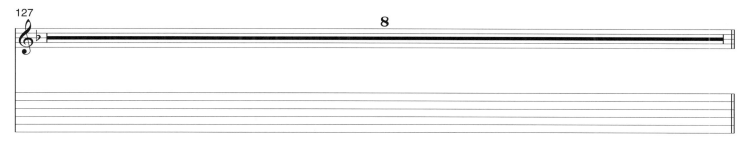

Piano Improv., 8 measures

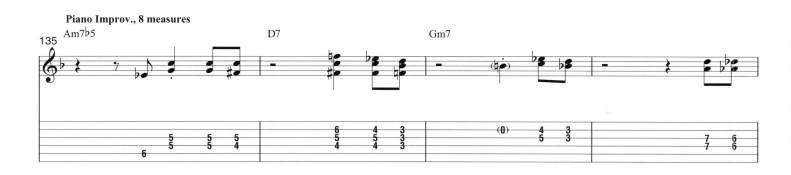

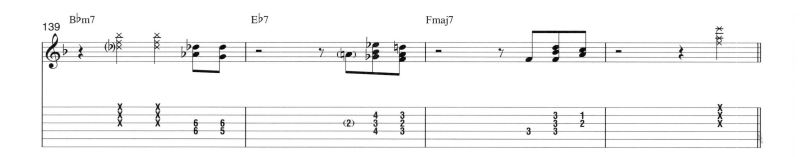

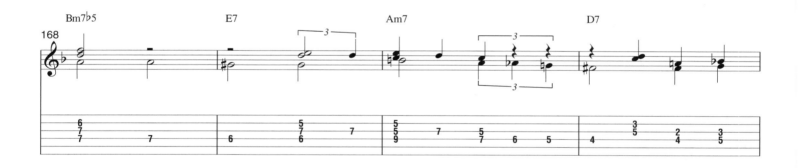

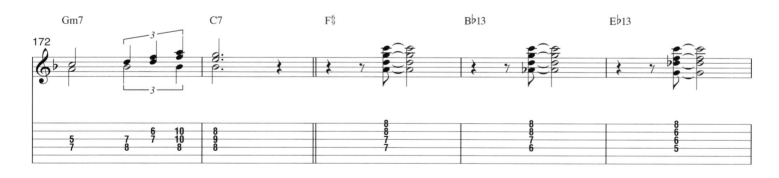

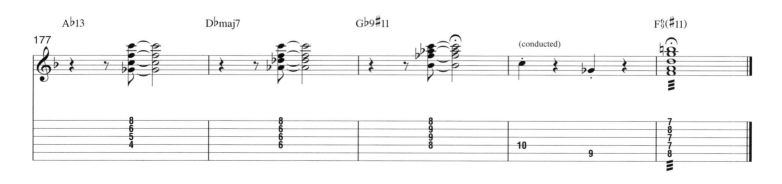

Meditation
From *Intercontinental*, 1970

Joe's classic trio version of "Meditation" offers a great chance to hear him taking the lead in a guitar/bass/drums setting, as well as playing on a song with a gentle bossa nova rhythm. The famously hard-swinging guitarist shows his great affinity here for this more even-8ths-based groove, while demonstrating his masterful handling of both melodic and chordal elements in the trio context. Aside from an intro and brief tag-plus-vamp ending, the whole performance is basically just three times through the 56-bar form of this famous Antonio Carlos Jobim tune (an AABA form with 16-bar A sections and an 8-bar bridge). The first and third of these are complete statements of the head (melody), such that it's really only the fully improvised middle chorus that would be called his guitar solo, per se. And yet, Joe is out front the entire time, and even while playing the written tune, he varies his interpretation of it along the way and improvises a good deal between its phrases.

Along the parameter of playing purely single-note melodic material versus simply playing chords, Joe does some of both—and just about everything in between—in the variety of textures he uses here. He certainly has a chord-melody approach to the song, though some of the melody's tones appear as individual notes between the chords, rather than every single one of them being harmonized. Sometimes he mixes that technique with independent bass notes so as to effectively have both a bass-chord and a chord-melody texture all at once. Chord sequences might be used as melodic fills or solo lines, or he might go into a simple chordal groove for a moment, in the middle of otherwise linear improvised material that itself beautifully outlines the chord changes.

Joe's rendition of the tune is essentially a piece to be played fingerstyle, but also one in which he distinctly makes use of a thumb-only attack for significant stretches (to somewhat gentler effect than famous thumb-wielder Wes Montgomery). Technical tips for the pick hand will be given here on this basis (with *pima* indications in the musical examples), though the song may be reasonably playable even if you're an insistent pick player. Some very basic fingerstyle technique, for those who may be trying to get a start with it, is presented in the "Essential Techniques" section of this book, and may help the uninitiated to approach "Meditation" in this authentic manner (which is indeed conducive to the feel of a bossa).

Bossa Rhythm

In gearing up to play the song, it's important to have a sense for the underlying rhythm of the style, which, far beyond just "even 8th notes" or "Latin groove," involves syncopations rooted in the musical tradition of Brazil. Without digging too deep at the moment, we can get a start by simply taking a hands-on look at Joe's own approach to these patterns. We'll start with a summarized version of this basic chordal bossa groove as he might apply it to a chunk of the tune's chord progression—first with thumb only and then with thumb plus three fingers on the repeat, in order to get used to the rhythm with both of these techniques:

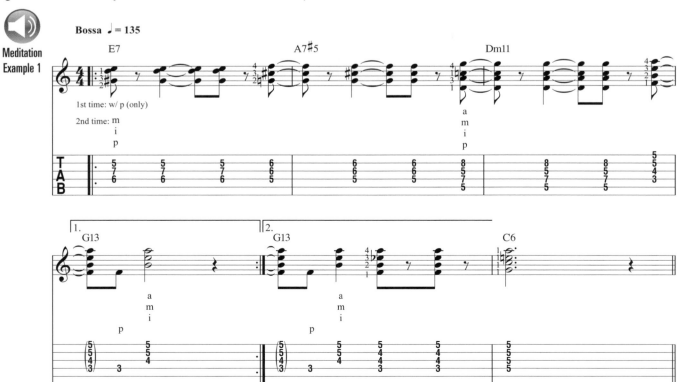

Meditation Example 1

Next, let's check out another typical way to play with that beat, busier and more 8th-notey, by trying a similar stretch of the progression as he plays it in measures 93–96 (notice that in the second ending of this repeated exercise, we will practice the actual way he concludes this section of his solo chorus and enters the bridge):

Meditation Example 2

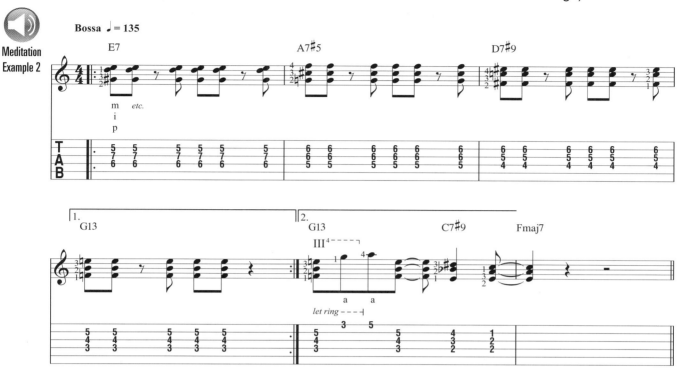

The following exercise is based on the recurring figure that he uses (with some variation) in the fifth and sixth measures of most A sections of the head, harmonically expanding what might otherwise have been another plain two-measure stretch of the tonic chord C. This is what seems like a bass-chord pattern on the guitar, but is really bass-chord-melody all together, in that the note A on top of each chord voicing is indeed the tone that is repeated through this segment of the melody itself. We'll try this one, too, with thumb only on the first go-around, and then using the *pima* indications on the repeat (which now include *c* for the pick-hand pinky). Also notice that two different voicings of F7 are used for further practice towards playing the whole song:

Meditation Example 3

Melodic Technique

Now we'll take a look at some of the techniques needed in either hand for getting through the largely single-note portions of this piece. Though Joe plays fingerstyle through most of the performance, there are large swaths of it where he uses the thumb alone, particularly during the head in (the initial full statement of the melody). This is generally more natural for chords than for melodic runs, so it's worth trying some single-note thumb downstrokes ahead of time, as well as checking out how he switches between all fingers and purely thumb. Measures 8–12, which encompass his transition from the intro into the first few measures of the melody, allow us to get a taste of these movements, with the use of the *pima* instructions here:

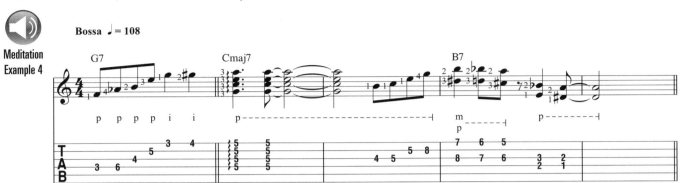

His melodic improvisation starts off gracefully and simply enough right at the top of the intro, but as early as measure 3, we encounter a quick figure that warrants some extra practice. He's still leaning towards use of the thumb at this point in the performance, which entails a quick downwards sweep within the phrase at hand. Notice that the fret-hand ring finger does extra duty here and must roll off of string 3 to cleanly move onto the next note on string 2:

*Downwards sweep w/ thumb

In measures 73–75 (early in his solo chorus), we have an example of his sudden use of chordal groove and thumb technique in the midst of melodic improvisation, as well as another fast, tricky, ascending arpeggio figure to navigate right as he switches back to fingers. (The fret-hand pinky is indicated for the first note here only because that's where it winds up at the end of the previous phrase in his solo, and it's from that position that we must jump for the chord that follows):

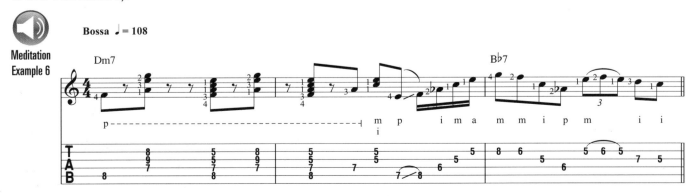

Immediately after this, in measures 76–78, is some linear material that nicely demonstrates how we may have to jump and stretch on the fretboard for certain spots in the piece. The jumping up between positions is really led by the pinky here, subtly at first at the beginning of the second measure, and more dramatically with the jump and slide early in the next measure:

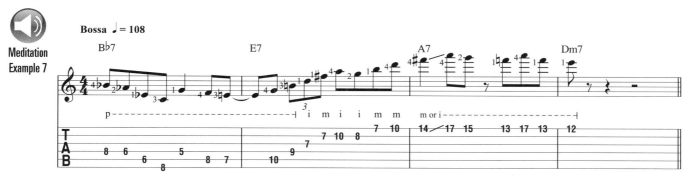

**Meditation
Example 7**

Another device which could be thought of as a Wes Montgomery–ism, but which Joe uses in his own sweet way, is the playing of melodic phrases doubled at the octave. This is how he delivers the solo line from measure 138 through the beginning of measure 141, a plenty long stretch of octaves for Joe (he tends to interject them into a line, rather than rendering whole passages or songs in this manner). To map out our fingerings and use of fingerstyle technique for this segment, we can exercise them ahead of time on that whole stream of octaves, taken out of rhythm as a slower, steady stream of quarter notes (note that when this exercise repeats, there will be a big jump up the fretboard which doesn't actually exist in the transcription—extra-rigorous practice!):

**Meditation
Example 8**

Chordal Movement Technique

Among places where Joe creates some particularly _melodic_ movement with changing chord voicings, a few key spots bear studying, both because they train our hands well to move smoothly from chord to chord throughout, and because they beautifully show how he uses this variety of chord shapes for musical fills and phrases.

Everything in the following chordal exercise, based on the material of measures 89–90, can be construed as some form of Dm7, or an extension of it. The pickup chords are both from a common Dm7 shape at 5th position, the stack of perfect 4th intervals right afterwards are all tones of Dm11, followed by a rootless Dm9 shape (same thing as Fmaj7!), and then another voicing of Dm11 without its 3rd. After starting to go back down through these same chord forms, we encounter two more voicings of Fmaj7 (or rootless Dm9) in the 3rd and open positions, as well as two double stops whose tones collectively fit into the concept of Dm11. In his solo, Joe intersperses single melodic tones between the first few of these chords (a common motif in his chord-melody work), but the last five chords here are in the exact sequence in which he plays them. This is effectively chord-melody soloing, with a sense of melodic motion created especially by the notes on top—and in this case, a sense of chordal motion created by the changing voicings altogether, while the actual chord in the progression (Dm7) remains the same.

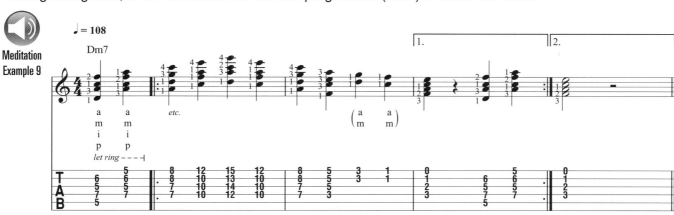

**Meditation
Example 9**

He delivers a similar sequence of Dm7-related shapes with a nice up-and-down melodic contour in measures 57–58 (midway through the final A section of the head in). But here, after the initial 5th-position Dm7 voicing, he makes his big switch from a mostly thumb-only approach to the full use of the fingers, and in the process, allows them to percussively land on the strings between the chords for another signature Joe Pass sound. We'll try that technique here using the same basic line of chord shapes. Technical tips: allow each chord to ring until the pick-hand fingers make their landing, and play around with the exact way those fingertips contact the strings—not much force is needed, just the right subtle amount of fingernail.

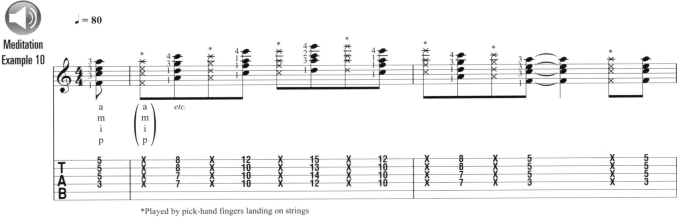

*Played by pick-hand fingers landing on strings

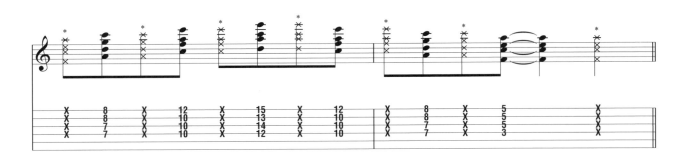

Joe often makes great use of the mobility of diminished 7th chords, as well as their strong relationship to certain dominant 7th chords. On a theoretical note, if a pure diminished 7th chord is moved up or down in minor 3rd intervals, it will actually remain the same chord, with its tones shuffled into a different order. This can be manifested by moving a diminished 7th chord shape three frets up or down along the same set of strings on the guitar. Take, for example, this diminished 7th voicing on the top four strings, and see and hear what happens when we move it up the fretboard by that increment, repeatedly:

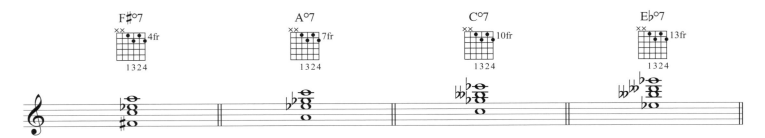

At each of these positions, the chord has been named (and spelled out in notation) as if the bottom note were the root. But if you look and listen carefully, you may realize that these are really the same notes each time, though stacked in different orders, not always appearing in the same octave, and sometimes enharmonically named in seemingly strange ways (because, for example, while we had an A in F#°7 and A°7, this tone is technically considered B♭♭ by the time it has become the 7th of C°7 or the 5th of E♭°7). So these particular diminished 7th chords are actually all inversions of each other, and each of them could potentially be named like any of the others.

We'll summarize a pattern he draws from in measures 67–68, 102, and 158 which involves a diminished 7th formation moving in this way. Notice that, in this case, it's only when we add in the single notes that appear on the upbeats between chords that we actually have the exact chord shape shown above. The top note of each of the full voicings is actually an extra tone added to the diminished 7th chord, belonging to the same *diminished scale* as its basic members (each one of the added tones could be found a whole step above or a half step below one of the regular chord tones). We'll call it E♭°7 this time, since that is officially the chord to which he applies this pattern in measures 102 and 158, towards the end of the bridge in either case (though now we'll be more casual about how the notes are spelled out on the staff). In the case of measures 67–68, he uses the pattern on B7, taking advantage of the fact that this diminished 7th chord is really the same thing as a B7♭9 chord without the root (think of E♭ being instead called D♯, the 3rd of B7).

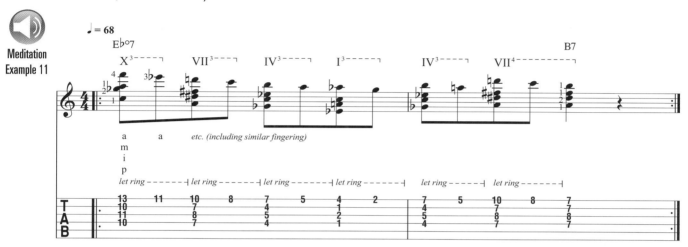

It's along a similar line of logic (even if a little more complex) that he manages to successfully bounce a dominant 13 shape up and down in minor 3rds for the A7 in measure 128 and the G7 in measure 160—though in the latter instance, he departs from that particular track by the highest point in the chordal gesture.

Tricky Chordal Figures

A few more particular figures are especially worthy of a detailed preview for their difficulty of execution, their harmonic interest, and their recurrence throughout the piece. During the melody, the A7 that leads up to the midpoint of the A sections (as in measures 16, 32, and 56 of the head in) is most often treated with a moving voice on string 2 that changes it from an A13 to A7♯5, then plain old A7, then A7♭5, and finally back to A7, before it resolves to Dm7 in the next measure. We'll take a look here at the fret-hand fingerings needed for this figure, and try it both with the thumb and with multiple fingers for pick-hand technique.

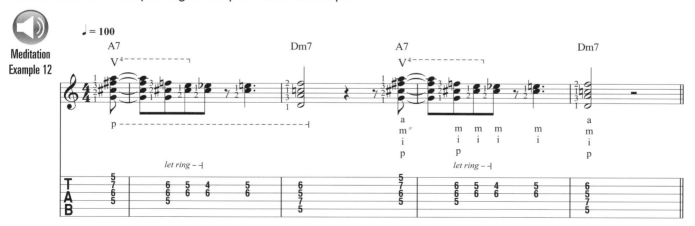

It should be noted that the only tones here that belong to the actual melody are at the top of the initial A13 and of the final Dm7 (the tones heard in between are all filler).

An extra-nice chord-melody segment that also frequently appears in this guitar trio arrangement is the one he uses, in nearly the same form, in the 11th and 12th measures of most A sections of the melody (such as measures 19–20 or 35–36 within the head in). The first three notes heard here, played over a sustaining Bb9 voicing, are the end of a phrase from the song which he answers with a five-chord descending fill of his own (the last three of those chords echoing the melody with their highest tones). The whole thing creates motion within the Bb7 harmony that is present at this spot in the progression; these last five chords are Bb13 (with the 9th on top), an Fm7 (creating a Bb7sus4 sound), another Bb13 voicing, a chromatic passing chord (the three-string barre at fret 2), and an Fm triad (part of Bb9, just like it was for the last melody note). Rhythmically, this is a distinctly dotted rhythm, with the beat subdivided into 16th-note time values. It can seem almost like a quarter-note-triplet figure, but it is not—the second note, for example, comes in on the last syllable of "one-ee-and-a" if we count out the beat and its subdivision in that way. To properly play the figure, it's good to get a feel for this type of syncopation and how it fits into the bossa groove. Don't work too hard to play the one-string slide at the end—it almost happens by itself just by relaxedly moving the index finger up to where it has to go next (string 3, fret 5)!

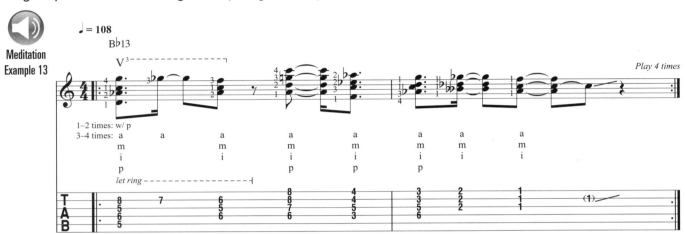

Meditation
Example 13

Once each during the head in and the head out, at the midway point of an A section, Joe plays an exceptionally pretty two-bar figure combining rhythmic *hemiola* (a two-against-three syncopation) and inner-voice motion of a chord. This is a place in the tune where a Dm chord is at hand for two measures, with an F sustained in the melody for most of that time. And in either case, he takes a common Dm7 voicing at 5th position, with the chordal 3rd (F) on top, and morphs it into different variations by moving the tone on string 4 (the chordal 5th [A], at the outset) up two frets and back down again, in half-step increments. Here are the chord shapes we wind up with along the way, and we might do well to try just moving back and forth between these fingerings out of tempo, before even venturing the complete figures with their actual rhythms (there's quite a stretch by the last voicing, and we want to carefully try to get used to it):

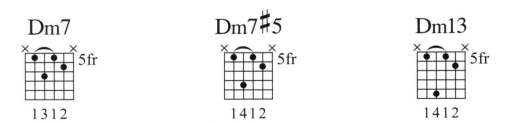

The last of these is an especially colorful sonority, perhaps technically a minor 13 chord with the presence of both the chordal 7th (C, on string 3) and the 6th tone of the scale (B, on string 4), but this 6th tone is right up under the 7th, just a half step away, resulting in an intriguing dissonance.

In the following exercises for playing this chordal device in tempo as it appears in the song, we'll in either instance try the rhythmic figure on Dm7 alone a couple of times, and then add in the changing chord tone (which we just now had opportunity to practice by itself, without the rhythm). In the first instance (measures 33–34), Joe is still using his thumb for the head of the tune. He accentuates the syncopation by alternating between single notes on string 4 and chord fragments on strings 2 and 3, and he settles into a pattern of one-and-a-half-beat units against the 4/4 time by the end of the first measure.

When he revisits this motif in the head out (in measures 169–170), he is playing fingerstyle. The alternation is mainly between the string 5 bass note and the remainder of each chord form, and the rhythmic effect of an accent every one-and-a-half beats doesn't really set in until the second measure. In the following exercise, note that the index-finger barre needs to briefly cover five strings once each time through the rhythmic figure (when the high A is played on string 1), and that the 8th rests between repetitions are good points at which to briefly relax your fret hand.

Listening to an early recording of "Meditation," such as by Brazilian vocalist Astrud Gilberto, one can further appreciate how Joe both honors the spirit of the tune and puts his own stamp on it within this tasty trio rendition… which we are hopefully better prepared to render ourselves, after all our careful preparation!

Meditation
Full Song

MEDITATION (MEDITAÇÃO)

Music by Antonio Carlos Jobim
Original Words by Newton Mendonça
English Words by Norman Gimbel

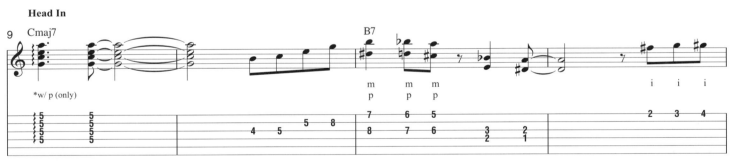

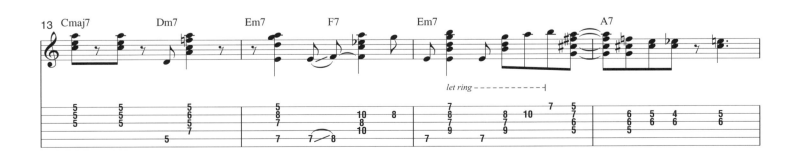

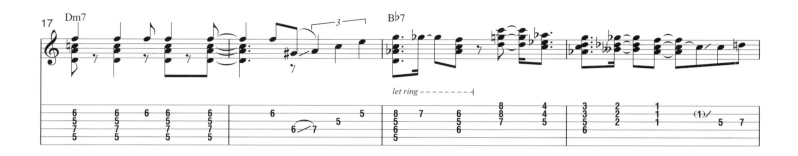

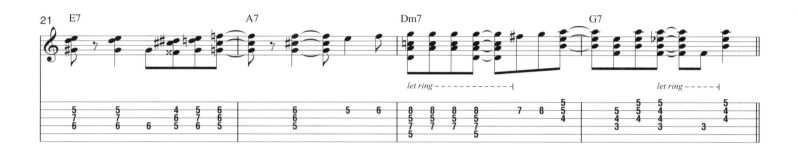

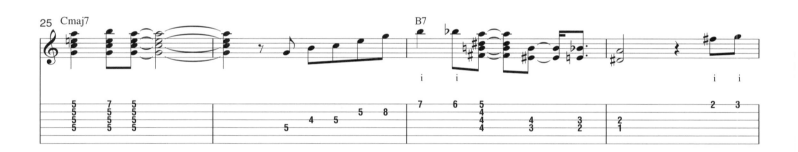

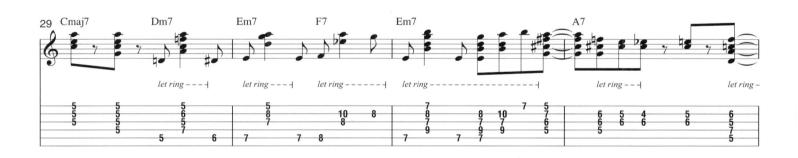

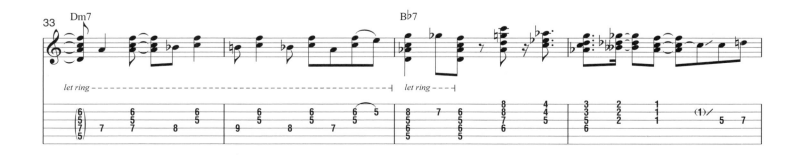

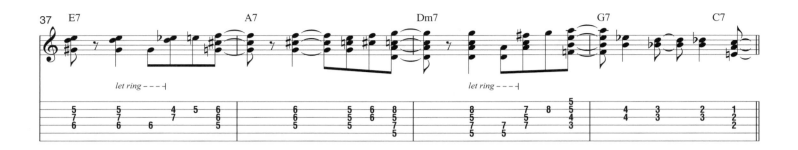

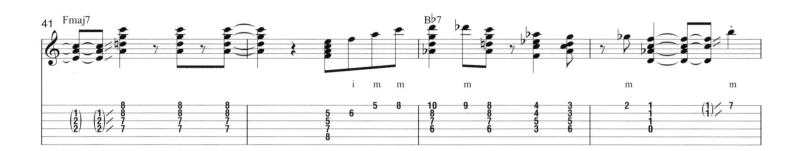

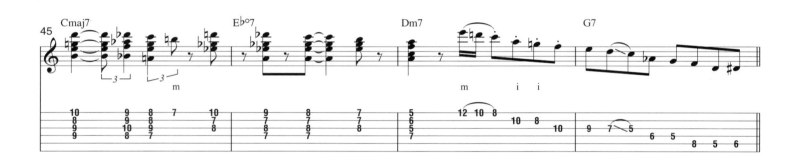

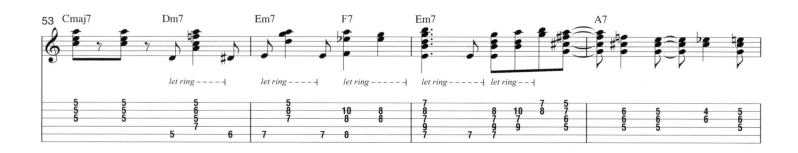

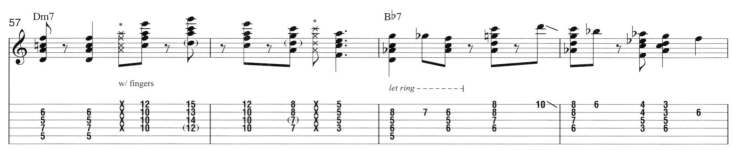

w/ fingers

let ring

*Played by pick-hand fingers landing on strings

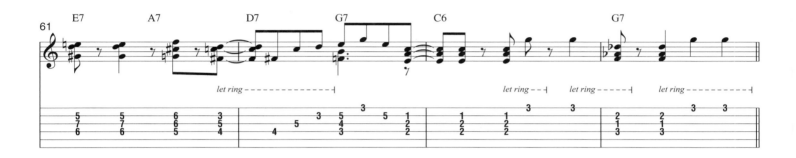

let ring

let ring

let ring

let ring

Guitar Solo

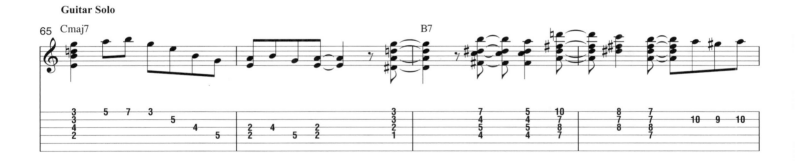

w/ p (only)

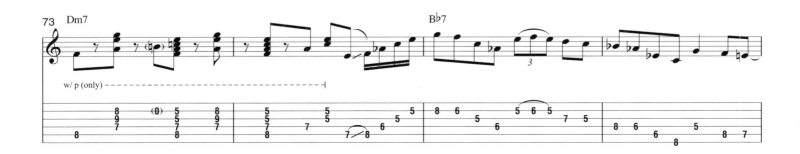

w/ p (only)

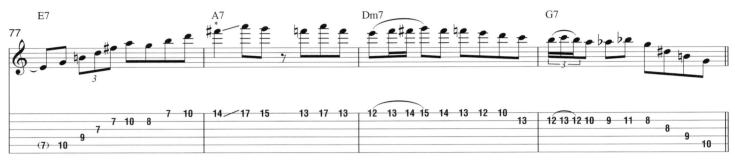

*Played behind the beat

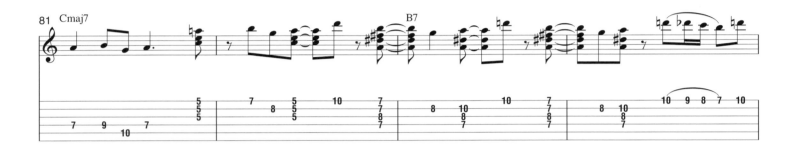

*Played behind the beat

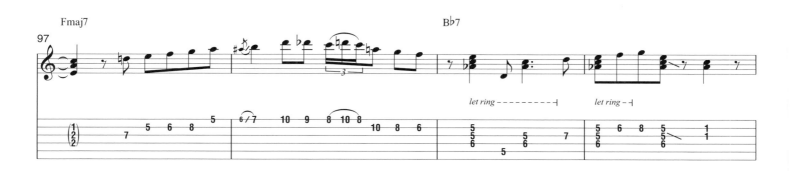

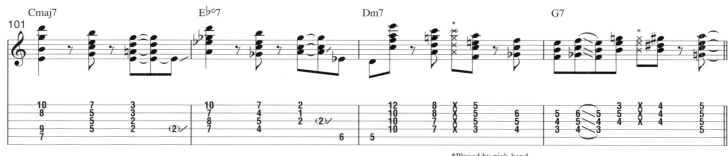

*Played by pick-hand
fingers landing on strings

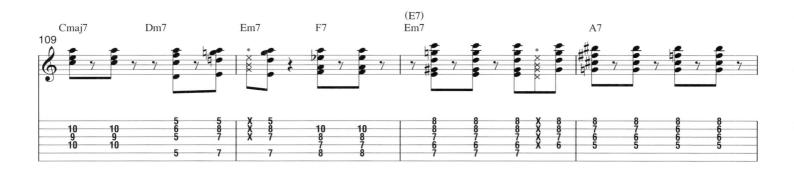

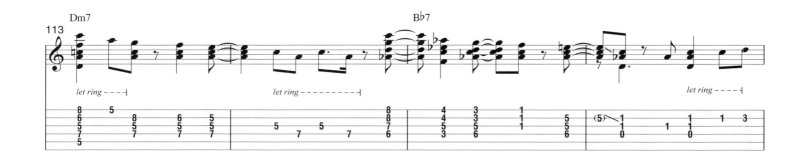

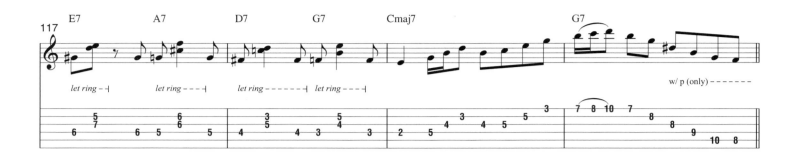

Head Out

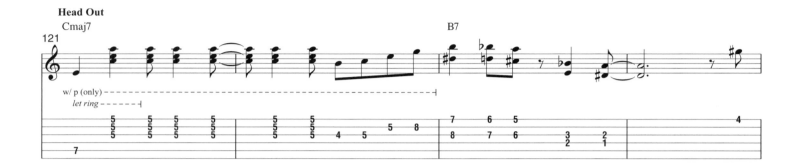

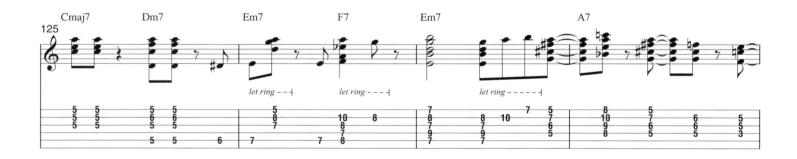

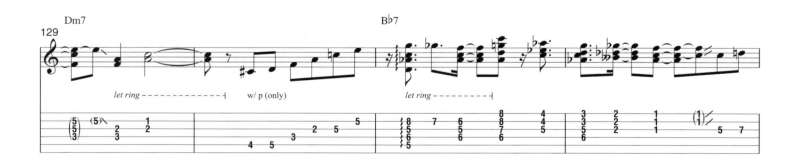

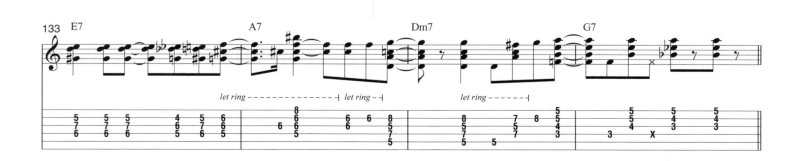

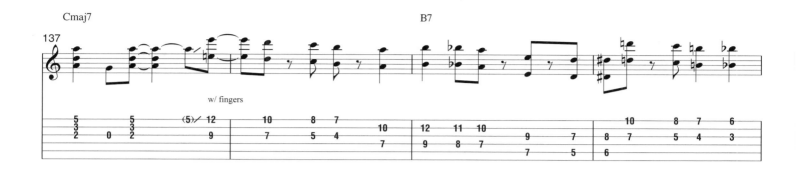

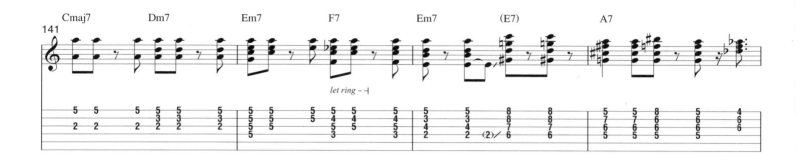

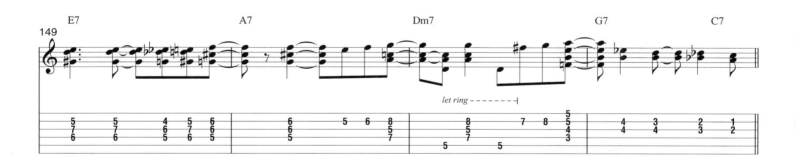

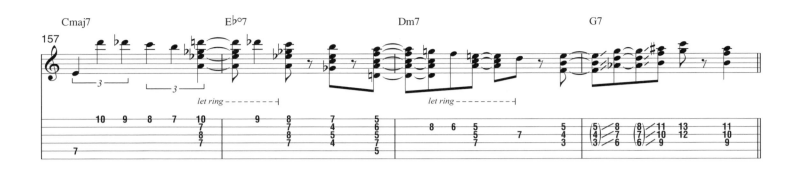

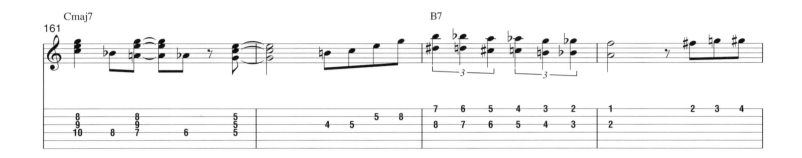

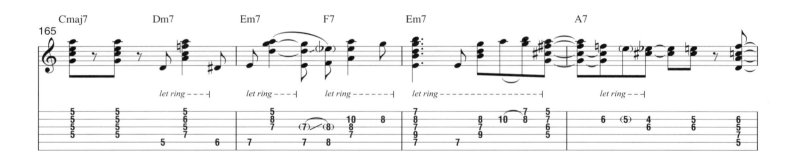

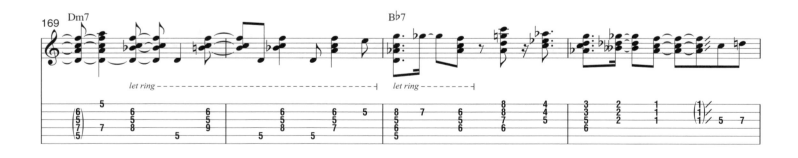

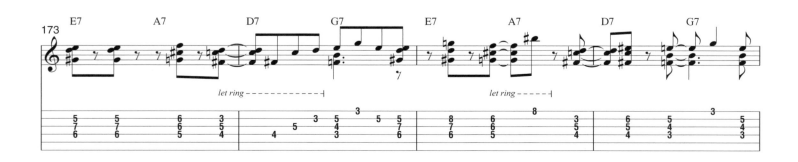

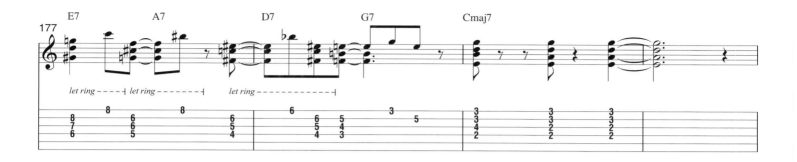

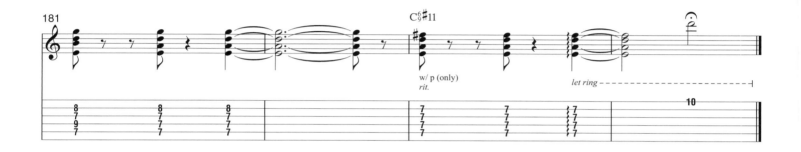

Blues for Basie
From *Virtuoso No. 2*, 1976

From the second in this acclaimed series of solo recordings, "Blues for Basie" is a great showcase for Joe Pass in a most familiar setting: going it alone on a relaxed, swingin', medium-tempo blues, and freely throwing in harmonic and textural variation while always maintaining a genuine, down-home flavor. It is an original song in the sense of coming from his hands and heart, with no other authorship, but it is based on a commonly used chord progression and really has no distinct melody that we could call the "head" to the tune. Rather, it is a set of largely improvised 12-bar choruses that tend to share a few recurring elements (especially a frequent ending figure)—a sort of theme-and-variations piece on this traditional form. In it, he starts off reasonably mellow, and subtly builds in intensity until arriving at a natural conclusion (there are eight choruses here, the last one extended by a tag ending, and they are numbered in the transcription). Along the way, he exhibits many of the key characteristics of his solo guitar approach, interspersing bits of chord-melody with single-note phrases, bass lines, chordal fills, and moments of pure rhythm guitar groove, often overlapping with one another. Like some other selections in this book, this one is basically meant to be played fingerstyle (perhaps even more so than "Meditation," though not as much so as "Summertime"), and that is how we'll approach it technically, even if much of it may still be viable for pick-only players.

A fundamental aspect of what Joe brings to the blues creatively are his choices of specific chord voicings and substitutions on this standard form whose harmonic progression famously lends itself to so much variation. To help understand what he does in this regard, it's good to know what he is essentially working off of as an assumed basic set of changes for each 12-bar cycle, and it would be fair to say it is this:

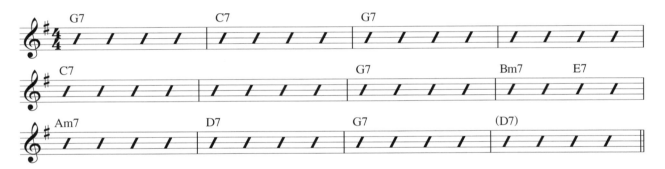

Specific chords that appear along the way in his performance, whether they are extensions of the chords named in this generic progression (like C13 used for C7) or seemingly different chords entirely (like C7 revisited late in the seventh measure of a chorus, or F7 where we're expecting Bm7), represent the ways in which he is playing around with the changes in his own distinctive manner, while still working within the norms of blues harmony.

Chordal Grooves and Moves

We'll start our breakdown of the piece with a look at some mainly chordal segments, especially those in which a shuffling blues rhythm is clearly laid out. The following exercise in rhythmic chording combines a classic boogie shuffle pattern like that in measures 25–26 with single repeated chords like those in measures 48 and 84. Take care to observe where a chord is played *staccato* (short) instead of being sustained for its whole time value. If you are using a pick or thumb only, fret strings 6, 4, and 3 for those first chords with fingers 1, 2, and 3 (or 1, 2, and 4) respectively, muting string 5 with the underside of the index rather than barring:

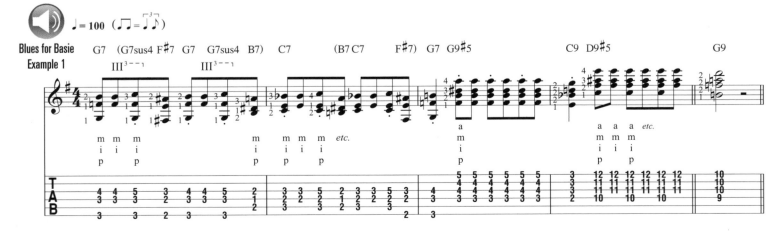

In measure 31 and just into measure 32, Joe uses a string of rising three-note chord voicings to create some movement within the essential G7 harmony, rhythmically bouncing off of the open D string on the upbeats in between. This is a common rhythmic pattern of his, and in measures 19–20, he similarly plays small chord shapes with single-note accents in between, in that instance using fretted notes on string 4 (from within the chords themselves, or nearby). Both of these segments are worth visiting ahead of time to get the feel of this groove, as well as to establish viable fingerings for the chord shapes involved, so we'll put them together here almost in their entirety for preliminary practice:

Blues for Basie
Example 2

In measures 73–75, he lays down an aggressive triplet groove of alternating bass notes and chords, made all the more edgy by the use of a sharp 9 chord for G7. It represents a bluesy hemiola pattern, with a sense of three beats felt for every two actual beats (thinking of each bass note as an accent that may be perceived as a beat). For part of the way, each bass note and chord is played short, not sustaining past its place in the triplet, but by the end he lets the bass notes ring under the chords. To get the hang of this rhythmic movement in which the pick hand must alternate quickly between thumb and fingers, we'll practice the pattern using only two different chords, while actually sustaining their tones progressively *less* as we go. This means that for the first repeated section here, we can just hang onto our chord shapes with the fret hand, and not bother muting the strings at all with either hand. Next step, we'll allow the bass notes to ring, but release the pressure off the remainder of each chord with the fret hand to silence it as we strike the next bass note. Finally, we'll mute everything (which is how Joe actually starts out this segment in measure 73) by also letting the thumb rest against string 5 or 6 when the fingers sound the next chord.

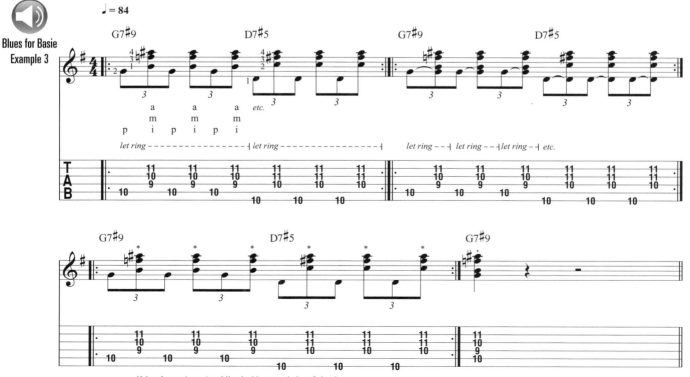

*Mute low string w/*p* while plucking remainder of chord.

In measure 58, we have an interesting pedal-tone figure with minor triads moving along the top three strings while the open D (the 5th, in our key of G) rings below. The effect is a bit harmonically "outside," as the tones wind up departing from the official D7 in the progression; the top notes of these triads trace a groovy little melody in the key, but it is only the Bm triad at fret 7 that really sounds like part of D7 (D13, specifically). After this quick departure from conventional harmony, Joe resolves to a plain G major triad on the next beat 1. The most natural fingering for this figure, which we will practice here, involves a partial barre with each of three different fingers:

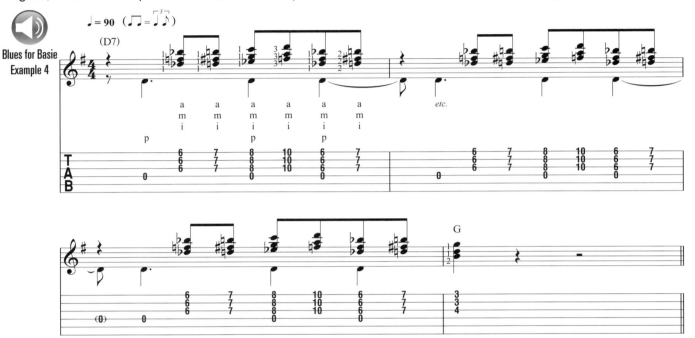

The sequentially descending chords of measures 79–80 bear looking at ahead of time for the sake of technique. Basically, a number of plain dominant 7th chords are each briefly turned into a 13sus4 and then back into a regular dominant 7th before moving down a half step to the next one in the series, all in a songful rhythmic pattern. The way Joe actually plays these involves an exception on the first chord, which is given a major 7th treatment, but our present exercise will be more homogenized. This can be a bit of a finger-buster, so be careful not to strain your fret hand on it. In part, we avoid undue effort by letting the index finger rock back and forth slightly in position, barring three strings for the chord and then releasing that pressure while fretting the interjected bass note, and then back to the barre only, etc. For the open E7, the pick hand mutes both chord and bass note by allowing the fingers and thumb, respectively, to touch their strings again a half beat after plucking.

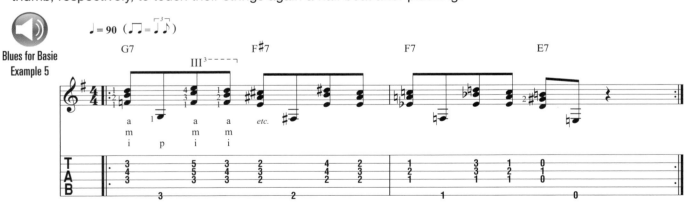

Mostly Melodic Maneuvers

Next, we'll check out some largely single-note stretches of this solo piece that may warrant a preview of their technical requirements, as well as a discussion of their musical significance.

In his fourth chorus, from the pickup through just past its halfway point (measures 36–43), Joe works within a classic call-and-response pattern. He plays a bluesy little bar-long phrase four times, each time varied slightly in its tones and/or rhythm, and each time followed by a measure of chordal material that has a particular melodic shape of its own. The repeating "call" phrase is more major than minor—even when the blue-hued flatted 3rd and 5th tones are thrown in—and involves a good deal of slurring from slides, hammer-ons, and pull-offs. Following are all four of his variations on it, with fingering suggestions that account for the surrounding context in each case (the *pima* suggestions may also be helpful, but are not so critical in this case).

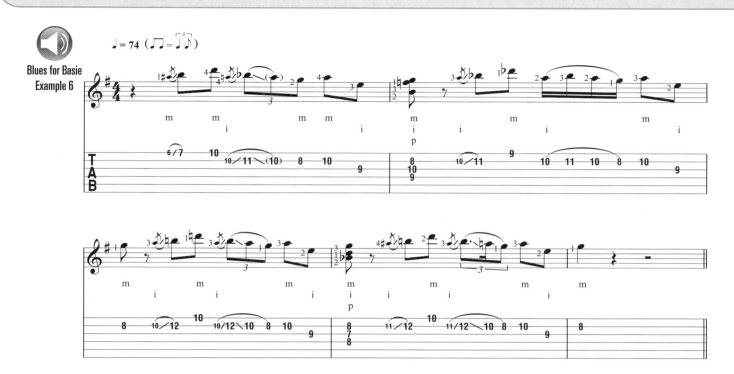

Measures 61–62 are packed with musical gestures and technical demands, starting with the super-quick slurring on the initial ascending figure (mostly a G7 arpeggio, with a half-step lead-in to the chordal 3rd and the addition of the 6th tone). After the declamatory G13 chords that conclude that phrase, a pair of sudden thumb-downstroke chords herald the arrival of a new one, made up of minor pentatonic triplets. We can try this segment a couple of times to get the hang of it with both hands:

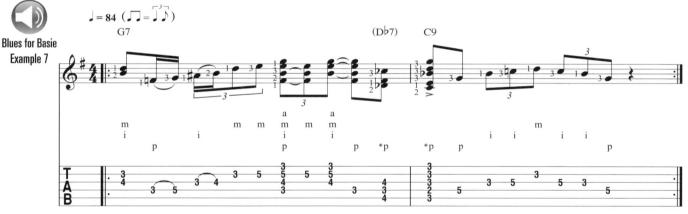

*Played w/ a downstroke of the thumb

The following exercise, a chromatically ascending and descending row of rising minor 10th intervals, can help us prepare not only for the similar motif of measure 67, but also for any of the numerous spots where bass notes rhythmically alternate with upper-string material (whether those bass notes are on downbeats or upbeats). This drill is also pertinent to measure 65 with its *harmonic* 10th intervals—in which the notes are played together—though in that case fingers 1 and 2 may be used. (This type of scalar movement with wide harmonic intervals gets some attention in the "Integral Techniques" section of this book.)

The angular figure of measure 69 is another Joe Pass–ism that breaks with traditional blues harmony and style, with a somewhat dissonant pattern that is both guitaristic and theoretical in its design. It's a series of rising octave intervals, altogether ascending by tritone intervals (A up to A, then Eb up to Eb, etc.), which lays on the fretboard in a fairly neat diagonal arrangement. With it, he is not only treating the II chord in the progression as dominant instead of minor, which is common enough (A7 instead of Am7 in this key), but also evoking A7b5 just by repeatedly playing its root and flatted 5th within this jagged contour of triplet rhythm. Our next exercise approaches this patterned movement in stages, to help us get used to each aspect of it: first with 8th notes moving straight across the neck, then with 8ths moving diagonally to go up in tritones instead of perfect 4ths, and finally, in 8th-note triplets (with most notes here occurring a third of a beat earlier than in the original).

Measures 70–72 contain another key segment for mastering the fretboard motion needed in this piece. After rhythmically bouncing off the open D string, Joe outlines a C major triad (which relates well to Am7 or D7sus4), jumps up to grab a high D13 voicing, and scoots back down again on beat 4 to land in 7th position. There his line largely traces a G major triad downwards and then upwards, before a chromatic ascending pattern works its way up string 2 (with the fret-hand pinky in the lead) until reaching an upper-range D7sus4 chord. After a high G at the very peak, he makes it back down slightly to 10th position for a blues scale–based descent. Try the whole thing using the tablature, fingering, and *pima* suggestions given, and keep in mind that after each of the two chords played here, a finger will just roll back from where it was in the chord to fret the next note with its underside (rather than jumping up to be on its tip):

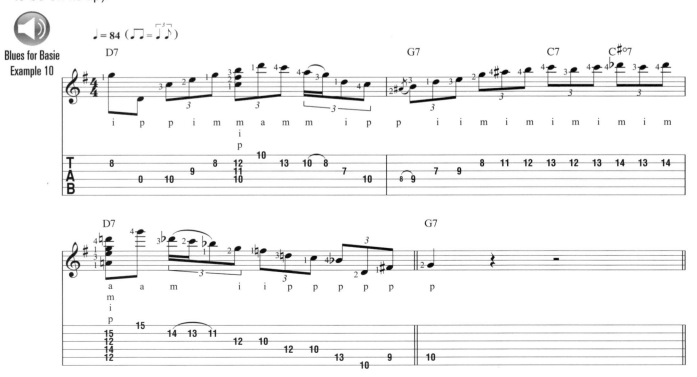

A particular line is used for C7 in both measure 17 and measure 89 (each being the fifth measure of a chorus), a line that moves significantly up the fretboard, in either case following a quick C9 voicing of some kind and leading up to a 10th-position Gm7 shape on the next beat 1. Harmonically speaking, what seems like a full arpeggio of B♭maj9 are really the upper tones of a C13sus4 chord (with a root tacked onto the top), and the Gm7 voicing fits into a C7sus4 concept as well. For the purpose of technical exercise, we'll take a closer look at this phrase as it continues from measure 89 through measure 90, where further vertical movement is needed for a series of high notes in octaves. Notice that the hand jumps up a couple of frets immediately after the initial C7 chord, and that the pinky effectively leads the way in further changes of position, both at the end of the first measure and as the octaves begin in the next:

Blues for Basie
Example 11

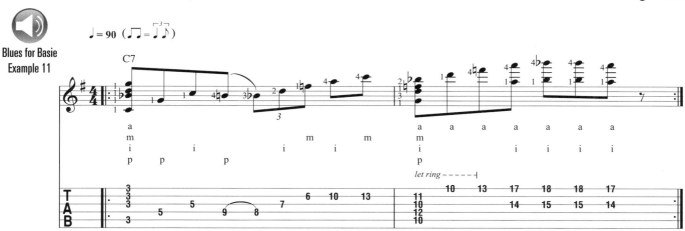

We pick up where we left off to check out the motif used in measures 91–92, involving a descending line of octaves in the upper range, with the open D string played between them as a pedal tone. We'll formulate this material here as an exercise to practice moving these octaves both down and up strings 1 and 3, while either allowing string 4 to ring or muting it with each new octave—an exercise which can also help us navigate spots like measures 24 and 77, where we find 6th intervals moving along this same pair of strings. Notice that the melodic line heads down a G7 arpeggio from a high chordal root, with the 4th tone of the scale (the octave on frets 5 and 8) thrown in for good linear movement. When it's time to mute the open D, let the index finger lightly touch it in the process of fretting string 3:

Blues for Basie
Example 12

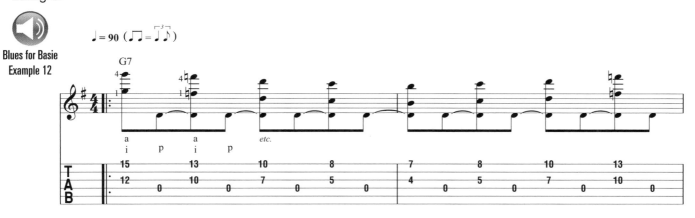

*Let index finger touch string 4 while fretting string 3.   **Let open string 4 sustain on repeat only.

Solo Guitar Chops Challenges

A few key spots in "Blues for Basie" require particular strategy, coordination, and agility to execute, often with elements of chording, single-note melody, and bass tones closely intermingled. Of greatest priority, for its frequency of use in the piece as well as the technical challenges it presents for both hands, is the contrapuntal figure which Joe usually plays at the end of a chorus (along with the phrases that typically surround it). It involves contrary motion of bass notes and melody tones that are numerous strings apart. Because of that, along with some of the chord fingerings needed, this segment is not really workable for playing with a pick only (a simple introduction to fingerstyle bass-melody movement is found in the "Integral Techniques" section of this book). With some variation in notes, voicings, and rhythms from chorus to chorus, it's never played exactly the same way twice, but here we'll look at measures 22–24 as a representative example. Some aspects to get used to may include the syncopated rhythm between bass and melody notes (which sometimes coincide and sometimes alternate), the fret-hand fingering with its odd stretches and twists (like for the G7/B or the octave on the downbeat of the third measure), and the sounding of the same note twice in a row but first on a fretted string and then with an open string (also within beat 1 of the third measure).

This figure generally appears in the second-to-last measure of the form where the progression comes home to the tonic chord (G7) and creates harmonic motion that leads back to the V chord (D7) for a turnaround at the end. In a musical gesture very characteristic of Joe, the official D7 on either side here is addressed at first with a cheerful descending G major triad, while the 5th tone (D) is played or implied in the bass. This is melodically quite natural within the key, and still serves to set up a tension that needs to be resolved (a few D7-specific tones do find their way in: in the brief tritone sub Ab7 towards the end of measure 22, or in just the note C on measure 24, beat 4, before he slides up into the next G7 from a half step below).

Big stretches can be involved for certain chord voicings, often with a need to quickly spread the fret-hand fingers apart. The following exercise is based on a certain stretch of this kind that is used in measures 29, 37, and 100 (the very end of the piece), in each case between a pair of dominant 9 voicings with no chordal 3rds. With the barre needed at fret 10, this is another instance in which fingerstyle technique is really required, in order to play the figure as is without sounding the unwanted note on string 5 (there are numerous other such cases where a barre necessitates a fingerstyle approach, as with the big, wide chords of measure 54). Notice that we land differently on the G9 chord every other time here, and also be very careful not to overdo your efforts if the stretch is tough for your fret hand:

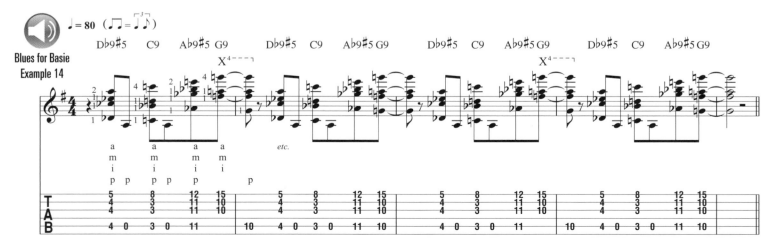

You may also notice that the first and third times we play G9 in the previous exercise, we start out with only the upper three tones, but the fret hand must at that point already be in position for the whole chord (with a barre on the middle four strings) so that we're prepared to add the bottom note on the next downbeat. There are several instances like this throughout the piece, where we must be nearly or fully in place for a chord voicing that is only partially being played, with the remaining note or notes soon to follow. Here we'll examine a few more such cases that are worth a preliminary look, drawn from measures 78, 41, and 43–44, in that order (though the same approach is useful also for the Eb9#5 formed in measure 9, and the piecemeal G9 played in measure 49). Refer to the chord diagrams above the staff for extra clarity on where the fret hand should take the shape of a particular chord, and note the use of *c* in addition to *pima* (for the involvement of the pick-hand pinky):

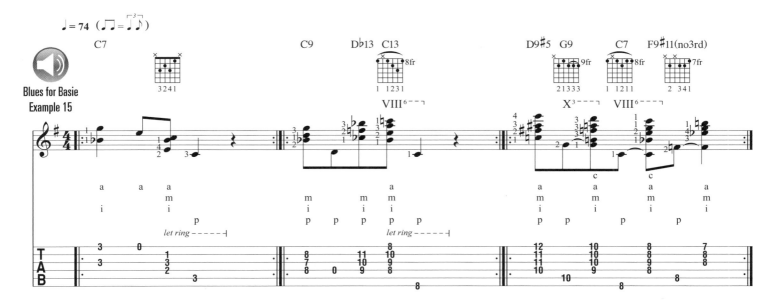

And finally, the last segment of the song is worth working out ahead of time, especially given the need to quickly jump into a substantial chord fingering right out of a melodic line. Instead of wrapping up the 12-bar form in the usual way when he gets to the final two measures of his last chorus (measures 95–96 of the whole piece), Joe begins to repeat the partly-chord-melody phrase he'd played in the previous two measures, creating a *tag* ending before finishing the performance. This winds up taking place over a I–VI–ii–V turnaround progression (in this case, essentially two beats apiece of G7, E7, Am7, and D7), with two slightly varied reiterations of the phrase, before he returns once more to his contrapuntal ending device and concludes the song. We exercise these tag variations here using the exact material of measures 95–98 (playing twice through the whole segment for practice). Watch out especially for the sudden grab of the E7#9#5 chords:

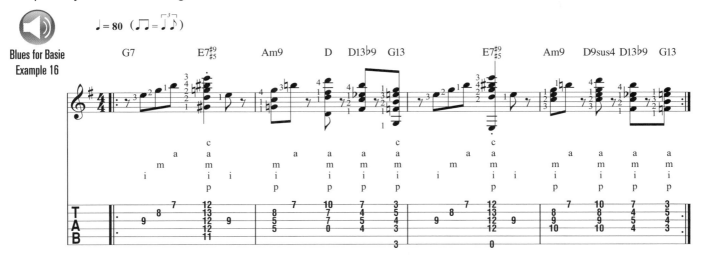

From the simple little blues lines and double stops that are highly idiomatic, to the surprising tone and rhythm combinations that are more idiosyncratic, Joe is joyously swinging throughout his rendition of this classic form… a factor we should not forget as we seek to put it under our own fingers.

Blues for Basie
Full Song

BLUES FOR BASIE
By Joe Pass

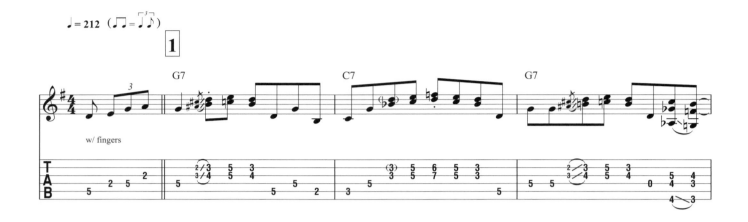

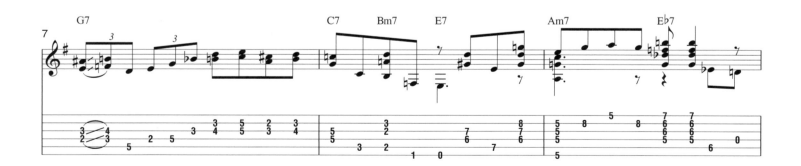

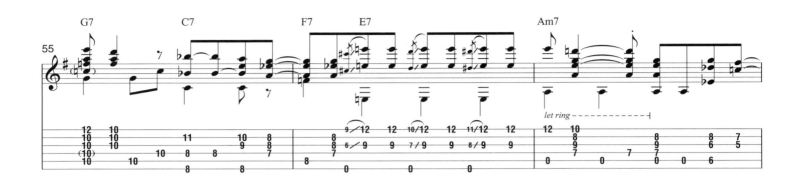

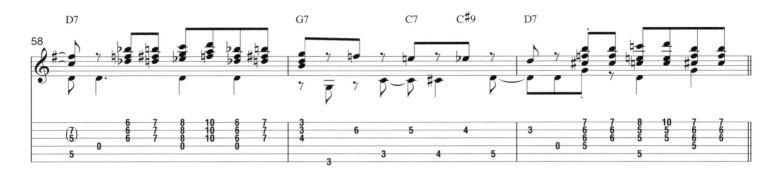

*Played with a downstroke of the thumb

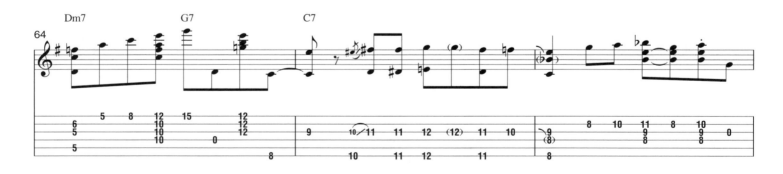

Tricrotism
From *Chops*, 1979

With "Tricrotism," from his tour-de-force duo album with fellow virtuoso Niels-Henning Ørsted Pedersen on bass, we find Joe in a classic setting for the display of his chops, a cookin' performance on a bop tune with plenty of room to stretch out. They begin right on the melody, with no intro, playing it in pure unison fashion (an octave apart, really) without a single chord or fill. After this, they run through a whole gamut of improvisational configurations: first a chorus of both of them soloing at once, then a guitar solo over walking bass, then bass solo with guitar accompaniment, and finally two choruses of trading eights on this 32-bar AABA-structured tune (each alternately soloing or accompanying, eight measures at a time). They then wrap up with another unison rendition of the head, this time with a tag and ending. Along the way, we get miles and miles of Joe's signature continuous melodic improvisation, a taste of his liberal embellishment of a chord progression, and a demonstration of his skillful accompaniment as a duo partner. We also have a chance to walk in his footsteps with both pick and fingerstyle technique in abundance, as well as some *hybrid picking* (pick and fingers used together).

[Editor's Note: this song has often been referred to as "Tricotism," without the second "r," but it is indeed properly called "Tricrotism."]

Melodic Movement and Technique

Mixed into his flowing scalar and arpeggiated lines are various melodic elements, including simple groovy ideas like the phrase of measures 65–66 (with its pickup) or the sort of rhythmically repetitive blues-tinged gesture of measures 57–58; pure bebop vocabulary, like the classic minor ii–V–i's found in measures 84–85 or 116–117; straight-up blues material, as in measures 69, 73, or 93–95; the building of tension with diminished scale tones, as in measures 101–102 (which start off with a complete ascending diminished scale, accentuating the G°7 in that part of the progression); and the sequential use of short melodic fragments repeated at different pitches, as in measures 77, 87, or (on a longer trajectory) 120–123. He also has a few regular habits or favorite ideas that seem to recur throughout the performance, such as bringing out the change from G♭7 to G°7 through a clear emphasis on their roots, in imitation of the melody itself, in the fifth measure of an A section (measures 37, 45, and 61 within his first improvised chorus); joyfully resolving into an A section from a high arching line like he does going into measure 73 or 105; or giving a minor/major 7 treatment to B♭m in the bridge, with an F major triad appearing along the way (as in measures 53–54 or 85–86); among other common devices, some of which we'll explore in the examples below.

Be aware, though, as you play, listen to, or analyze his work on this song, that on rare occasion something will not exactly make sense with the chord progression (neither in a direct nor in a blues-tone sort of way), probably due to a simple misstep. At the most severe, he spends all of measure 115 as if he is outlining D major—which could normally be a natural point of resolve for the preceding A7, but not here in this tune, where we are supposed to come back to D♭ major! He nearly does the same in measure 211, but in the second half of the measure he sequentially moves his triadic arpeggio down a half step, giving the overall effect of simply resolving to D♭ major from a half step above.

It can be useful, in considering how he approaches both the complex melody and his linear improvisation on this key of D♭ tune, to be familiar with some common D♭ major scale positions on the fretboard. Much else goes into playing on these chord changes, as just noted, but this is a start for seeing how Joe might have located many of his fingerings and phrases. After checking out these basic scalar shapes, you can see in the tablature how parts of the melody, in particular, are situated nicely in these areas of the neck (and a helpful hint: the multiple scale and arpeggio positions examined in the "Integral Techniques" section of this book are conveniently also in the key of D♭):

Common D♭ Major Scale Positions

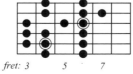
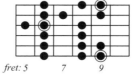
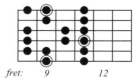
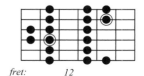

fret: 3   5   *fret:* 3   5   7   *fret:* 5   7   9   *fret:* 9   12   *fret:*   12

The bridge of the tune, in its first two measures, makes a visit to the more distant chord A7, at which point the relevant scalar positions are more like this (thinking of A dominant or Mixolydian as a corresponding scale):

Common A Dominant Scale Positions

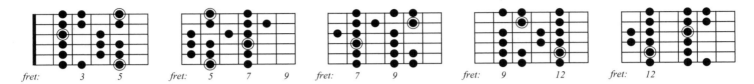

fret: 3   5   fret: 5   7   9   fret: 7   9   fret: 9   12   fret: 12

Mobility in Fingering and Picking

While some segments of the melody or guitar solo lie neatly within such scale configurations, many others may be fingered in a more "stretchy" or "jumpy" sort of way, often shifting rapidly between these positions. For starters, let's look at the concluding phrase of the melody with a fingering that shows how to navigate through the slight shifts of position required on the fretboard:

Tricrotism
Example 1

More radical jumps up or down the fretboard are often used throughout the piece, as exemplified by the movement in measure 72, leading up to the next downbeat. Follow especially the locations of the 1st finger to see how this may work:

Tricrotism
Example 2

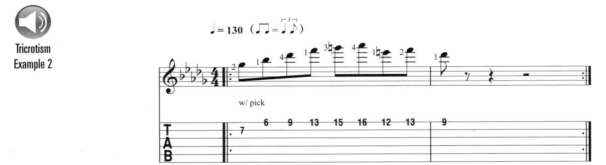

Sometimes, such quick jumps are made while avoiding the use of any fret-hand finger twice in a row, as in the example above. But on other occasions, they may be carried out by simply scooting along (almost sliding) with the last finger that was used in the original position before the jump. Notice how this may occur in a line like that of measures 113–114, where the index and pinky do double duty in the ascent up strings 2 and 1 (the "hammer-on from nowhere" that occurs in the actual solo has been eliminated here for simplicity's sake):

Tricrotism
Example 3

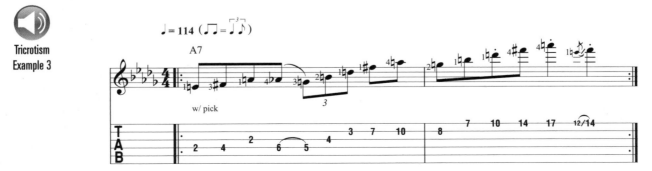

This line, as well as the similar one in measures 81–82, is reminiscent of a favorite Wes Montgomery device in its treatment of a dominant 7th chord, evoking the 7sus4 sound with arpeggios of a minor 7th chord rooted on the 5th of the dominant 7th at hand (using Em11 tones here to suggest A7sus4).

The ability to move rapidly *across* strings is also helpful in executing this material, as seen in the arpeggiated lines of measures 111 and 199. We'll combine these here for the sake of exercise, with picking as well as fingering indications (the jump that results on the repeat, from the last note back to the first one, is a challenge that doesn't exist in the actual solo, and we can allow that last note to be a little short to help out). Harmonically, Joe plays on the upper extensions of the Eb7 chord, creating an Eb13#11 sound. Compare these phrases with a common Eb9 shape at the 5th position, especially with the 13th (the C on string 1, fret 8) or #11th (the A on string 1, fret 5) on top:

Tricrotism
Example 4

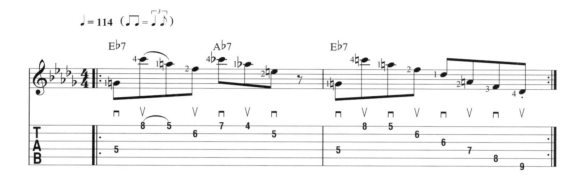

Some of the fastest playing Joe does in this performance—and certainly the fastest in which he articulates every note—comes with the burnin' 8th-note triplets he lays down in measures 192–195 to kick off the trading. To prepare for this segment, let's isolate the material of measure 195, including its pickup, and leading into the next measure (a yet-more-focused exercise on picking triplets is found in the "Integral Techniques" section of this book). After trying it at this easier pace, remember to gradually increase the tempo to work towards full speed:

Tricrotism
Example 5

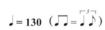

Slurring Technique

A degree of hammer-ons, pull-offs, and slides is common in the work of many guitarists, not least among them Joe. But a few segments of his linear improvisation on "Tricrotism" are especially thick with notes he doesn't pick, sometimes within a particular repetitive pattern, and these are worth some preliminary practice. The rolling triplets of measure 245, for instance, may seem fast, but really roll off the tongue (so to speak) when we're at home with the corresponding pattern of picking, fingering, and slurring, which can be exercised in concentrated form:

Tricrotism
Example 6

He makes frequent use of decorative turns such as the one in measures 40 and 42. Notice that such a figure is often rhythmically played according to a certain *feel* within the jazz vernacular, rather than following the exact time values that are most naturally written to represent it. This group of four 16th notes, for example, tends to come across as if the first one were a grace note, and the last two squeezed into a short second half of the beat (like we normally get with swung-8ths division), like so:

Let's try an exercise for this figure, based on measure 40. In the middle of the second measure, take care to roll with the 3rd finger from string 4 to string 3 (from its tip to its underside):

Tricrotism
Example 7

In measures 120–123, towards the conclusion of his solo, Joe cooks through a particularly challenging pattern of repeated slurs with a four-note figure that twice moves down in pitch (along string 2) after being played several times in a row in one spot. It should be noted that he plays these 16ths a little more evenly than those in measure 40, but also that he does not quite manage to execute the pattern cleanly, at least not at those points where he's about to jump down the fretboard! We can prepare for this segment by first practicing the repeating slurred group of tones at each of its three positions separately, and then putting them all together in a continuous sequence:

Tricrotism
Example 8

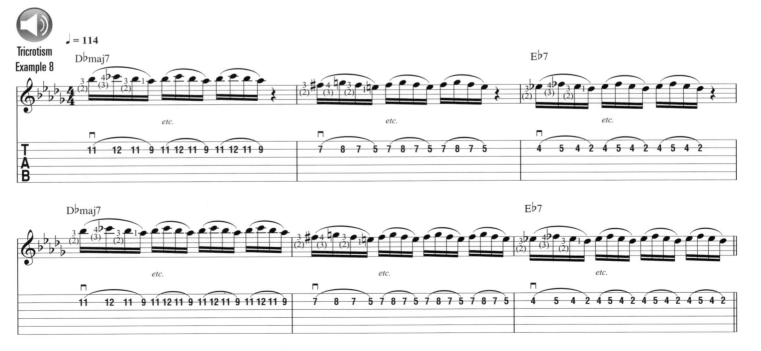

Harmonically, he is playing through these measures with a purely Db blues approach: the first group of 16ths bringing out a Db7 sound, the second group coming straight out of a Db blues scale, and the third group emphasizing a minor 3rd tone, relative to Db (even though, by that time, the official chord in the progression is Eb7).

Joe's work on "Tricrotism" includes a fair number of instances in which these slurring methods are compounded in one phrase, that is, where we need to slide right after a hammer-on, or vice versa, and so forth. The following exercise combines material from measures 246, 244, and 46, in that order, for specific practice of this sort (note that here we'll slide into the downbeat of our second measure, while a hammer-on is used for the actual corresponding place in measure 46).

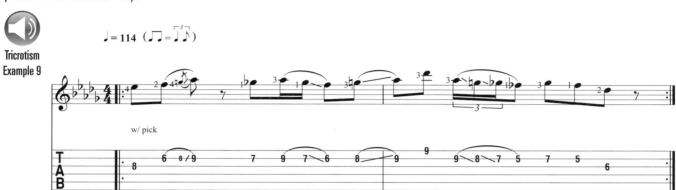

Some Other Tricky Spots in the Soloing

We'll take a detailed look here at a few other spots in the guitar solo, or within the trading, for which some mapping out ahead of time of one's fingerings and picking could be especially helpful. First off, consider measures 93–96, at the conclusion of his first solo chorus, where he gets down and dirty with a blues-flavored double-stop motif. One note is often sustained while another one is repeated or changed, and as he moves on from this figure in the last measure, the pinky winds up leading the way in a dramatic reach up the fretboard (similarly to how it'll need to move up from the last note of measure 53 for the first few notes of measure 54).

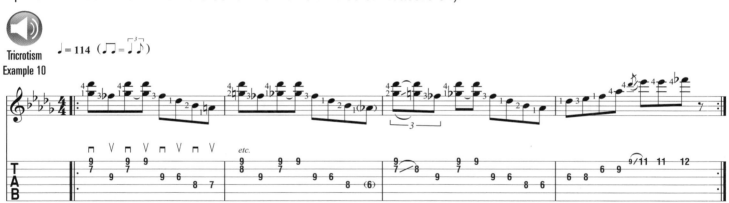

Measures 125–129, at the conclusion of his second solo chorus (and of the whole solo), provide a solid dose of fretboard movement both up and across the strings. The diminished scale pattern of the first measure accentuates the G°7 and serves as a launching pad for the subsequent leaps up the neck. The whole thing culminates in an almost purely Db minor pentatonic run down and across the 9th position (bringing out an aggressive blues vibe), through the third and fourth measures. Notice that the index finger will need to roll from its tip onto different spots on its underside for the three notes in a row at fret 9, as happens in reverse at places like measure 91 (and in the actual solo, Joe avails himself of a couple of pull-offs in the first two measures of this segment).

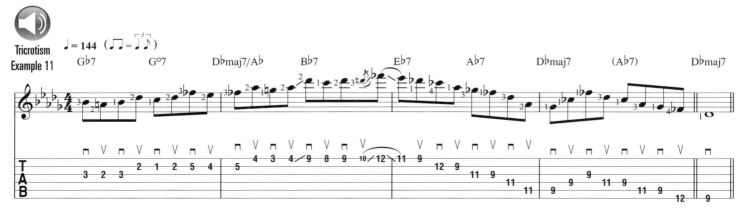

In measure 232, it is a bit tricky to either hear or reproduce Joe's actual tones, with part of the line *ghosted* (barely heard) and some less-conventional technique involved. But to check out how that sound came about and get an idea of what he was going for, we can try our hand at this segment (through the phrase's ending in the next measure) using the fingering and picking indications below. Be aware that within the quick upwards sweep here, the last of those three notes should feel like a clear downbeat on beat 4, while the next note (on the swung "and" of 4) comes in with different pacing, and thus is not really part of the sweep, even if it too is played with an upstroke. Also notice that the index finger needs to move into place above the middle finger, replacing it at fret 6 to roll from string 3 to string 4, for the last two of these sweep-picked notes.

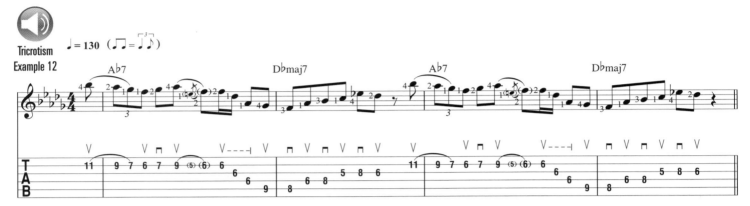

The melodic material here is really all pure D♭ major scale tones (aside from the grace note), with a pretty clear outlining of the tonic chord in the last measure.

Chordal Movement and Technique

Through two choruses of N.H.Ø.P.'s bass solo and four 8-bar segments featuring the bass in the trading, Joe demonstrates a variety of duo accompaniment textures including sustained chords, lively bass-chord figures, repetitive rhythmic grooves, and brief double-stop segments that are basically like harmonized melodic fills. He also takes ample opportunity to keep things fresh through chordal substitution, such as the use of a dominant 7th in place of the major tonic chord, as in measures 161–162 (perhaps also making it an altered dominant, as with the sharp 9 chords of measures 153–154); the occasional replacement of a regular dominant 7th with a dominant sus4, as in measures 145–146 or 177; or even the alteration of a chord that we would very much expect to be a natural dominant, as with the E♭7♯9♯5 voicing used in place of E♭9 in measure 203. In a couple of instances, he goes yet further afield by chromatically moving into the actual chord in the progression from a distance away (fret by fret along the neck) as he descends into the E♭13 of measure 171 with a fixed chord shape, or targets the E♭9 in measure 236 with a change of voicing along the way. We'll take a look in the following examples at some pertinent technical tips for these chordal passages, and also discuss some further harmonic points of interest.

Recurrent Figures

During the bass solo (and in part, the trading), Joe plays a similar figure for the last four measures of the second and last A sections of each chorus. He usually approaches this cadential sequence (the busiest part of the progression, with its IV–♯IV–I–VI–II–V–I motion) using a combination of bass notes and small chords, in a way that exemplifies his accompaniment technique throughout the whole piece. To help us get a handle on this kind of movement, our next exercise is a representative version of how this segment may be played. It's a good idea to practice it both fingerstyle and with hybrid technique. Either the thumb or the pick (held by thumb and forefinger) sounds all the notes on strings 5 or 6, while the next available fingers are used for strings 3 and 4.

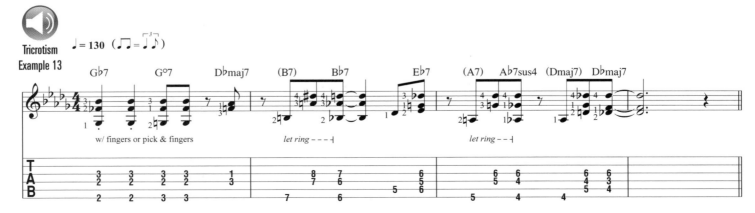

Typical of his harmonic movement in the song is the way in which a chord may be approached from a half step away (especially from above), as with the B7 or A7 briefly heard here (which respectively lead to B♭7 or A♭7sus4). Such a chord may often be considered a tritone substitute for one that would lead to the same destination in V–I motion, and may itself have just been played—that is, the A7 here could be a tritone sub for E♭7, interjected into the normal E♭7 to A♭7 movement. In a way that is typical of jazz comping altogether, the chords tend to be anticipated on the preceding "and" counts. Of a little more particular interest in this segment is the use of a sus4 chord for A♭7, and even a Dmaj7 where we'd more likely expect the tritone sub D7, in either case to harmonize the tonic tone D♭ through the last couple of measures of the sequence. (Effectively, this time a major 7th chord is replacing a dominant 7th, instead of the other way around.)

The rhythmic figure found in measures 153–154 and 165–166 (in each case including a pickup chord from the previous measure) is representative of the sort of chordal groove often found in his accompaniment. In the following exercise, we first get used to the rhythm with the stable D♭7♯9 chord found in the earlier segment, and then apply it to the changing double stops and single notes of the later segment, with their trickier fingering (realize that E and F♭ are enharmonic, both of them giving us the same note on the guitar, although they are each used here according to what is theoretically correct at the moment):

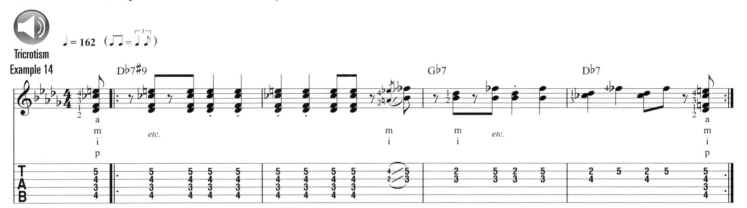

Special Chording Techniques

One chordal device that is worth checking out is actually found within Joe and N.H.Ø.P's chorus of simultaneous melodic improvisation, where Joe briefly interjects a chords-and-bass pattern at the start of the bridge in measures 49–52. This next exercise repeats the material from the first two of these measures (with a recurrent harmonic motion of A7sus4 to A7) to help get a feel in both hands for the syncopated alternation of the two-string chordal shells with each other, and with the open A in the bass:

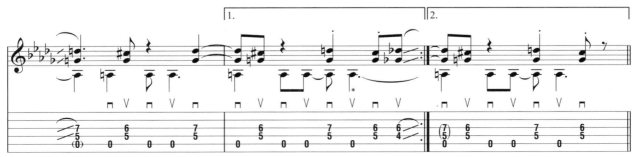

*Let open string 5 sustain on repeat.

A colorful feature of Joe's chordal vocabulary, one that really depends on the involvement of the pick-hand fingers, is the use of wide voicings with more than one large gap between tones. This often requires a barre across more unwanted strings than can be gracefully muted by the fret hand, and is sometimes followed by a chord change or alteration in which one or more tones are sustained from the original chord. Check out this condensed version of such material from measures 148–149 and 168–169, involving full index-finger barres at frets 1 and 4:

Tricrotism
Example 16

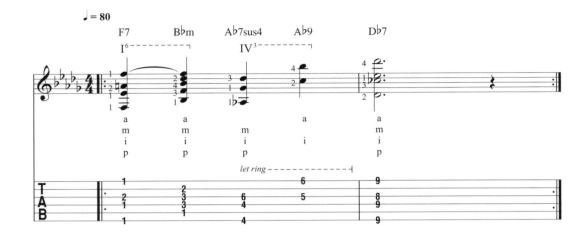

An aspect of Joe's playing that is demonstrated nicely in this rendition of "Tricrotism" is the preference he often shows for playing fast single-note lines with the pick, while going fingerstyle for chordal work, and making the switch as needed in the middle of a tune. After using the pick for the head in, the chorus of in-tandem improvisation, and the guitar solo, he puts it aside to accompany the bass solo with fingers only. But he picks it up again just ahead of time for the trading and hybrid picks most of his accompaniment figures from that point on (keeping the pick between thumb and index finger, but using it like the thumb in conjunction with the remaining fingers). Notice that he gives himself some time to put it down with the held note in measures 129–130, and a bit less time to pick it up during the sustained chord in measure 187. The very skill of managing these transitions is worth a look, if we are to try playing like Joe Pass! He himself might have kept the pick between his teeth when not in use, for an easy grab, if he didn't have it in his pocket. It's up to you whether or not you are concerned about essentially putting it in your mouth, but there are other options, such as placing it on an amp, music stand, or other nearby surface. In any case, the following exercise helps us prepare to make the switch one way or the other, by walking us through the very points of transition (described above) that are actually found in this performance. Take care to play the first non-pick chords here with the fingers, and the next group of them with thumb only (noticing that a pick-like upstroke with the thumb will be involved):

Tricrotism
Example 17

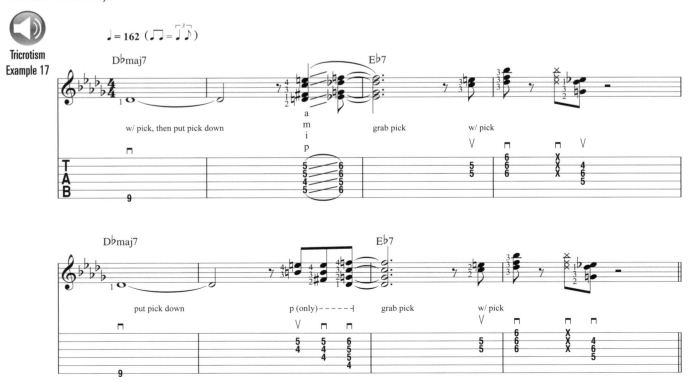

Perhaps the trickiest spot in all of Joe's accompaniment work here is the percussively rhythmic—and deceptively simple—strumming of a chord with a sustained bass note in measures 145–146. Here, he strums with downstrokes and upstrokes like one might do with a pick, except that he's using one or more pick-hand fingers to go through the strings with this motion; this is executed a bit loosely so that he sometimes hits the continuously ringing A in the bass, and sometimes not. You may want to have these fingers generally positioned for fingerstyle playing, that is, slightly curved, roughly perpendicular to the face of the guitar, and turned a little so basically the corner of the nails contact the strings. And indeed, keep them loose enough to go back and forth through the strings without getting jammed up.

This is a common enough guitar technique, even if it's a departure from most of his playing, but the main challenge lies in the chord fingering. It's the same A13sus4 voicing he slides into in measure 177, where it is likely fingered like this:

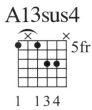

However, that fingering relies on using the separate fingers of the pick hand so as not to sound string 5, on which an unwanted note is fretted due to the barre at fret 5. In measures 145–146 though, string 5 must be muted since we're strumming through all those strings together, even while not using a pick (the low A will remain on string 6, since it is slid into from two frets below). There is no really easy solution; barring with the index would make it very awkward to mute string 5 (or string 4 for that matter, when most of the chord is silenced), and using all the fingers results in a big stretch. A thumb-over-the-neck player could possibly fret the bass note (and mute string 5) that way, but a more likely fingering for the whole chord involves a short barre with the pinky on strings 2 and 3 (with caution to avoid also barring string 1):

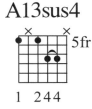

For all the potential technical effort, this is still a bass-and-chord figure that is played with a freewheeling, strumming-in-rhythm kind of feeling. Be careful not to overdo your practice with this unusually tough job for the pinky, but it could be helpful to spend some time with this exercise to get used to the strumming pattern as well as the chord fingering (keep in mind that the middle finger and pinky will have to release their pressure to stop most of the chord for each rest, while the index holds onto the A on string 6):

*Perform downstrokes & upstrokes w/ fingers.

TRICROTISM

By Oscar Pettiford

Tricrotism
Full Song

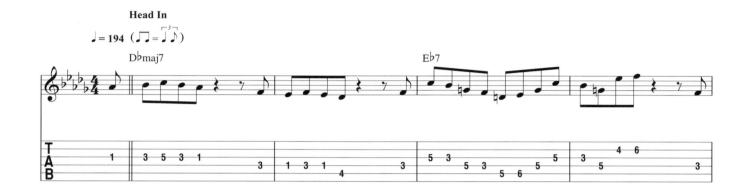

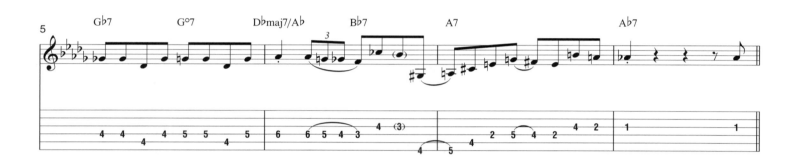

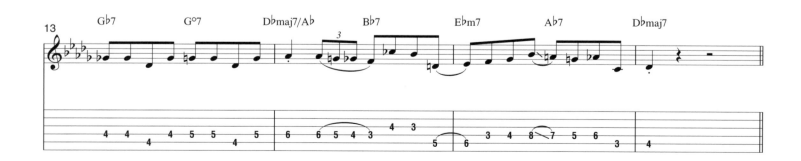

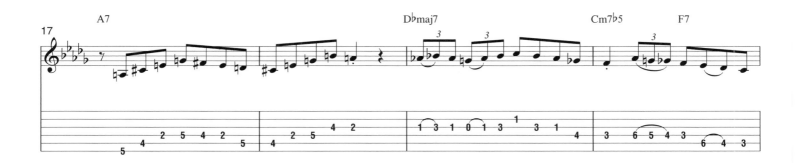

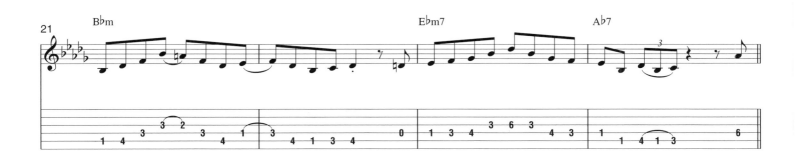

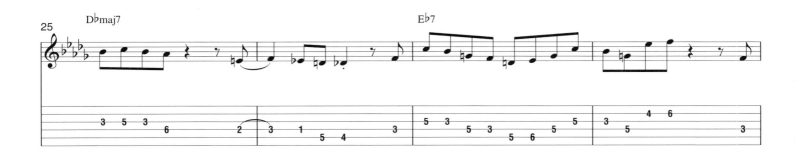

Joint Solo

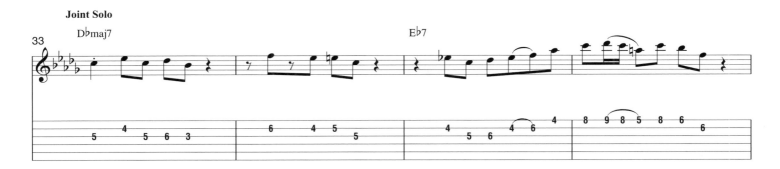

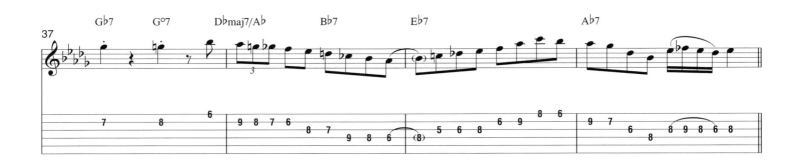

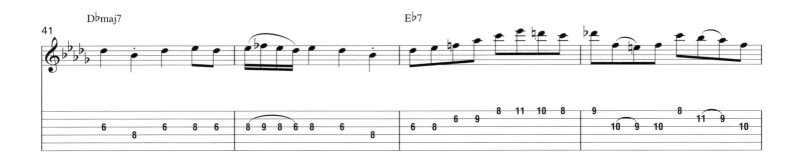

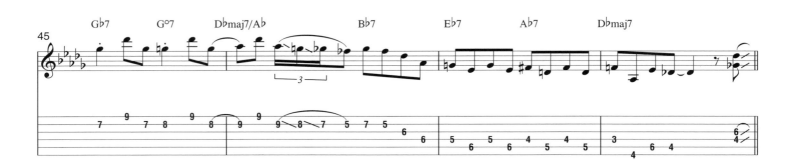

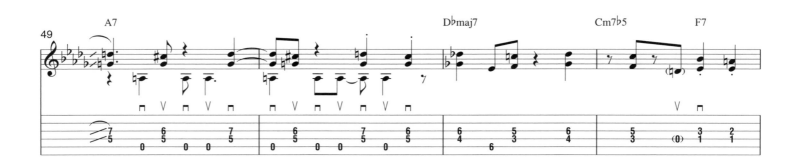

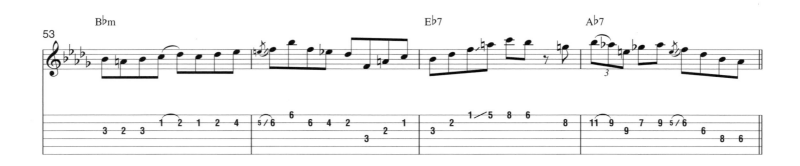

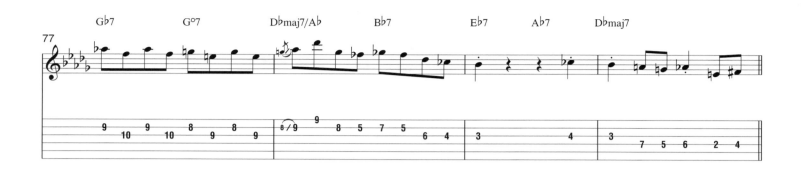

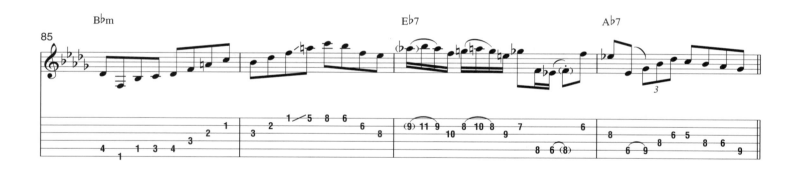

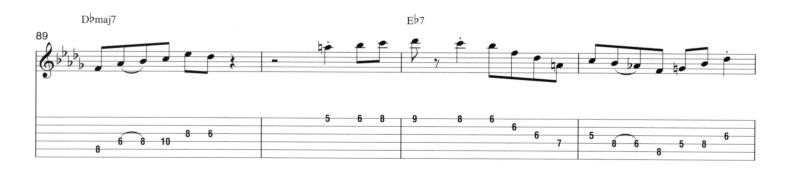

Guitar Solo (2nd Chorus)

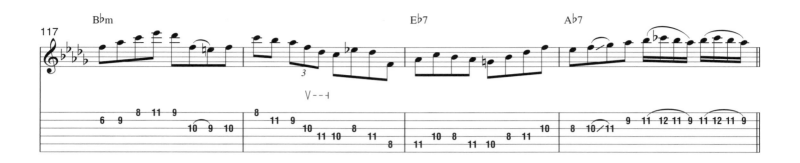

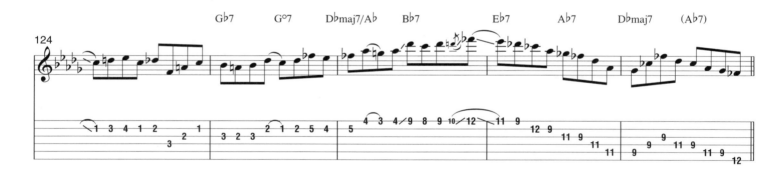

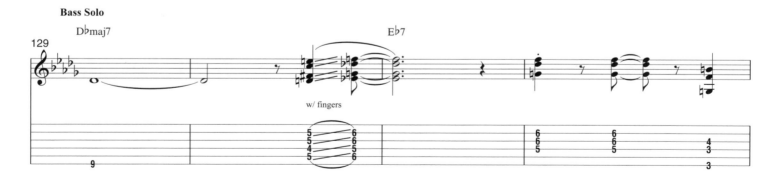

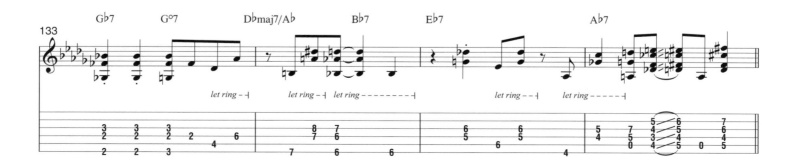

*Pick up/down with thumb.

**Perform downstrokes & upstrokes w/ fingers.

***Played by fret-hand
fingers landing on strings

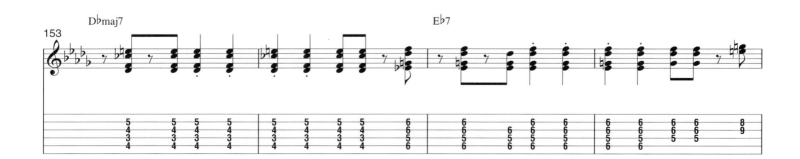

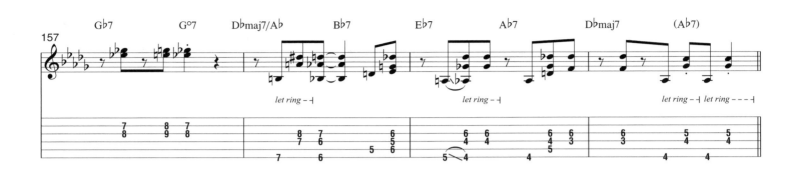

Bass Solo (2nd chorus)

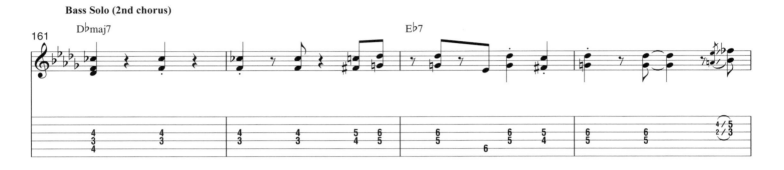

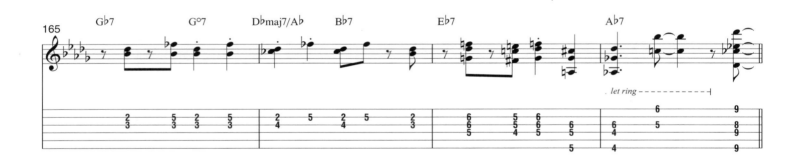

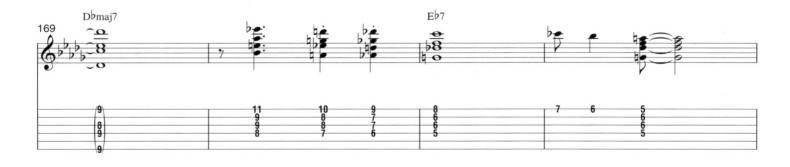

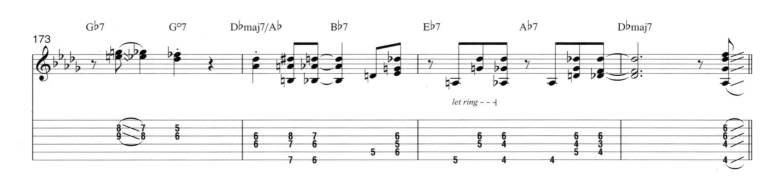

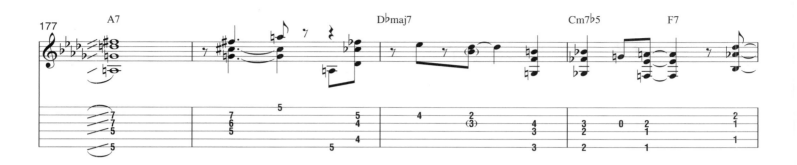

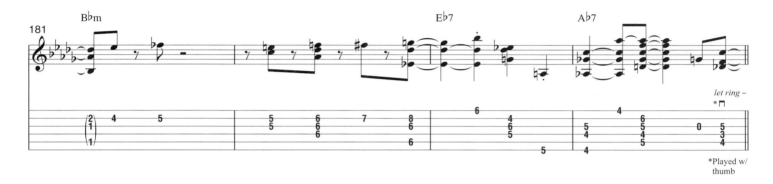

*Played w/ thumb

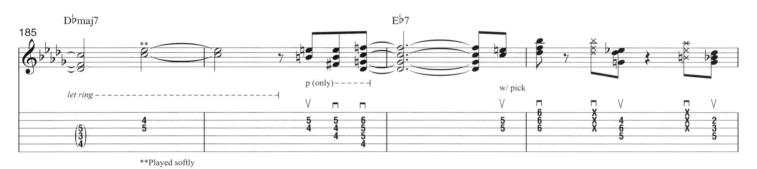

**Played softly

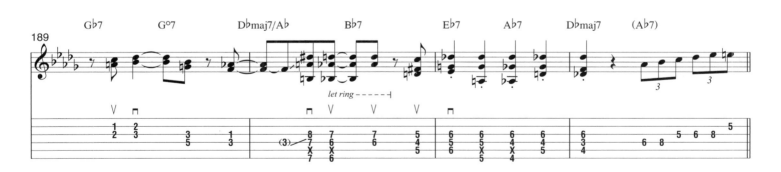

Trading Eights

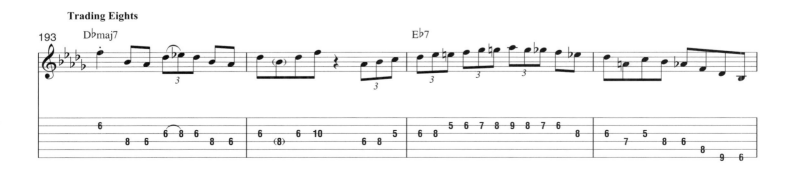

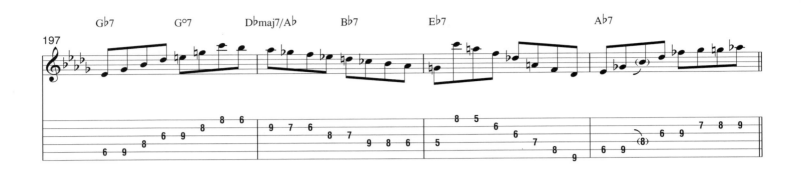

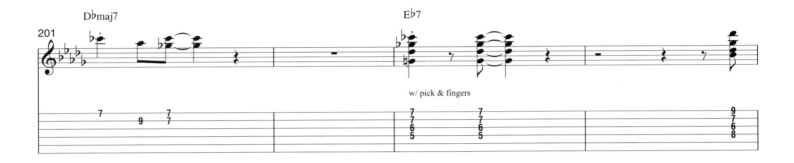

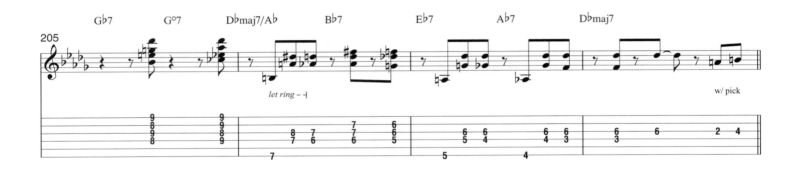

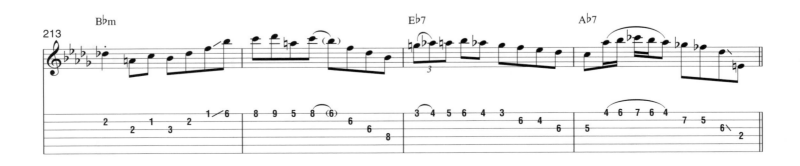

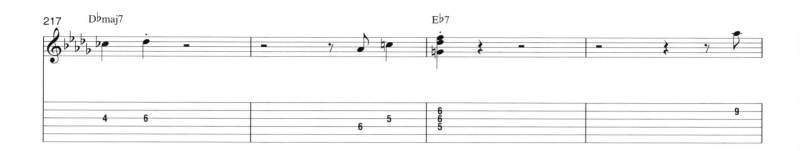

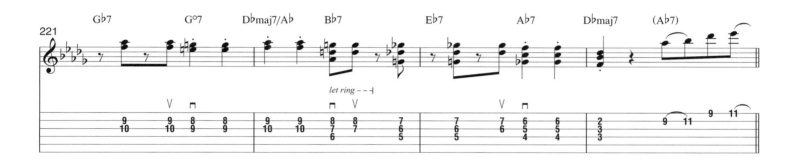

Trading Eights (2nd chorus)

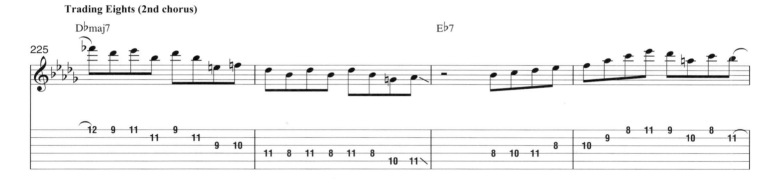

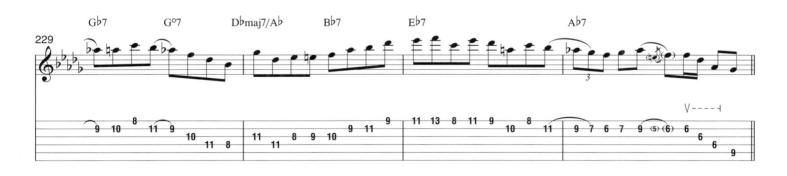

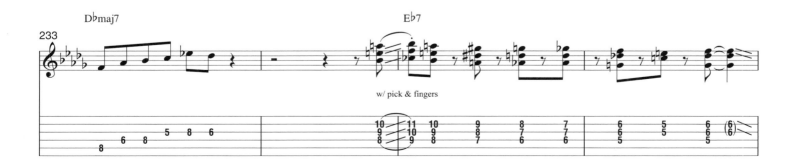

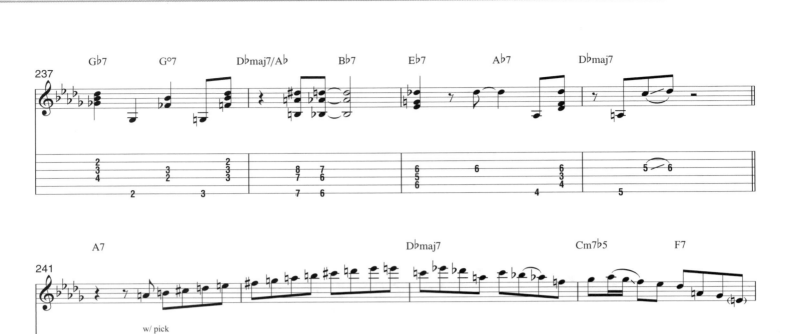

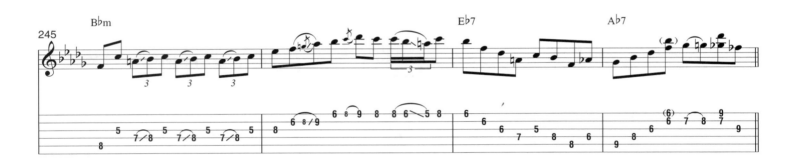

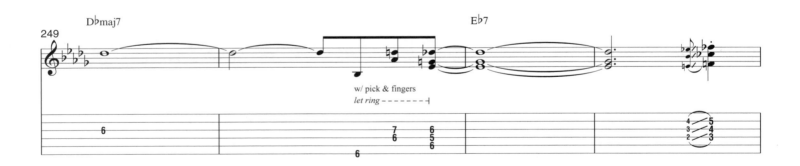

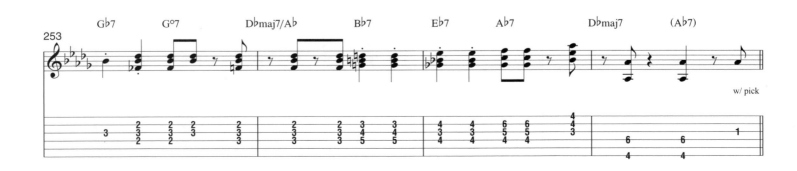

Head Out

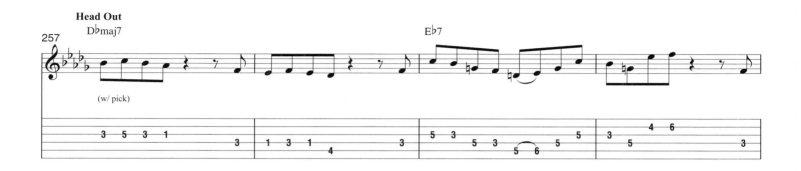

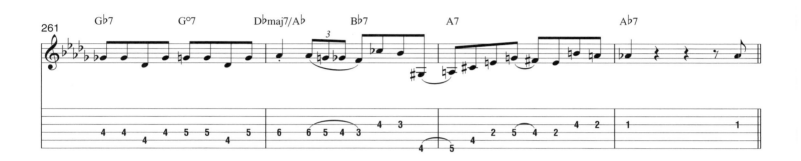

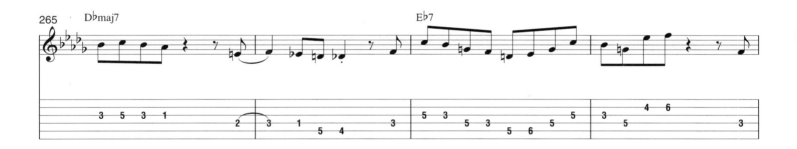

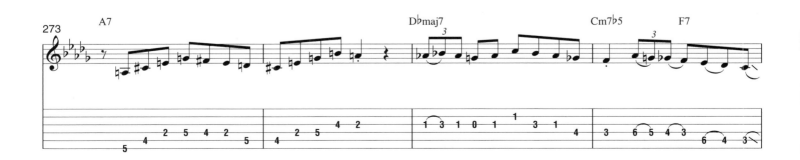

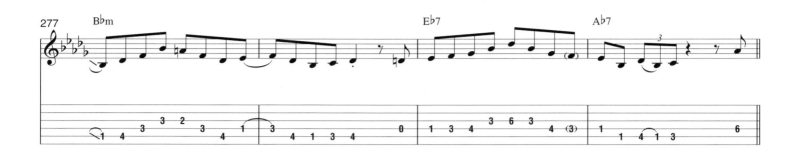

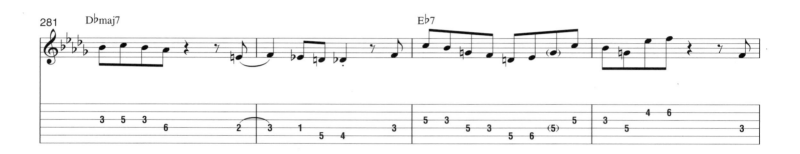

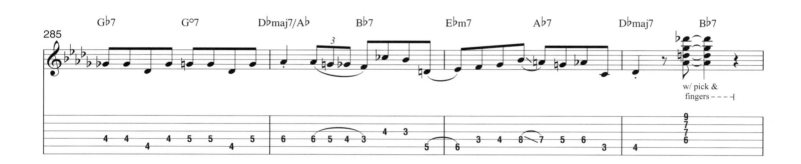

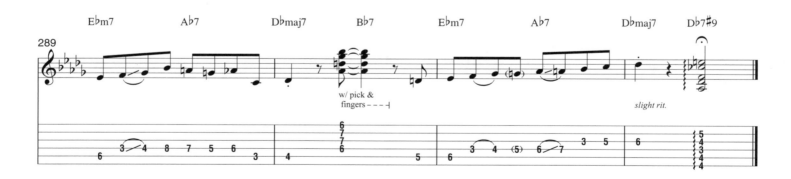

Summertime
From *I Remember Charlie Parker*, 1979

This solo nylon-string version of "Summertime" is a uniquely beautiful piece in the Joe Pass catalog, a stand-alone performance even within the work of this superlative solo artist. It is a compositionally elaborate arrangement of the well-worn standard, occasionally drawing from elements of classical guitar, and essentially meant to be played fingerstyle. Although much of it was surely improvised or left open to the spontaneous interpretation of the moment, there is no real "solo" here between statements of the melody, and relatively little linear improvisation. Rather, it has more of a theme-and-variations format, as he delivers five multi-faceted choruses (five times through the form of the tune), bookended by a lovely introduction and ending. It is also among the most intensely *rubato* of his recordings, as he moves freely in and out of tempo, never settling into swung time for more than eight measures in one shot. Besides creating a huge contrast between the aggressively swingin' and the slow or mysterious, he also gracefully and slickly moves between four different keys, with rich harmonic substitution applied to the original progression.

It should be noted that this is fundamentally a song in 4/4 time, but because of his very free approach to time here slowing down and speeding up, jumping ahead or adding tones between phrases, this rendition will be notated in changing meters (including odd meters) to most closely approximate the rhythms heard. This does not mean that "Summertime" is an odd-metered composition, either generally, or in his conception!

Note also that almost all our preliminary exercises will be presented in steady time, even if they pertain to a rubato section of the full song. That is, the idea will be to practice them in tempo, and that is how they'll be heard in the provided audio (this doesn't preclude odd or changing meters in some of the examples, however).

Joe's Interpretation of the Song

Depending on your familiarity with this ever-enduring classic, it may help to hear it in a very basic, simplified form as a point of reference, in order to better appreciate what Joe has done with it. This brief demo of the song (fundamentally just a 16-bar tune when not played in repetition), shown here in A minor, is reflective of the way in which it is played by many jazz musicians, both in the particular chord progression used, and in its medium swing tempo (as opposed to the original ballad feel):

In several ways though, Joe pays greater tribute to the original Gershwin composition, starting off similarly slow and melancholy, and making reference to a couple of its distinctive elements: a rising two-chord background motif (Am6 to E9 in the key of A minor, as heard in his intro), and an instrumental phrase that appears between halves of the sung melody (paraphrased in measures 32–33 of the transcription, a spot that corresponds to measures 7–8 of the song demo in Example 1). Also, at one point where a minor 7th chord is typically used in the generic jazz version of the progression, as the ii7 of the relative major (the Dm7 in measure 12 of our demo, heading via G7 to Cmaj7), he might plug in a dominant 7th instead, which is more authentic to the original piece (like when he implies G7 instead of Gm7 in measure 40, as the II7 instead of the ii7 of F major, while fundamentally in the key of D minor).

Some of his own recurring devices include the fingerstyle arpeggio patterns of the intro and of measures 13–16, a particular chord sequence for the point in the progression where it resolves to the relative major (as heard from measure 19 to measure 20, beat 1), and a string of quarter-note chords that essentially moves along the circle of 5ths (to wind down the second chorus or kick off the coda). An especially frequent and significant chordal substitution is that of a dominant III7 chord where the minor tonic is expected, as if he had not only gone to the relative major tonic chord instead (the III in a minor key) but also turned it into a dominant 7th, as in measure 13 with C7 chords in place of Am, or measure 35 with F7 sonorities replacing Dm.

And then there are those clever modulations! Where one would normally resolve home to Am as the chorus comes to an end in measure 22, he instead colorfully harmonizes the tonic tone A (the final note in the melody) with an Eb6/9#11 chord, which resolves smoothly to Dm7 for a seamless transition to the key of D minor. The A in the melody is repeated, now as the 5th in the new key and the first note of the melody for the next go-around. At the end of the chord sequence with which this second chorus concludes in measures 42–44, he arrives at Ab7b5 (a tritone substitute for D7), perfectly poised to move into G minor… which he effectively does, though Bb7 is used right away as a dominant III7 sub for the tonic chord Gm. He even makes another key change halfway through the third chorus, quickly moving to a G7 in measure 52, with which he pivots into C minor. We'll detail other modulations yet, which are found in the transition to the fourth chorus (discussed before Example 8) and in the coda (described at the very end of this text).

Introductory Chordal Motif

He begins his performance with an introduction based on the original two-chord background motif, using pretty combinations of fretted and open strings, and a classical-esque arpeggio pattern that involves all the fingers of the pick hand (*c* is added to the *pima* instructions to denote the pinky). The following exercises can help us get down the repeated hand movements needed for this intro figure or the variations of it that briefly occur later in the piece. If you are not yet accustomed to fingerstyle technique altogether, you might benefit from the brief primer found in the "Integral Techniques" section of this book.

For starters, let's try the basic motion in both hands without worrying about muting any strings, but with a change in the movable-shape part of the chords after two measures (as occurs in the actual intro). While generally allowing all the strings to ring freely, we will indeed release the fretted strings to move our fingers up or down two frets during the rests on each beat 1 and 3.

Summertime
Example 2

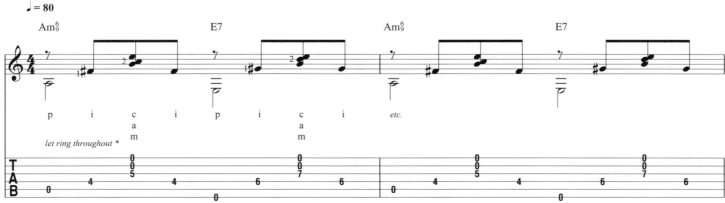

*Fret-hand fingers will move on 8th rests.

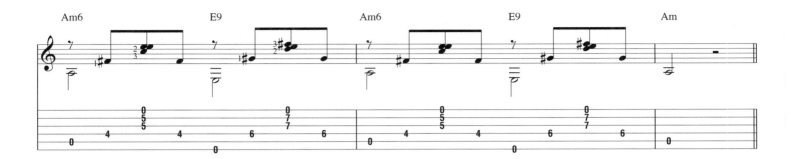

Now for a greater degree of control that will be helpful in playing the intro as it actually appears, we add the muting of each bass note after two beats (making sure they are literally just half notes), as well as the muting of the upper strings on beats 1 and 3. This is easier when it comes to silencing the open string 5, since the thumb is simply allowed to land on it with a rest stroke after plucking the open string 6. Muting string 6 then requires a deft touch with the side of the thumb right as it's about to pluck string 5 again. In order to mute the remaining strings, allow the pick-hand fingers to land on them again at the very moment you play the next bass note with the thumb.

Summertime
Example 3

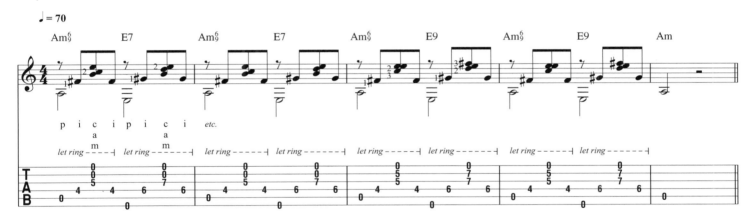

As the pattern continues into the first full measure of the first chorus (measure 5 in the whole piece), the open bass notes are muted after one beat, and a passing tone is added on string 4 between chords. Here the thumb must land right back on string 5 or 6 to silence it right as the fingers pluck strings 1, 2, and 3 each time. The other notes will still be allowed to ring for as long as they can within their half of a measure. Notice that we're now working with only the first of the original movable shapes from within the chords, and realize that it's getting more difficult to avoid a squeak when moving the index finger along string 4 of a classical guitar.

Summertime
Example 4

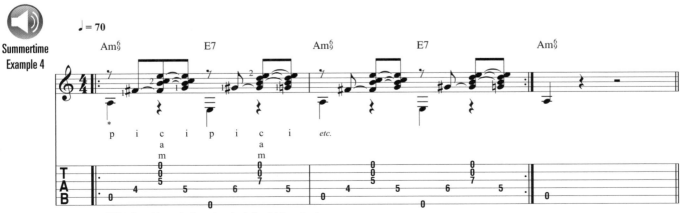

*Mute low strings w/*p* for rests on beats 2 and 4 throughout.

The figure momentarily returns at the top of both the fourth and fifth choruses (measures 64 and 82, respectively) with yet further modifications. In either case, it is played in swung time and with part of the fingerstyle arpeggio pattern reversed, in a way that calls to mind a stride piano rhythm. By the latter instance, the tempo is cookin' (relative to the rest of the piece), only the second of the original fret-hand shapes is used (without open strings this time), and the string 4 passing tone slides into its destination within the next chord. To get the hang of the basic movement here, which involves coordinating the slide-slurs on string 4 with the attack of the bass notes on string 5 or 6, we'll try it more slowly at first, in repetition:

Summertime
Example 5

Other Patterned Motion

Aside from the distinct and prominent intro motif, there are numerous other types of patterned movement throughout the piece that are worth preliminary practice. These may be either more melodic or more chordal in nature, but they often blur the lines between the two.

The melodic climb of measure 70, from the top note of the chord on beat 1 through to the top note at the beginning of the next measure, lies entirely along a diminished scale (with alternating half and whole steps), lending itself to a regular fingering pattern much of the way. The 1–1–3–4 finger sequence that moves upwards from string to string here (from string 2, fret 5 to string 1, fret 10) is indeed part of a classic diminished scale form. This is also a good situation for the steady alternation of *m* and *i* in the pick hand. In the exercise below, note that the change to 2/4 meter for the second measure is not authentic to the full transcription, but rather has just been put in to make this work as a repeating exercise:

Summertime
Example 6

Starting where we just left off, Joe essentially takes the chord shape from the beginning of measure 71 and moves it down in minor 3rds (increments of three frets) along the neck, though he is inconsistent as to whether he plays a three- or four-string voicing. The tones on the top three strings alone, as heard at the outset on beat 1, form a second-inversion major triad, but the full four-string chord is a complex diminished unit (akin to the one detailed in "Stylistic DNA" Example 17 later in this book) in which the note on string 2 is an added tone with regard to a regular diminished 7th chord. The whole pattern, using the whole chord, gives us a series of closely related diminished sonorities whose tones are all pertinent to an altered E7 (though with a natural 13th). To exercise this motion, which involves a single fret-hand shape shifted quickly to different positions, we'll try this chordal sequence both downwards and upwards with just the triads at first, and then with the full four-note shape.

Summertime
Example 7

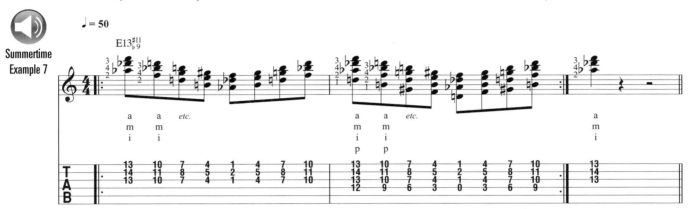

In the brilliant harmonic transition from the third chorus, which ends in C minor, to the top of the fourth chorus in A minor, Joe uses what is at base a simple, steady fingerstyle arpeggio pattern on a dominant 7th chord, alternating between a common three-note voicing (omitting the 5th) and its sus4 version:

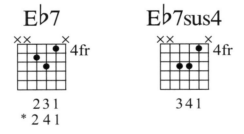

Eb7

231
*241

Eb7sus4

341

*Fingering needed in passage

Measure 60 is the point near the end of the third chorus where the progression would normally come home to the tonic chord Cm, after briefly moving to the relative major Eb two measures earlier. But instead, he arranges a return to Eb here, additionally substituting Eb7 for the usual major chord (another dominant III7 sub for a minor tonic). It seems then like a common half-step-up modulation when he moves to E7 two measures later, but this turns out to be the V7 chord in the new key, resolving to the tonic Am at measure 64. The initial four-8th-note *p–i–p–a* pattern gets metrically turned around when he jumps to the tones of E7 after an odd number of beats, so that the part of the figure that previously fell on beats 2 and 4 now really belongs to beats 1 and 3. To get a feel for both the basic arpeggio pattern of measures 60–63 and the rhythmic/harmonic changeup that happens midway, we'll practice this odd-metered modulation in both directions:

Summertime
Example 8

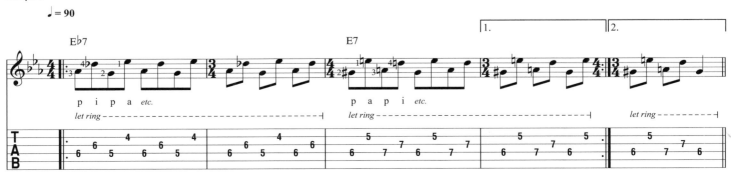

In measure 81, he sets up the climactic fifth chorus, and the fastest in-tempo part of the performance, with a series of downward augmented triad arpeggios that altogether move up by whole steps (before heading back down), all in triplet rhythm. The first and third of these could be considered different inversions of an E augmented triad. These three tones combined with those in the second triad make a complete whole tone scale and also comprise the members of a chord that could be called E9 with both a raised and flatted 5th. (Be aware that some of these notes are spelled enharmonically in order to make the triad shape clear on the page, that is, we see C and not B♯ for the raised 5th, and initially A♭ instead of G♯ for the 3rd.) Thus, this whole-tone pattern altogether suggests a particular version of the V7 chord in A minor, which will indeed once again lead home to the tonic in that key. It is also another instance in which the same basic shape is moved sequentially (and quickly) along the fretboard, and the following drill expands upon this motion for the sake of exercising it through a wider range, from 1st position on up to 9th position and back.

Summertime
Example 9

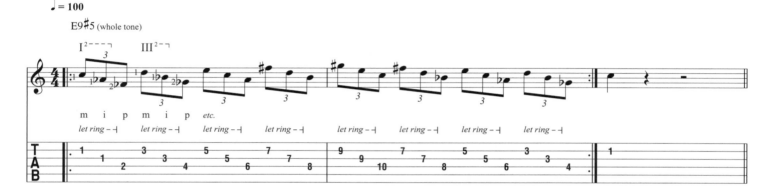

A favorite chord-melody textural pattern in the Joe Pass playbook is one in which full chord voicings on downbeats are each followed by a change of their top note on the upbeat, such that the top notes collectively form a melodic contour. It can be found, among other places, in measure 49, where it is used in conjunction with another of his frequent chordal motifs, that of moving up or down through a series of different voicings for the same basic chord (as explored in "Stylistic DNA" Example 12). In order to try our hand at both types of motion, and be better prepared for that measure in particular, here's an exercise based on its first half. The chordal content is the same as in the transcription, but the time values have been streamlined for our present purpose (with all the chord-note pairs rendered in 8th notes). Notice that each time a new top note is played for an already-sounded chord, it too is a viable chord tone—in these three instances, the 9th, 3rd, and root, respectively, of Cm.

Summertime
Example 10

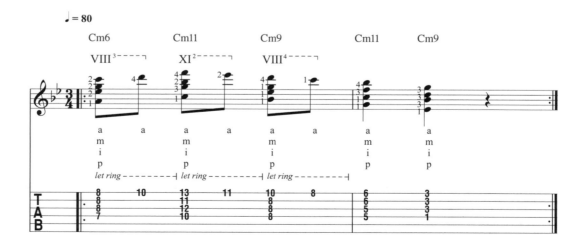

Measure 69 features a very guitaristic rhythmic pattern that Joe often likes to use for a series of chords. In this fundamentally swinging chordal motif, a chord is played on each downbeat, and just one note from within the voicing is echoed on the swung upbeat, quite typically the note on string 4 (a pattern demonstrated in "Stylistic DNA" Example 13). The pick-hand pattern is not too complicated—largely similar to the one in the previous example, except for being applied in swung rhythm and using *i* for the in-between notes—but it's important to have it down well enough so that it flows naturally and we can simply groove with it as we play. Let's try the contents of measure 69 in repetition and at a reduced tempo to get the hang of this pattern, and also to smooth out the fret-hand movement required here. Notice that the chord fingerings involve an index-finger barre that progressively moves down in position along the fretboard while sometimes adjusting slightly to cover different strings (the parenthesized F after the Cm7 results from lifting the ring finger a little early in preparation for the move to F13).

Summertime
Example 11

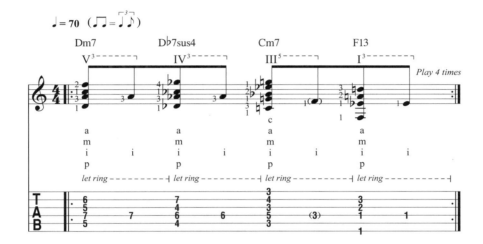

Sustaining Melodic Figures

The need to sometimes sustain one or more notes while others are played in melodic sequence, beyond the bounds of an arpeggiated chord shape, is among the aspects of this piece that are reminiscent of classical guitar repertoire and technique. Doing so often requires extra balance and precision in the fret hand, as the fingers may have to work quite independently of each other without inadvertently touching or releasing the wrong string.

One of the most challenging of these instances occurs at the beginning of measure 40, in the middle of a lengthy, fast phrase that altogether merits some study and preparation. To this end, measures 39–40 are detailed here, almost in their entirety, for specific finger usage. Carefully map out your fingerings and slurring through the first of these measures, making sure to shift down from 5th to 3rd position on the next beat 1 to plant the middle finger on B. The real technical crux of the matter is that this note must then be sustained on string 3 while the other fingers fret and slur the notes above on strings 1 and 2. The last note on string 2 (D) is fretted by the flat of the index finger, such that it can be rolled up onto its tip for the next note on string 3 (B♭) as the middle finger finally lets go from its spot one fret higher.

Summertime
Example 12

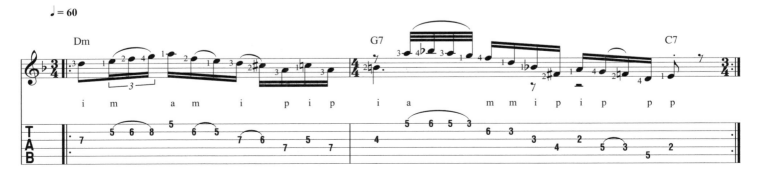

Harmonically, this line beautifully evokes the change from Dm (the tonic chord in this second chorus) to G7, using a classic melodic device from the jazz vocabulary. Notice, towards the end of the first measure here, how the tones on string 3 move chromatically down from D (the root) through C♯ (the major 7th) and C (the minor 7th, implying a Dm7 chord), while bouncing off of a lower A (the 5th), to lead to B (the 3rd of G7) at the beginning of the next measure.

Measure 31 presents two types of this playing-while-sustaining action rolled into one. Let's first isolate the cascading six-note figure from the end of the measure, where the top four strings are allowed to ring together in an additive process. The last note on string 4, the last one on string 3, the open string 1, and a note on string 2 all sustain, as they are played in turn, until they essentially form this chord shape (which by itself is an incomplete E7♭9♭5):

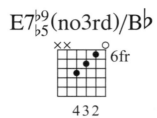

$$E7^{\flat 9}_{\flat 5}(\text{no3rd})/B\flat$$

In order for all these tones to be clearly heard together, the pinky, ring, and then middle fingers have to be accurately set on their tips—as they would be if they were placed all at once to fret that chord shape—and neither they nor the palm of the hand (near the bottom edge of the guitar neck) may touch any of the other strings involved. Here's a drill in 3/4 time to exercise the motion of this segment:

Summertime
Example 13

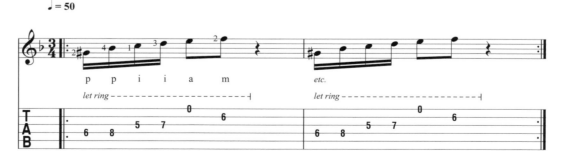

In the actual piece, those stacking notes are played with the open string 6 still ringing in the bass, following a brief chord-melody figure of both sustained and changing tones earlier in the measure. We'll add that part back in for this next exercise (which, like measure 31 itself, is in 5/4 time, though the content has been metrically shifted). Notice that after the initial B♭9 chord, the partial index-finger barre is maintained at the 1st fret, and only strings 1 and 6 are plucked to form E7♭9 together with the sustained strings 2 and 3, while the thumb is allowed to mute string 5. Also, be ready right after this to move the fret hand quickly up to 5th position for the part we already practiced (and note that the resultant chord is now technically in root position, with the open E ringing below).

Summertime
Example 14

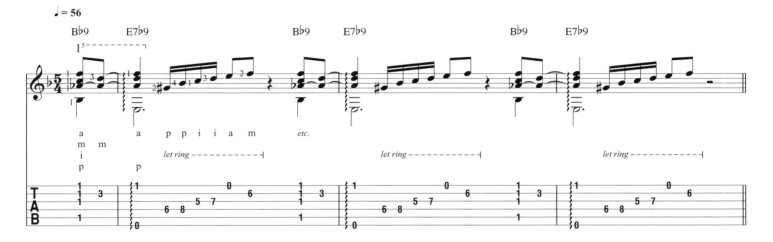

Joe plays a pair of pretty and elegant filler lines in measures 94–95, a poignantly expressive place of quietude within the overall livelier fifth and final chorus. Each of these phrases takes off above a sustained note in the bass for the ascent of a graceful arc, and here we'll take a close-up technical and harmonic look at a slightly abbreviated version of this segment. Leading up to it, he begins at measure 90 to wind down from the quick-paced first half of this chorus (measures 82–89, along with the pickup in measure 81), switching from an old-style swing feel to a more classically derived contrapuntal texture in rubato time. He slows down most pronouncedly at measure 94 as he lands on the melody note A on beat 1. Instead of the tonic chord Am that would normally be heard here (this spot corresponds to the downbeat of measure 11 in our Example 1 demo of the song), he implies a G9sus4, between the G in the bass, the A in the melody, and the tones that follow. This temporarily sets the progression in a new direction, leading to F#m7b5 in the next measure. Notice that by the "and" of 1 in the first phrase, as multiple notes begin to ring over the sustained bass, the fret hand has already assumed the shape of a G9 chord with an open string 2. Even though string 4 is released on beat 3, the A on string 3 is still held while the next two 8th notes are played on string 2. The fingerings indicated towards the end of this measure allow for a smooth transition out of the sustained tones and set us up nicely for the next measure, which begins similarly: the fingers, one by one, forming the shape of an open F#m11 chord (before releasing it on beat 3).

Summertime
Example 15

Big Chord Movement

Several times throughout the arrangement, Joe plays a consecutive series of sizable chord voicings, sometimes arpeggiated and sometimes solid, sometimes as a chord-melody phrase and sometimes not. We'll look in detail here at a select few of these chordal segments, which will give us a good idea of the kind of motion generally needed in their execution, as well as the type of harmonic embellishment they may represent. Notice that many of the specified chord fingerings necessitate a fingerstyle approach, as they involve a barre across unwanted strings (though some of these shapes can be given alternative fingerings for playing with pick or thumb only).

First, let's try the string of chords that runs through measure 103 and the early part of measure 104, at the start of the coda or "outro" to the piece (this is the ending passage he adds on after the final full chorus of the tune). We'll consider the first chord here to be the Dm7 formed by the melodic A on the downbeat of measure 103, plus the tones that sustain from the previous measure. Along the way, two different fingers must lay down a partial barre that will at least once move down a fret from one chord to the next (the index finger for the first three and last two chords, the ring finger for the other two), similarly to what we saw in Example 11. Also be aware that quite a stretch is required for the final F13 shape. Joe plays these chords in an arpeggiated manner, rolling quickly from one pick-hand finger to the next (rather than plucking all the strings at once), but especially spreading out the tones of the F13. We'll practice this sequence in 4/4 time, first without the arpeggiated attack, and then adding it in.

Summertime
Example 16

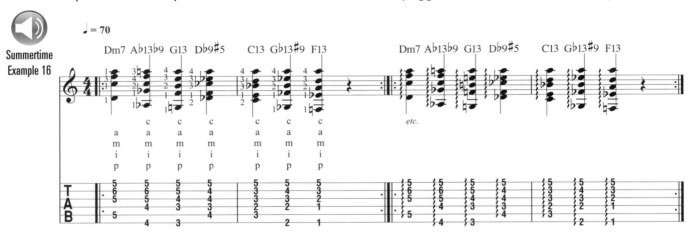

Though a similar chord sequence appears earlier in the arrangement (in measures 42–44), a particular pattern of harmonic movement is demonstrated most clearly in this instance: the chordal roots are moving along the circle of 5ths (down in perfect 5ths or up in perfect 4ths, like from D to G, G to C, etc.), but with a tritone substitute interjected at every step along the way. That is, after the initial minor 7th chord on D, the next chord is a dominant 7th rooted a tritone away (meaning three whole steps away) on Ab, which will resolve down a half step to a variant of G7. Likewise, this is followed by its tritone sub Db7, which then moves down by half step to C7, etc. This typically makes most sense with dominant 7th chords, which almost all of these are. Clearly, different versions of this basic chord type are being used, in large part for the purpose of harmonizing a single note that is kept on top of all the voicings (the A on string 1, fret 5).

The chord-melody phrase of measures 23–26 involves another such row of chords, nearly the same as those we just looked at in measures 103–104, though here they are mostly played in a more pronounced, classical-inspired pattern of arpeggiation (with the tones rendered as 16th notes or in 8th-note triplets). Also, we can see in this case how he has used them as substitutions within the progression of the song. This is the first phrase of the second chorus, in the new key of D minor. But where the tonic chord Dm would normally return for the last two notes, the harmonic pattern has instead led to F13 and Bbmaj7 (the relative major tonic chord turned into a dominant 7th, followed by its IV chord). Before trying a segment of this kind of texture with its actual rhythm, it can be helpful to focus on one's fret-hand movements first, as we'll do in the exercise below (for which the meters shown in the transcription have been simplified). Here too, an index-finger barre will progressively move down the fretboard from chord to chord, but we should take particular care as of the pickup note to the F13; it should be fretted with the underside of the index, close to its base, due to the lower-string barre needed in both the preceding chord and the upcoming F13 shape (see photo). To move smoothly into the partial Bbmaj7

voicing, maintain the barre but let the pick-hand thumb mute string 6 (alternatively, you could efficiently release the barre to place the index on its tip on string 5, fret 1). Notice that, in either this or the previous example, the use of the ring finger in fretting the initial Dm7 (where either the middle finger or pinky would normally come into play) is due to the way the fret hand would be situated in the process of playing the whole piece.

Summertime
Example 17

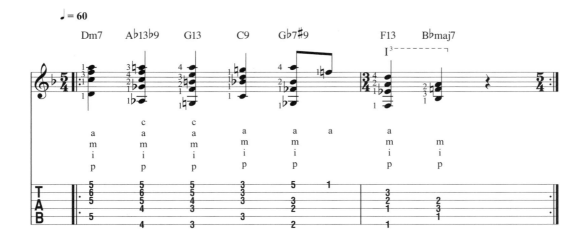

Finally, let's try our hand at the sort of arpeggio pattern found in measures 13–15, which involves sounding the top and bottom notes of a chord on a downbeat and then sustaining them while the other tones are plucked one by one. We'll do this using a simplified version of the material in this segment (including its pickup), so we can get the hang of these chord movements as well as the fingerstyle pattern, and be better prepared for this and other similar parts of the piece. To navigate this tricky sequence, carefully observe the fingering, barring, "let ring," and *pima* indications shown here:

Summertime
Example 18

Bass/Melody/Chords Together

In addition to the figures that challenge us in the ways we just explored are some more contrapuntal moments within the piece, where a melodic phrase is played against a bass line, or where the whole texture becomes a jumble of bass notes, melodic fragments, and brief chords. Here we'll work through a few such spots that nicely illustrate the technical demands typically involved.

The following double exercise combines paraphrased material from measures 66–67 and measures 92–93, to give us a taste of Joe's basic bass-melody motion (albeit with a couple of chords thrown in) as it appears in this arrangement. Keep in mind that while you don't need to barre with the index finger for the initial E7♯9 chord, you should be prepared to lay it across the strings immediately afterwards to fret the next note with its underside. The real switch of hand and finger position occurs on the next beat, where the index jumps down to string 6, fret 4. Similarly, in the next repeated sample, the main change of position is on beat 2, where, in this case, the ring finger quickly stretches to reach string 6, fret 4.

Measures 84–85 are mostly filler material following the first phrase of the song as it appears in the fifth chorus. After landing on beat 1 with a momentary power chord (the tonic [A] doubled at the octave with the 5th [E] in between), he lets the open A continue ringing in the bass and spins off into a blues-flavored line higher up. The tones of this phrase are soon harmonized, in chord-melody fashion, with dominant 7th chords (all in the same three-note voicing with the chordal 3rd on top). These twice lead by half-step motion to an A7, which is in both cases sustained while a higher tonic A is played above. The fingerings required to manage this flurry of activity are detailed below; notice, in particular, the efficiency with which the pinky must get to the A on beat 2 and slide up from there, and the use of *three different fingerings* for the same three-string chord shape as it moves around, in order to make this work out smoothly:

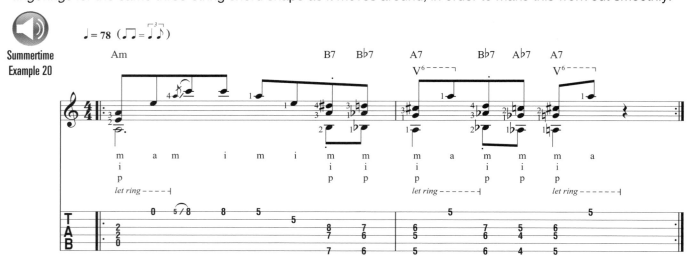

The second half of the second chorus begins in a jagged, irregular 8th-note rhythm of melodic tones interspersed with bass notes and midrange double stops, running from measure 35 (including its pickup notes) up to measure 38. In the following exercise, we'll focus on this segment (with slight modification of meter), both to get used to how it feels rhythmically and to practice the movements needed in jumping between parts. Be aware that the last pickup note (F) should be fretted with the underside of the index finger, positioned almost as if it were about to barre fret 1, so that it is ready to seamlessly move up onto its tip for the low F that follows on string 6 (the higher F will be played twice more in this sequence, in one case with similar technique and in the other with an actual barre).

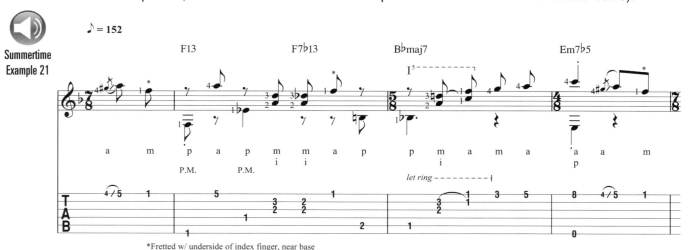

*Fretted w/ underside of index finger, near base

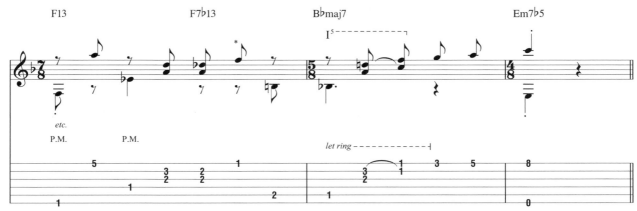

*Fretted w/ underside of index finger, near base

After briefly alluding to the intro motif at the top of the fourth chorus in measure 64, Joe continues the newly established stride piano–like rhythm with another mix of melody, bass, and chords. Our next exercise serves to solidify the technical elements from the end of measure 64 through the first half of measure 66, such that we can more easily relax and settle into the stride groove (which is evoked especially in measure 65, with the clear alternation of bass notes on beats 1 and 3 and midrange accents on beats 2 and 4). Take care not to overly articulate the initial hammer-on in the pickup (with the index finger), as this glissando figure should feel like a continuous slide up from the open low E. Also, as the index frets string 4 to begin the triplet at the end of our first full measure here, have the other fingers ready to quickly get into place for the whole E7♯9♯5 shape.

Summertime
Example 22

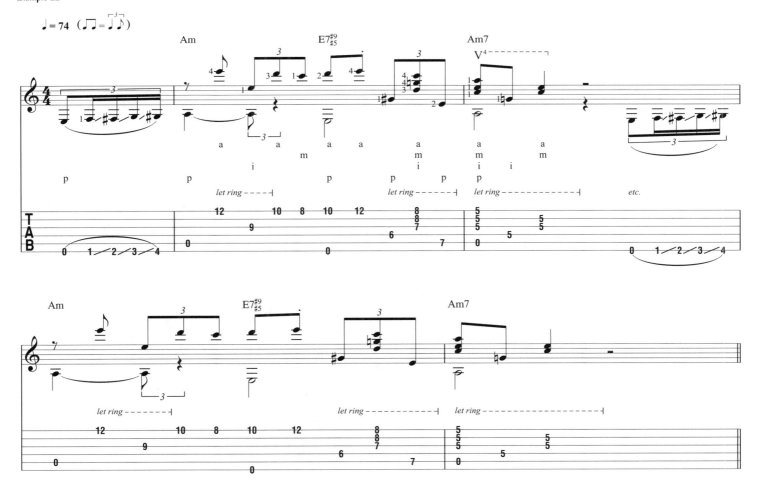

Tricky Melodic Movement Towards End

Right after the dramatic series of arpeggiated chords that usher in the coda comes a pair of blazing, sweeping lines (in measures 104–109) that we would do well to break down for close-up study, and our next three examples help to do just that.

The first of these dense, arching phrases, from the middle of measure 104 through measure 105, is perhaps the most technically demanding part of the whole piece when played up to speed. But keep in mind that Joe's own execution of it, in the heat of performance, isn't entirely clean. Besides a couple of unintended notes being sounded by an inadvertent pull-off or hammer-on (not shown in the transcription), a couple of notes that are actually part of the line are missed by the pick hand and heard only from the fret-hand fingers landing on the strings. Work through this segment carefully and slowly at first with the fingerings and *pima* suggestions given, being prepared to jump up and back down between fretboard positions along string 1 (following the locations of the index finger) and to reach up the neck slightly with the pinky for its note on string 6. Also be aware: the first note here is shown as coming in at the second 16th-note position in the beat, in keeping with how it appears in beat 2 of the 3/4 measure in the transcription, but it is really felt as a downbeat when played in context of the passage in free time.

Summertime
Example 23

Harmonically, the line plays on the close relationship between Cm and F7. It starts off ascending straight through the five tones of Cm(maj9) (which fit right in with the sound of the F13 that was just played) and then repeats this arpeggio an octave higher. After descending largely through tones of Cm(maj7), we come to rest momentarily on a low B—which, though it could be considered the major 7th of our Cm chord (or the sharp 11th with regard to F7), is actually suggestive here of B7#9#5 (which can be a tritone substitute for F7, and which sets up some expectation of movement towards an E chord of some kind).

It is with the phrase that immediately follows, however, that Joe seems to take a bigger harmonic turn, implying Fmaj7 through the wide arc of the next three measures. We'll look first at the initial rapid ascent (measure 106, plus the next two notes), which here again involves an arpeggio repeated at the octave, this time Fmaj9 (starting off with the 7th tone leading up into the root). And again, it is only with a little imperfection that he himself manages the line when going for it at full steam—the fifth note is really felt more than heard, since it is fretted but accidentally not plucked. Practice your fingerings carefully for this segment as well, and be ready to roll the ring finger onto string 2 after its slide up to fret 10

on string 3. Also be aware that to reach high enough on the fretboard on a standard classical guitar (which has no cutaway), the hand needs to turn to let the fingers point in a more up-the-neck direction as it jumps up for these last two notes (which is why the ring finger is indicated instead of the pinky for the last of these notes).

Summertime
Example 24

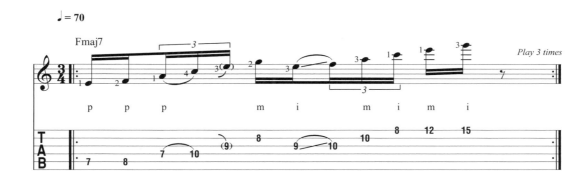

Finally, he makes a grand descent, in measures 107–109, from the entire performance's high point of pitch, speed, and energy, down through the whole range of the instrument to its lowest note, with a dramatic slowdown along the way. The mechanics of this run are detailed below, starting with the final two notes from our previous example. In the provided audio demonstration, it is played rubato rather than in steady time, though a count-off is given to get started; the big ritard is very much part of the point here, and after some review of our fingerings, we should include it in our practice of the line (the 16th notes towards the end will have much longer actual durations than those at the beginning). Except for the jump down to fret 9 for the fourth note, all the substantial position changes are taken care of by a downwards slide or slide-slur with the index finger, as you can see from the fingerings shown.

Summertime
Example 25

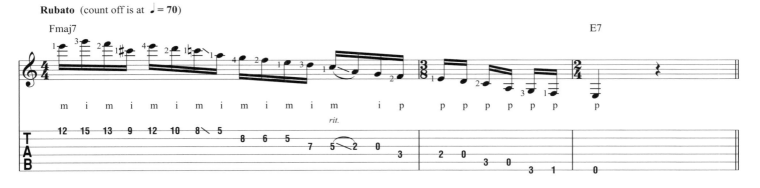

The sustained low E on which he lands (on the downbeat of measure 109) gives the impression of another tension waiting to resolve—it really implies the V chord of A minor (E7), thus setting up a return to the original key, and the conclusion of the piece. A brilliant feature of this coda is that it is essentially a reprise of the first phrase of the melody, divided into two parts that are separated by a half-dozen measures of chords and lines… and that are in two different keys! The two pickup notes to measure 103, plus the A on beat 1, seem to begin the melody anew in D minor, but when the phrase truly recommences with the upper-range notes of measure 109, after all the in-between material, we are back in A minor.

SUMMERTIME

from PORGY AND BESS®

Music and Lyrics by George Gershwin, DuBose and Dorothy Heyward and Ira Gershwin

Intro
Rubato (starts off at ♩ = 75)

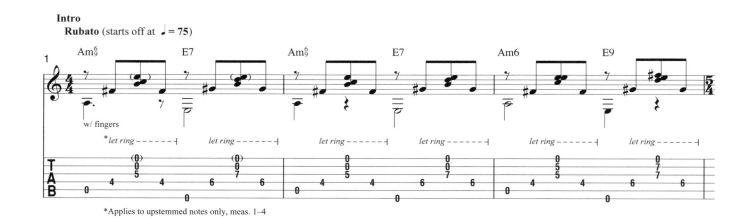

*Applies to upstemmed notes only, meas. 1–4

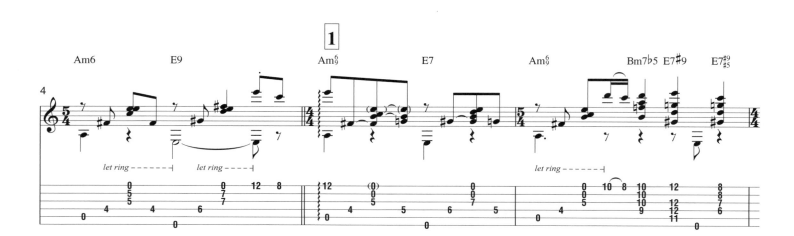

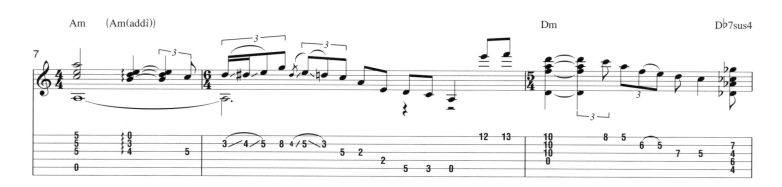

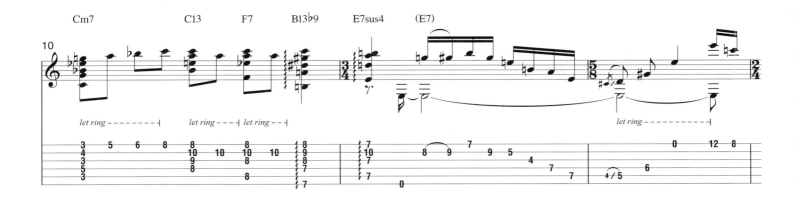

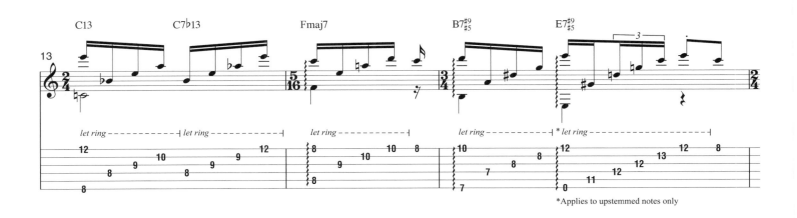

*Applies to upstemmed notes only

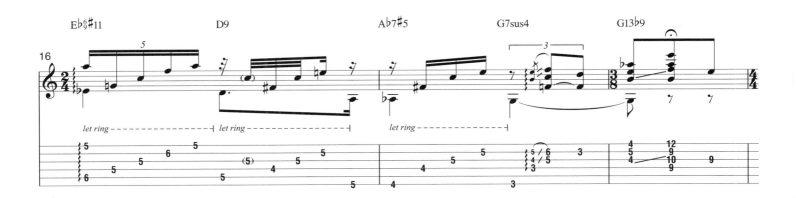

2

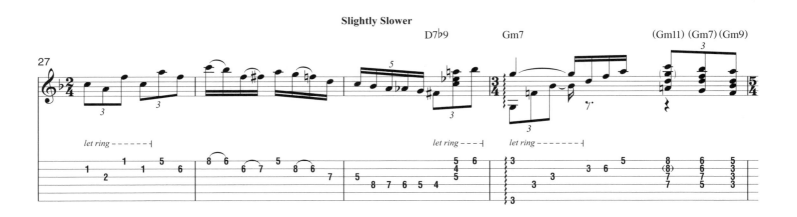

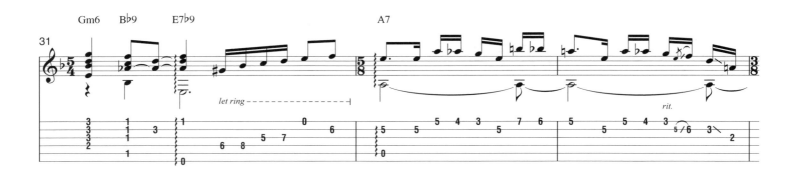

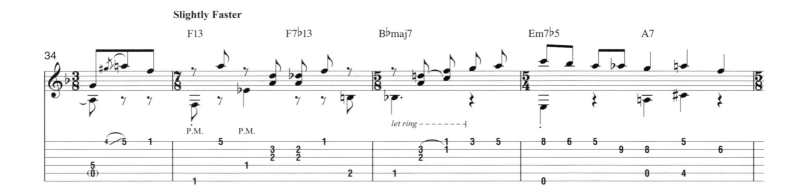

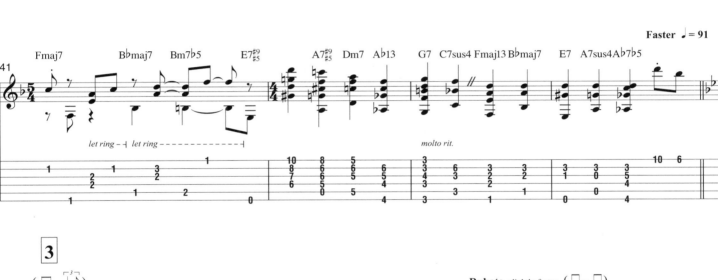

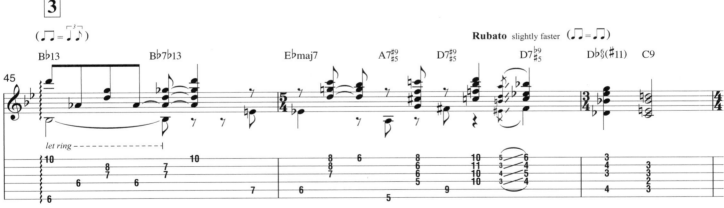

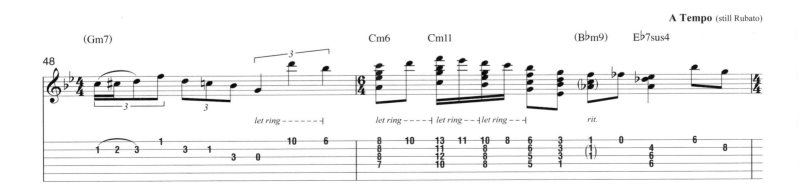

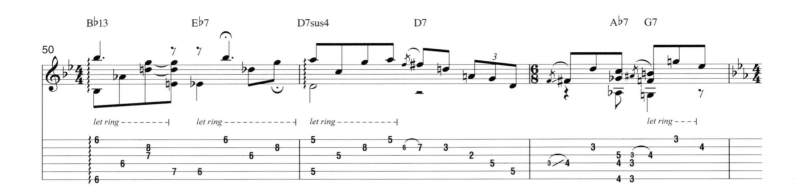

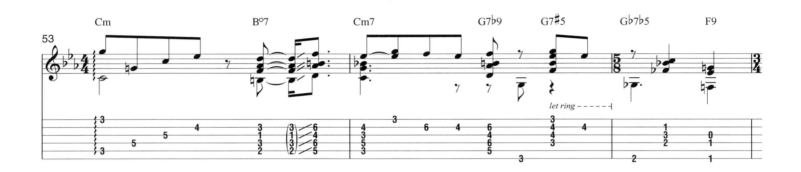

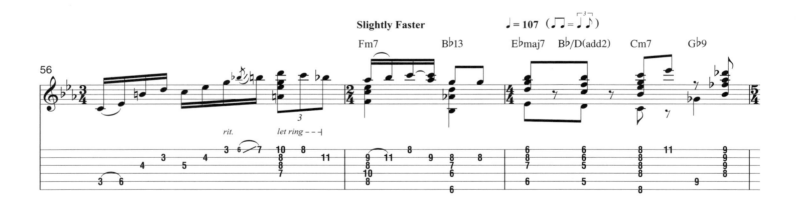

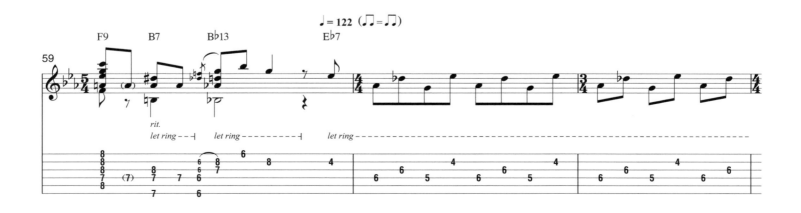

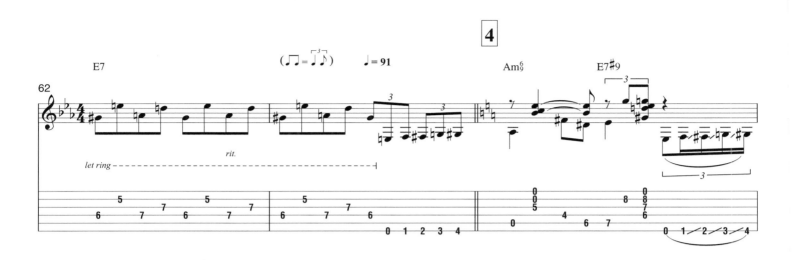

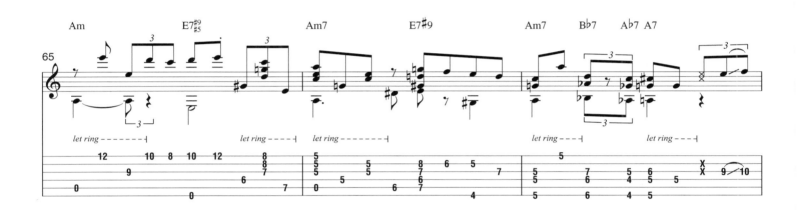

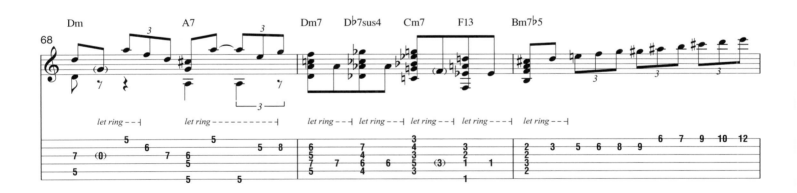

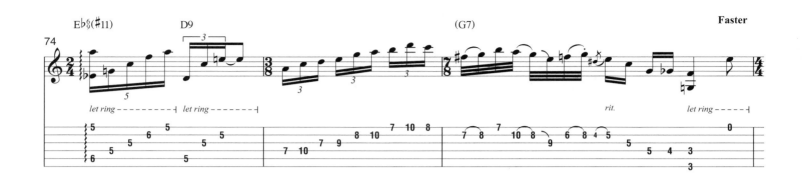

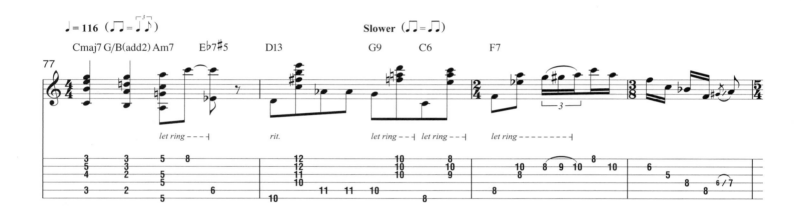

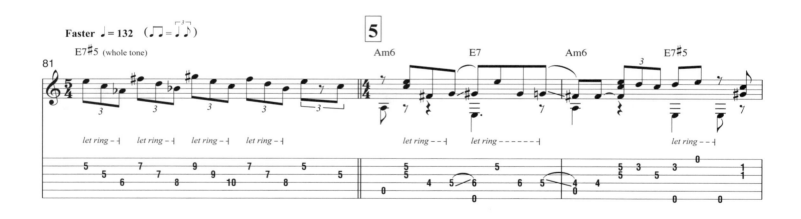

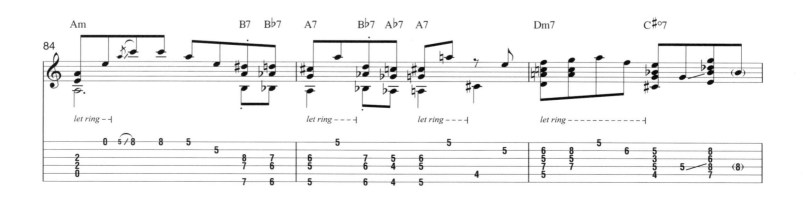

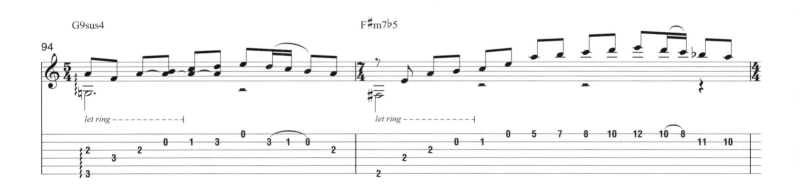

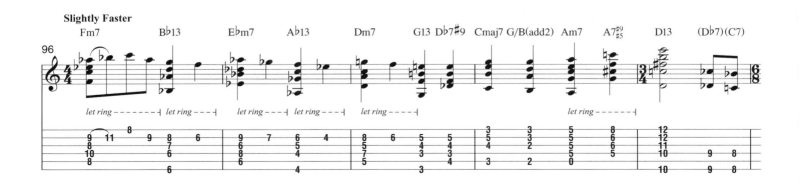

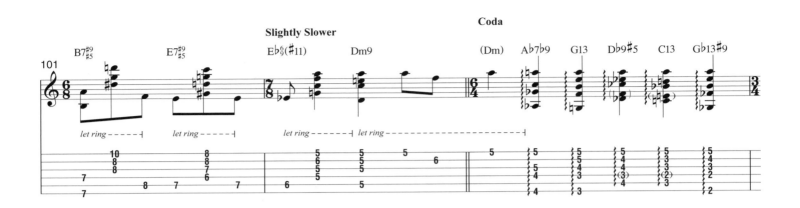

ESSENTIAL LICKS

Here we take a focused, hands-on look at the kind of musical phrases and gestures that typify Joe's improvisational style and approach!

Bop Vocabulary

The language of bebop, the style of jazz pioneered in the 1940s by figures such as alto saxophonist Charlie Parker and trumpeter Dizzy Gillespie, is an integral part of Joe's own musical identity. He absorbed it in part through firsthand contact with the New York scene of that time, hearing these and other musical heroes up close. To this day, it pervades much of the jazz world, and legions of players still internalize it through studying the songs and solos of the greats. Generally based around complex 8th-note lines that very specifically address the chord changes, bop encompasses some common phrases and devices that can be heard in the playing of most of its practitioners, each using them in their own individual way. Following are some of the ways this is manifested in the work of Joe Pass.

Here's a classic example of a bop-style line played on a minor ii–V–i chord sequence (shown here in A minor), a common part of many harmonic progressions. This phrase starts out with stepwise motion down a B Locrian scale (suitable for the Bm7♭5 chord), and proceeds through arpeggiated tones of the E7♭9 chord before concluding with a rough outline of the tonic chord Am. Each new chord is introduced with a typical movement into its 3rd tone, from the 7th of the preceding chord.

Lick 1

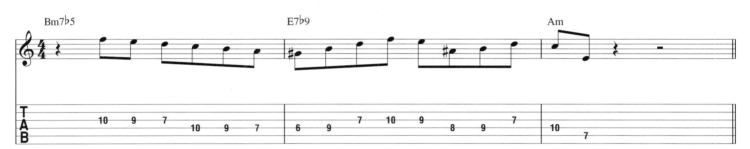

A very common harmonic and melodic device found in bop—and in music generally, from classical to rock to Afro-Cuban—is a short chromatic descent from the root of a minor chord, which has the effect of implying different types of minor harmony along the way (if not different chords altogether). The descending tones may be bounced off of other chord tones in between, as in the following lick, where the essential movement is actually traced by the notes on beats 1 and 3 of each of the first two full measures. Within Joe's linear playing, this timeless musical idea might very well appear in this way. Keep in mind, as you try the lick you'll want to roll with the index finger, from its underside to its tip, through the consecutive notes at fret 8:

Lick 2

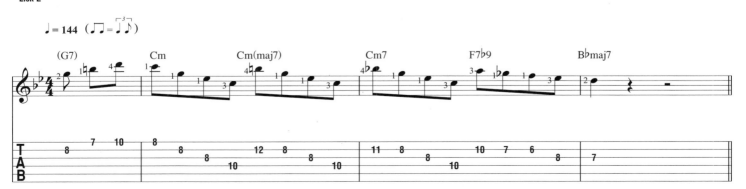

Next, we have a line that moves through an elongated version of what we could call *turnaround changes*, typically a I–VI–ii–V sequence that resolves back to I (the tonic chord), but varied here with the iii chord (Em7) preceding the VI chord (A7), and a dominant 7th used in place of the usual minor ii (D7 instead of Dm7). It exemplifies Joe's way of keeping a line going and going with a strong melodic flow, and as in Lick 1, each chord change is marked by a movement into the new chordal 3rd (usually from the previous chordal 7th). Twice in the third measure we'll need to roll off the tip of a finger to fret the next note at the same fret (with the middle finger at fret 5, and the pinky at fret 7), and as this measure moves to the next, we'll want to use the middle finger twice in a row on string 3 to be in the right position.

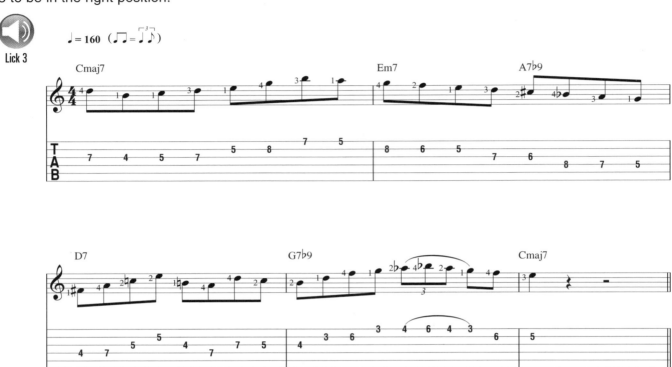

A common rhythmic variation amid the prevalent 8th notes of bop is the mixing of 8th-note triplets into a line, and this is characteristic especially of Joe's playing. Within the following phrase on a ii–V–I in F, we get a taste of this rhythmic habit of his, as well as some further examples of how he might move melodically through chord changes. The line involves a mix of arpeggiated and scalar motion, the *chromatic enclosure* of the 3rd of C7 (the E on beat 1 of the second measure being immediately preceded by the tones a half step above and below it), and further chromatic movement in the descent by half steps from the high Eb on beat 3 of the second measure (effectively a descent from the #9 tone down to the root of C7). Try also slurring that chromatic descent, with a multiple pull-off from fret 11 down to fret 8, for another variant of the interspersed-triplet effect.

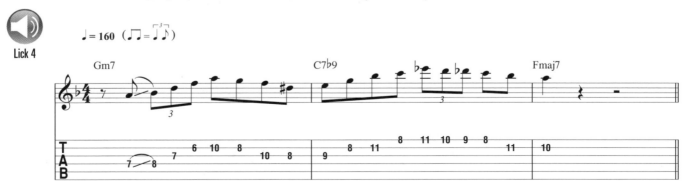

Blues Licks

Another fundamental aspect of Joe's style (as well as that of many a soulful jazz musician) is the blues element, which he injects plentifully into his playing, whether or not it's on a blues-related tune in particular.

This next characteristic line combines a greasy slurred entrance (one that imposes a minor sound on a dominant 7th setting), a bold descent through C blues scale tones across the fretboard, and a couple of typical gutbucket double stops on strings 2 and 3 (resulting in the brief inclusion of the major 6th note [A] on string 2, fret 10):

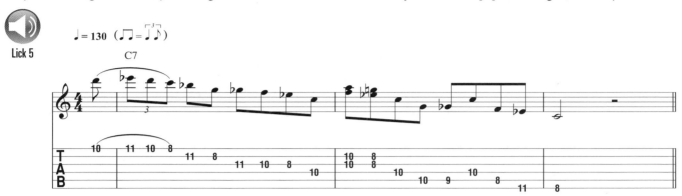

Joe often ventures to the twangier side, especially with repetitive motifs like the one in this next lick (which could potentially be played at the beginning of a 12-bar blues in B♭). Notice that the tone material here involves all the notes of the B♭ blues scale, but with the 2nd and 6th tones of B♭ major thrown in (appearing on fret 8 of strings 1 and 2, respectively). Alternate picking works best for the repeating pattern, with downstrokes on downbeats and upstrokes on upbeats, and to get it going this way, it's helpful to start the whole lick with an upstroke (on the very first note in the pickup).

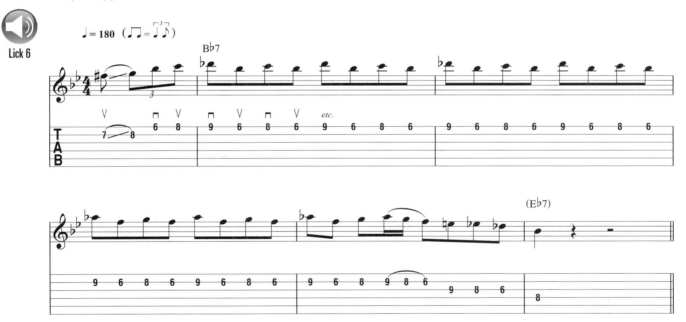

Though a blues flavor is often evoked in part by the imposition of certain minor tones in a major context (especially the minor 3rd and minor 7th), Joe is a master of bringing forth the blues while actually playing in a minor key, often in a *pretty* sort of way, as in the lick below. The use of the flatted 5th tone here (the A♭ on string 2, fret 9) contributes to the blues effect (as it also would in a major key) but so do the more subtle elements of phrasing and articulation.

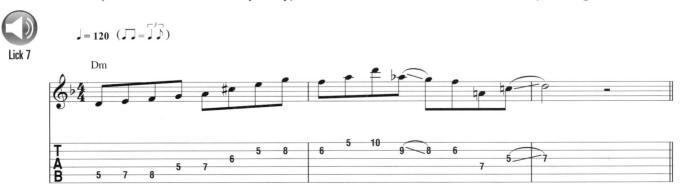

Beyond 4/4 Swing

The majority of the material covered in this book (like the majority of Joe's recorded work) is in 4/4 time, with a swinging rhythm. And indeed, even when he plays in 3/4 time, or with an even-8ths feel, many of the same principles apply to his approach. But it's worth looking at some examples of how he might adapt his improvisation for these different situations.

The following line, for instance, could for the most part be played with a swung-8ths feel on a swing tune. But it lends itself especially well to being delivered with even 8ths, and with the kind of relaxed feel that is suited to a gentle bossa nova setting. Also, it includes a couple of double stops of the sort that Joe might throw in for decoration on such a tune (in 3rd intervals, this time sounding pretty rather than bluesy or aggressive). The degree and manner of slurring here is also typical of his bossa approach, especially with the graceful multiple pull-off at the peak of the line in the fourth measure. This is another example, by the way, of continuous playing à la Joe on elongated turnaround changes, like in Lick 3 (except it's in the key of G). Of particular harmonic interest are the four notes in the last half of the fourth measure (especially the G on beat 3), which bring out the sound of Cm while in official D7♭9 territory, to lovely effect (the minor iv imposed on the V7, arguably turning it into D7♭9sus4).

Swinging in 3/4 time, as opposed to the more common 4/4, can certainly affect the shape of a line (or shapes within it), and our next lick shows how Joe might accentuate the waltz meter with a three-beat-long motif that is repeated every measure (with some variation), always starting on beat 1. Once again, we have a line on a turnaround progression, back in the key of C this time:

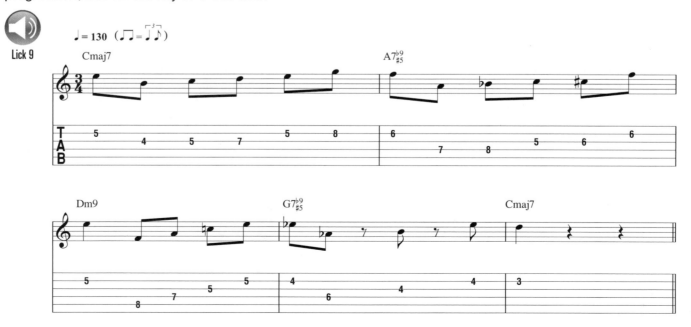

In the following line—another one in 3/4 time over turnaround chords in C—the motivic emphasis is on a descending arpeggio or scalar shape, whether or not it begins on beat 1, for almost every chord (and measure). Twice for these arpeggiated segments, we'll need to roll from the underside to the tip of the index finger to descend through three notes in a row at the same fret.

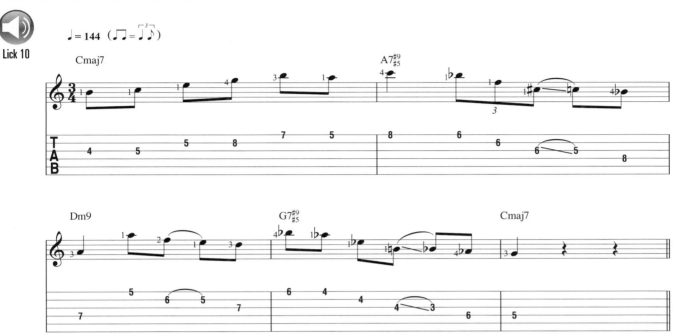

Intervallic Licks

We've already heard a couple of licks where Joe interjects double-stop 3rds into a mostly single-note line, but he may similarly mix in other harmonic intervals (in which the two notes are played together), or use a linear motif based on a single kind of *melodic interval* (meaning the two notes are played in succession).

A special case is the involvement of octaves, since a note doubled at the octave really just gives us the same note in different ranges rather than any harmonization, per se. But as in the work of Wes Montgomery, Django Reinhardt, and others, lines played in octaves do have a particular kind of thicker sound. And Joe has his own way of lapsing in and out of octave-doubled notes midstream, for variety of texture, as in this next lick. The line itself is one that works for the beginning of a 12-bar blues in C, and we could play it with either a pick, the fingers, or hybrid technique (keeping in mind that if using a pick alone, we have to make sure to mute string 2 while hitting those octaves in the third measure). For further textural variation, the whole thing wraps up with a couple of triads, landing in a way that suggests an F9 chord.

The following lick, also suited to the beginning of a C blues, makes use of both melodic and harmonic 6th intervals. It begins with a series of falling 6ths, both major and minor, moving down through a C dominant scale. As we hit the second measure, they become harmonic 6ths, with tones that initially fit F7, before a blues-tinged return to C7. These double stops are on non-neighboring strings, and probably best played fingerstyle (here again, if using pick-only or thumb-only technique, take care to mute the in-between string).

Lick 12

The intervallic licks we've heard so far—and for that matter, all of the licks we've heard so far—have been of a very harmonically straightforward nature, clearly relating to the specific chords of a progression and/or bringing out the sound of the blues in a given key. And this is fitting for Joe Pass, very much an "inside" player who showed great freedom and creativity in his improvisation without going in an avant-garde, "free jazz" direction. Once in a while, however, he'd play something that would strike the ears as "outside," departing from tones or phrases that entirely seemed to belong with the chord or key at hand. And he would generally do this by way of an *intervallic pattern*, like the one that runs through most of the lick below, which involves a series of rising perfect 4ths altogether going down in whole steps. Most of the tones here could actually be part of some kind of Bb7 chord (all but the A♮ on string 4, fret 7), but as the pattern progresses through the first measure, the overall effect is one of moving away from the originally implied harmony, until the phrase reaches a bluesy ending in the second measure that speaks much more plainly again of Bb7. The suggested fingerings will help to navigate this somewhat twisty lick—keep in mind, you'll often need to roll with a finger between two strings (from tip to underside, or vice versa).

Lick 13

It should be noted that such an intervallic pattern can certainly also lie more fully within the present chord, and can appear as more of a clear visual pattern on the fretboard—both of which are the case with the series of rising octaves, altogether going up in tritones, that he plays in measure 69 of "Blues for Basie."

Large-Scale Melodic Contours

Within the famously long lines that so profusely emanate from his guitar, there are some distinct contours, both in pitch and in movement on the fretboard, that Joe tends to create. A classic example is the kind of stretched-out melodic ascent and descent that appears as a big wide arch on the notation staff, as seen in the following lick (which is designed for a ii–V–I–VI–ii chord sequence in F major). When playing it, watch for the jump you'll need to make towards the end of the second measure, up to 8th position:

Lick 14

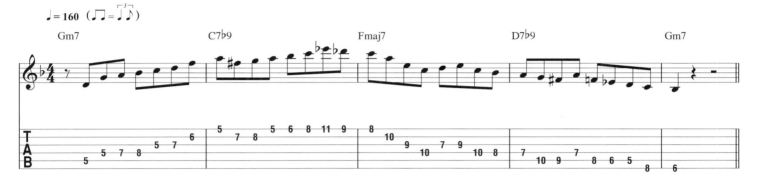

Joe often adds excitement to his lines with a big and/or sudden jump up to the highest range of the guitar, as seen in the following bop-infused lick for a ii–V–i in E minor. This may entail a physical jump along the fretboard as well, and in this case it needs to happen on beat 4 of the second measure. Here the fret hand, which has been comfortably situated in 7th position the whole time, will leap up for the pinky to reach the high note on fret 15. Note that you'll want to roll with your index finger across the three notes in a row at fret 12.

Lick 15

One particular motif he uses on occasion, to very pretty effect, is a quick chromatic descent to a targeted held note, as can be found in both "Summertime" (measure 29) and "Moonlight in Vermont" (at the end of the passage). In this next lick, as in those songs, the line concludes with such half-step motion after a more diatonic scalar beginning, and lands on a tone that marks the arrival of a new chord (in this case, the 5th tone of Fmaj7). Most of the notes here lie neatly in 5th position, but at the end, let the index finger keep moving down for the last couple of notes.

Lick 16

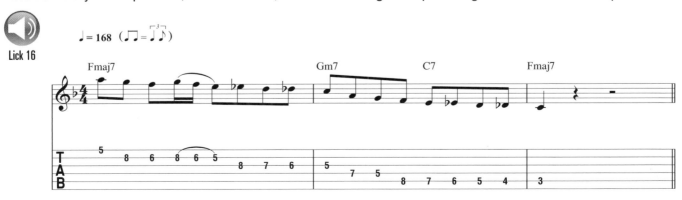

In a more general way, he often likes to involve some chromatically descending tones within a line—he even begins his solo on "Secret Love," from *The Trio*, with a quick descent through a complete chromatic scale, from B♭ to B♭ (at a later point in the track than the passage featured in this book)!

An expert at covering lots of ground on the fretboard, Joe has a penchant for nifty melodic patterns that work their way up or down the neck through the whole range of the instrument. The following lick, by way of example, winds upwards through three octaves of Gmaj7 arpeggios (linked by two snaky enclosures of the root), in a pattern that is almost (but not quite) uniform. In the last two measures (the last two cycles of the pattern), the major 7th (F♯) is preceded by its lower neighbor (F) to make things metrically work out. This was not the case in the first measure (the first cycle of the pattern), and this contrast makes for a more organic phrase altogether. Observe the few finger numbers given, as they will direct you to the optimal positions for the trek up the neck.

Lick 17

Our next lick moves *down* the whole scope of the fretboard in similar fashion, using a one-bar repeating pattern with a bit of variation and in different octaves. In this case, the first cycle involves only tones of the G harmonic minor scale, while the next two have a blues scale tone thrown in (D♭, the flatted 5th, as on string 3, fret 6) and follow a slightly different contour, both for musical variety and for smoothness of motion on the instrument. Like Lick 7, it exemplifies the prettiness that can come about with such a mix of blues and minor tone material. Follow the indications of where to place the index finger, and the appropriate shifting down of positions will fall into place.

Lick 18

SIGNATURE PASSAGES

In this section, we'll look at ten excerpts from recordings by Joe Pass, in order to explore specific aspects of his playing that are nicely demonstrated within them. Elements of his technique, his musicality, and his writing all come shining through in these abbreviated selections.

Catch Me (Forward Pass) [excerpt]
Up-Tempo Hard Bop–Styled Composition and Soloing

An early original among the recordings of Joe Pass, "Catch Me" has a remarkably hard-bop flavor in comparison to much of his work, sounding almost more as if it were a Wes Montgomery tune or a classic from the Blue Note Records catalog of the day. A fast and driving swing groove is established right from the bold minor pentatonic riff and firm rhythmic kicks of the melody, and his soloing follows in the same spirit. Replete with in-the-pocket 8th notes and slick melodic movement, his burnin' lines hint at how a young Pat Martino was influenced by the elder master. Our excerpt begins with the last 8-bar A section of the head (melody) to this AABA-structured song and continues through the first A section of Joe's first improvised chorus, to give a taste of both song and solo.

Originally entitled "Forward Pass" and released as a single (opposite "Days of Wine and Roses") after a January 1963 session, the tune was recorded again a couple of months later on a date led by pianist Les McCann, resulting in a track entitled "Catch Up (Forward Pass)," which would not be released until decades later on the Mosaic box set *The Complete Pacific Jazz Joe Pass Quartet Sessions*. It was laid down in the studio once again in July of that year as "Catch Me" for the album of the same name. We are dealing here with the first recording, which has itself also come to be known as "Catch Me," often followed by a parenthetical "Forward Pass" to set it apart from the album version (you may notice, too, that piano can be heard in the original rendition, while there's an organ instead on the LP's title track—in either case played by Clare Fischer).

An important factor to note while trying to walk in Joe's footsteps on the earliest incarnation of this tune is that he recorded it on a Fender Bass VI—a true *bass guitar* (as opposed to electric bass), a long-scale instrument with six strings tuned an octave lower than normal. So to deliver this material at the pitch heard on the recording, he was actually positioned on the fretboard where it would've sounded an octave higher on a standard guitar (in standard tuning). And later in his solo, he will go down to a D below the usual low E on the instrument, not by using an alternate tuning like drop D or DADGAD, but by taking advantage of the low range of this special axe. For the purposes of our study, we will look both at how to play the excerpt at pitch on a conventional guitar (most of us not being in possession of a Bass VI!), and at how he himself approached the fingering on the more unusual instrument. Suggested fingerings for the lower octave will correspond as much as possible to the way these lines were actually played in the higher position.

The repeated phrase that makes up the melody to "Catch Me (Forward Pass)" can be played in the lower range of a regular guitar as follows:

Catch Me
Example 1

Guitar (standard tuning):
(low to high) E–A–D–G–B–E

On this occasion, however, it was physically placed in the upper register of the bass guitar fretboard, in this manner (the provided audio is in the higher octave, like this will sound in standard tuning):

Catch Me
Example 2

As played on Bass Guitar
(6 strings, tuned one octave lower than standard guitar tuning):
(low to high) E–A–D–G–B–E

Keep in mind that if you actually have access to one of these quaint low-range instruments, you can read Example 2 using the audio for Example 1 as a reference in the right octave.

The riff seems much more intuitive or "guitaristic" in its fingering in the upper-range version, due especially to the initial double stop being played on strings 2 and 3 (instead of on strings 3 and 4). And indeed, if we check out for comparison how he handled it on the album version, it was modified to lay more naturally on the fretboard while being played in the lower octave at standard pitch. That time, he placed it neatly at the 5th position with no double stops, most often no grace-note slide, and sometimes an ascent to a tonic note D at the end (basically every other time the riff is played):

Catch Me
Example 3

Guitar (standard tuning):
(low to high) E–A–D–G–B–E

Interestingly, on the Les McCann session, he actually does play it an octave higher (on a normal guitar), but again varies it from the way it originally appeared, using a couple more double stops that sit easily on the B and G strings.

The opening salvo of the guitar solo is ablaze with speed and precision, especially in the picking of the downwards arpeggio at the beginning of measure 9. One might be tempted to sweep-pick to catch the four consecutive strings with a single upward movement, but alternate picking may lend itself best to the rhythmic definition of the line. This requires well-timed motion of the pick hand down across the strings while the pick itself moves in either direction, followed by a quick jump back to string 3 (in our lower-register fingering) for the next note. It should be practiced slowly at first before incrementally increasing the tempo.

**Catch Me
Example 4**

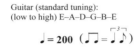

The whole eight measures of soloing in this passage (measures 8–15) can call for some careful mapping out of one's fingerings. Here are his phrases from that section (integrating the downward arpeggio we just focused on), as we could play them at pitch with the original recording, while in standard tuning. Fingerings are given, alternate picking is recommended, and we'll take it a bit slower than full tempo, at least to begin with:

**Catch Me
Example 5**

Guitar (standard tuning):
(low to high) E–A–D–G–B–E

To better see how Joe was actually thinking and moving on the fretboard on this session, let's take a look at the way he placed these lines in the area of a Dm barre chord at the 10th position, while he was playing in the upper range of the Bass VI. The same 8-bar solo segment will be detailed below for this higher position, but it wouldn't be a bad idea to isolate the first five notes of its first full measure for some preliminary practice, like we did for the same chunk an octave lower (keeping in mind that, this time, the index finger will need to roll across strings 1, 2, and 3, from the flat part up onto the tip, for the first three of those notes). Notice that within beat 3 of this measure, as shown here, a reach with the index finger that was likely intended for the G♯ on string 2, fret 9 eventually lands on G at fret 8 instead—probably an overreach as Joe tried to compensate for the longer scale of the bass guitar neck (this was simplified in our previous lower-range version, and will be also in the full transcription, to avoid awkward fingering and better reflect the musical intention).

Catch Me
Example 6

As played on Bass Guitar
(6 strings, tuned one octave lower than standard guitar tuning):
(low to high) E–A–D–G–B–E

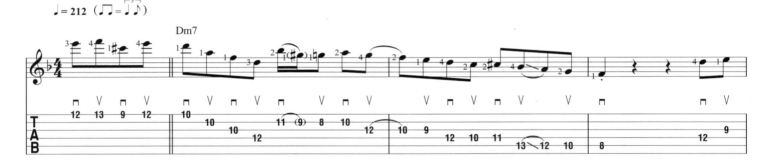

Here again, if you happen to have a Bass VI or similar bass guitar, you can read this upper-range notation along with the lower-range audio (from Example 5 in this case).

The harmonic structure to the A sections of "Catch Me" is rather static, essentially just based on Dm7 rather than involving any real chord changes. But Joe creates movement with the suggestion of repeated V–i motion in his first phrase of cookin' 8th notes, and in the next one he makes various colorful note choices for a hip and snaky sound. Referencing the full excerpt, shown next: the pickup notes to his solo in measure 8 imply an A7 (V7 in the key), while the four-note arpeggio that follows goes straight down a D minor triad (the basic i chord). The first half of measure 10 is clearly in Dm7 territory, while the second half invokes the sound of A7♭9, before resolving to the note F (the 3rd of D minor) on the next beat 1. The second phrase, beginning with the pickup at the end of measure 11, takes off from a starting point of D minor scalar material. He then throws in some chromatic movement (second half of measure 12), the blues-tone inflection of the A♭/G♯ (especially on measure 14, beat 1), and a quick but startling F♯ (the *major* 3rd tone relative to D, on measure 13, beat 4) that lends a bit of a harmonically "outside" feeling to the line—all before landing emphatically on B♮, the major 6th (bringing a Dorian sound to Dm7).

Here then is the full passage in the lower register, and thus, readable on a normal guitar in standard tuning, at pitch with the original recording or with the audio for this book. The kicks played by the rhythm section during the melody are included below the guitar part, for a more complete picture of the tune itself:

Catch Me
Excerpt

Guitar (standard tuning):
(low to high) E–A–D–G–B–E

$\boxed{0:20}$

Bright ♩ = 284 (♫ = ♩♪)

For Django [excerpt]
Graceful Jazz Waltz Composition and Soloing

In the beautifully melancholy "For Django," we have a chance to check out all at once Joe's linear improvisation on a mellow jazz waltz, an early instance of his fingerstyle playing on single strings, and beyond that, a unique example of his compositional work. The title track of his classic 1964 tribute to Gypsy jazz guitar legend Django Reinhardt, it moves with a mysterious prettiness and some less-common chord motion that set it apart from most of his writing, and from much of the jazz repertoire altogether.

The quartet on this record includes fellow guitarist and frequent collaborator John Pisano, who holds down a strictly accompaniment role while Joe renders the melodies and takes the improvised solos (Pisano's rhythm guitar part is heard on our sound-alike recording but not notated here). For this conventionally structured 32-bar AABA tune, our excerpt begins with the last 8-bar A section of the head in (the melody at the beginning of the track), and continues through the first two A sections of his first solo chorus, allowing us to sample both his writing and his soloing on this rarefied gem.

Throughout the performance, he plays with a particularly relaxed, songful feel and phrasing. The occasional even 8th notes heard in the first eight measures of this passage, along with the triplet figure in the pickup, result in some notes that come in a little earlier than expected on the upbeats in swung rhythm, but which paradoxically make for a greater impression of laid-back timing here, rather than a sense of rushing. The subsequent streams of 8th notes in his solo are played almost (but not quite fully) legato, with just a little space between the notes (though only a few of them wind up truly staccato).

Joe's improvisation moves in a very direct way with the 3/4 meter, with phrases or melodic shapes that tend to emphasize the downbeat of each measure. Notice the one-measure motif of measure 9 (more fully formed in measure 10), which repeats with its tones changing as needed for different chords, initially for the dramatic shift from the C#m7/F#7 zone to Am7/D7. For the solos, the progression is simplified from the way it appears during the melody, and resolves in each A section to Emaj7 (an interesting move within this overall minor-sounding tune).

His fingerings here involve a lot of playing in position, like at the beginning of the solo (basically in 4th position in measures 8–12, before a slight jump or stretch to get to fret 9 at measure 13), but also require some quick jumps, like from the end of measure 1 into measure 2 (from 8th position down to the 4th fret), or slight stretches as in measure 19 (pinky reaches to get to the 9th fret).

Those of us who prefer to use a pick can certainly play this passage in that way, although his use of the pick-hand fingers instead contributes to the mellow sound that permeates his playing on the tune. By way of example, we'll take a look here at how we can navigate the phrase of measures 16–18 using either fingers or pick. Regarding fret-hand fingering (also shown here), this is one of those spots where everything almost fits neatly into one position on the fretboard (all the notes here lying in 4th position, aside from the very last one).

A conventional fingerstyle approach to this line could involve the thumb covering string 4, while the index and middle fingers basically alternate for the notes on strings 2 and 3. Pass, however, has somewhat of a tendency to let a single finger handle all the plucking on a given string, at least at moderate tempos, as shown in the *pima* indications here. (More detail about a fingerstyle approach to single-note lines is found in the "Integral Techniques" section of this book.)

For Django
Example 1

With the pick, strict alternate picking may be the way to go, probably starting with an upstroke for the first note since it comes in on an upbeat (the "and" of 1).

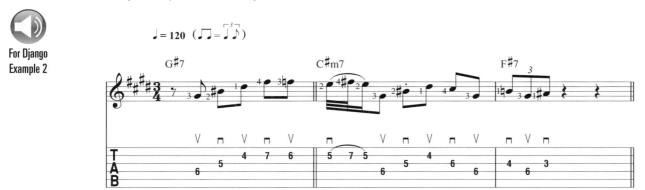

For Django Example 2

Either way you play it, here's our complete sampling of this elegant song and solo:

For Django Excerpt

Night and Day [excerpt]
Melodic Interpretation of a Standard Song

Another selection from the landmark 1964 album *For Django*, this rendition of "Night and Day" allows us to hear how Pass might reinterpret and vary the written melody of a standard tune. Here again, close colleague John Pisano takes care of rhythm guitar duties behind Joe's linear playing in a quartet setting (and again, this chordal part appears in our sound-alike recording but not in the transcription). Pass recorded the Cole Porter classic on other occasions as well, most famously as a stunning solo piece on 1973's *Virtuoso*.

Our excerpt consists of the first two 16-bar sections (the A sections in this AAB song form) of the head in, or initial presentation of the melody, as played on the *For Django* session. To better understand what he has done with the tune, by way of both rephrasing and arrangement (Joe's version also entails some chordal substitutions and a particular bass figure during this part of the melody), let's take a look here at a more "vanilla" rendering of the A section:

Night and Day
Example 1

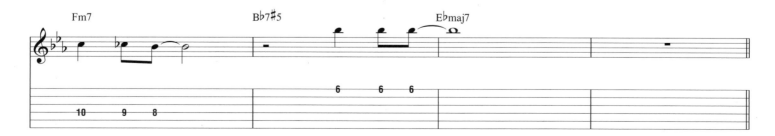

Comparing this basic lead-sheet version with the actual excerpt, we can see where he—in a manner fairly typical of jazz musicians, generally—has played around with the rhythm of the melody, added or changed a few notes, or interjected an entirely new ending figure (the embellishment heard in measures 14–15, and again in measures 30–31). Additionally, his performance through two A sections provides a good example of the extent to which he may either stick to a certain way of playing part of a song, or vary his own interpretation from one repetition to the next. Notice how measures 16–31 are indeed the same material as in the pickup measure through measure 15, but with slight variation, especially in rhythm.

A line like the one in measure 7, which involves three notes in a row on the same fret but on neighboring strings, requires a little sleight-of-hand to execute. In this instance, let the 2nd finger take string 2, fret 8 while the 1st finger prepares to roll, on the same fret, from string 3 to string 4 (see photo)—positioned like it's going to barre, but really only fretting one string at once, and winding up on the fingertip on string 4 (to catch the note at fret 8, the slide down to fret 6, and one more note just below that).

Night and Day
Example 2

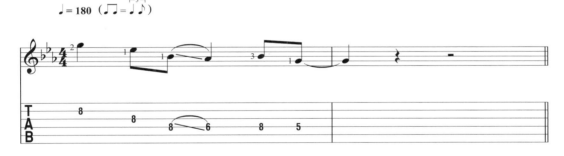

The quick figure that appears in both measure 14 and measure 30 is a particularly tricky one to execute with accuracy. In fact, on the original recording, Joe himself slightly misses it each time, in different ways. In measure 14, besides rushing a bit, he winds up sliding into an E on string 2, fret 5, where E♭ on fret 4 is clearly enough intended (as shown in this transcription); in measure 30, a couple of the notes wind up ghosted, just barely "ticked" instead of clearly sounded. To play it, we need to time the downward sweep of the pick so that it begins on the swung "and" of 1 (a late upbeat) and covers the first two notes of the following triplet, while the subsequent upstroke catches the last note of the triplet (akin to a swung "and" of 2). Let the pick be angled for the sweep, with the tip pointed slightly up (see photo).

Though it can obviously help to slow the phrase down for practice and then increase the speed, the timing of the sweep may actually be more natural at full tempo. Follow the pick-stroke and fingering indications shown here (though pick direction is not so crucial for the last note), and perhaps try it first at half the original tempo (which is how it is presented on the provided audio for this example) before taking it incrementally faster.

**Night and Day
Example 3**

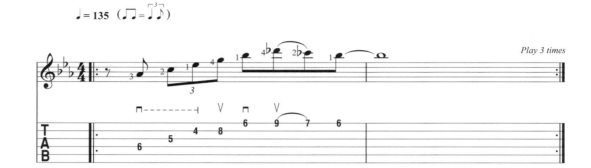

And here is Joe's complete rendering of the first 32 measures of the melody to "Night and Day," as it appears on the recording:

**Night and Day
Excerpt**

*Played behind the beat

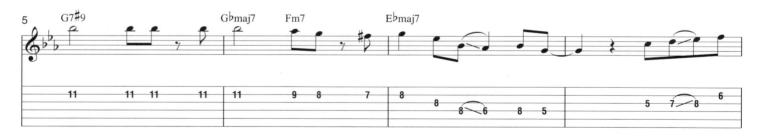

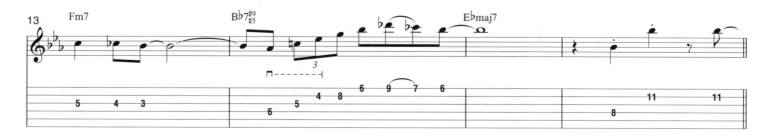

*Played behind the beat

**Played as even 8th notes

Secret Love [excerpt]
Finding the Spaces to Fill

One of the most famous and remarkable group settings in which Joe Pass appeared was the trio with pianist Oscar Peterson and bassist Niels-Henning Ørsted Pedersen, a meeting of supreme virtuosi who matched each other in swinging drive and technical dazzle, and whose monumental 1973 live album was simply entitled *The Trio*. The opening passage of its fifth and final track, "Secret Love," exemplifies how Joe might use the guitar to augment a song, even while both melody and harmony are being rendered on the piano. Unless he were to have adopted a strictly four-to-the-bar rhythm guitar role, he needed to find the right spaces to fill amid Oscar's notes and chords.

Our excerpt begins a very short way into the track as the trio finishes up its intro to the tune, involving a pedal figure with B♭ (the 5th tone of the key) in the bass. While Oscar plays changing chords on the swung "and" of beat 2 for each measure, Joe adds tone color each time with just the note B♭, in a higher register and generally doubled at the octave. As the intro winds down to resolve into the top of the melody at measure 5, he morphs this octave into dissonant 7th intervals that blend with the Fm7 and B♭7 in the piano (treating them as Fm11 and B♭7♭9) before quietly landing on a midrange B♭ (now the 5th of the tonic chord E♭ major). You may notice that Joe is indeed a little rhythmically off with Oscar on these last two chords of the intro, which were likely meant to be on the "and" of beat 2 in their respective measures rather than on the downbeat of beat 3—but that's part of the organic nature of live performance!

We continue through one 16-bar A section of the tune, whose usual AABA structure the Trio has reduced to an ABA form, such that this first section ends with a transition to the initial Cm7 chord of the bridge. Looking at and listening to the piano part shown above the guitar transcription, you can see how Joe's groovy little melodic fills in measures 7–9, 11–12, and 19–21 (largely harmonized in 3rds) each serve to *answer* a phrase of the song itself, played by Oscar. These mostly double-stop figures are similar to each other in motif (helping to create a sense of simple *arrangement* of the tune), with the notes modified to fit the chords at different spots in the progression. Through these segments, Eb major is treated much like Eb6, Fm7 and Bb7 are handled a bit interchangeably, and measure 20 is approached like it's all G7 on the way to Cm7, with fragments of a 3rd-position barre chord used for the harmonized melodic figure at that point:

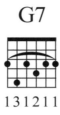

G7

131211

These harmonized fills lend themselves to being played with the pick if one is using combined pick-and-fingers technique. Check out this fingering and pick-stroke approach that works well for measures 7–9 (noticing that the slide with the index finger does not connect to another note on the downbeat of measure 8):

Joe also interjects a few three- or four-string chords in measures 13–18, taking care to play them sparsely and lightly, especially right when Oscar is laying down part of the melody. He again treats Fm7 and Bb7 (the ii and V of the key, respectively) as different sides of the same coin, and a couple of times along the way he throws in a form of F7 as a quick substitute for Fm7, one that will strongly lead back to Bb7. You can see how he uses all or part of each of these chord shapes in the process:

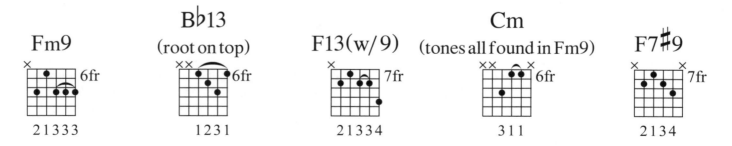

These chords, and the whole passage for that matter, could be played purely with the pick or with the fingers if you prefer (or with the thumb only, at least for the chords). If using pick and fingers, the pick is held by thumb and index, and all the other fingers of the pick hand (including the pinky) will be involved in sounding the strings, since all of them will be needed at once for any of the four-string chords here (such hybrid picking is discussed further in the "Integral Techniques" section of this book).

Here's the complete excerpt, putting all these elements together, with the basic piano part displayed above for reference:

Secret Love
Excerpt

All the Things You Are [excerpt]
Changing Textures Within Solo Guitar Improvisation

Joe Pass' 1973 album *Virtuoso* stands as a milestone in the art of jazz guitar, a manifesto of its possibilities as a solo instrument in the genre. Famously produced, for most of its tracks, with his archtop guitar heard only by its miked acoustic sound (due to some mysterious trouble with the amp or amplified signal), it consists mostly of standard tunes that he spins into brilliant solo performance pieces, moving in a freewheeling manner between rubato and in-tempo passages, and between colorful statements of the theme and more purely improvised material. This chunk of the perennial standard "All the Things You Are" nicely exhibits the kind of textural pastiche he might use to flesh out such a solo guitar arrangement, especially during an improvisational passage.

This song has a 36-bar AABA structure, with each section being eight measures long except the final 12-bar variation of the A section, and we join him at the bridge of an improvised chorus in the middle of the cut. By the time he reaches the end of the chorus, he has used a moving line of triads against an open-string pedal tone, a segment of chord-melody playing, and chords interspersed with melodic fragments. Also, much of the time he is flat-out *soloing* in the single-note manner of a soloist in front of a band, and all of the time he is solidly keeping time, making the beat, meter, and groove readily apparent the whole way through. He is also, in typical straight-ahead jazz fashion, explicitly outlining the tune's harmonic progression as he goes (an especially complex one that visits different keys), occasionally throwing in a substitute for the usual chord.

An over-arching principle that generally applies to playing like Joe Pass is especially pertinent here, within this kind of dense, constantly shifting texture: being ready to *move wherever and however you need to on the fretboard*, *quickly*, to execute the intended musical ideas, even as they come in spontaneous bursts. This may mean a jump up or down the neck, or a sudden reconfiguration of fingers in one area.

Within this solo format, for which he might use either pick or fingerstyle technique (or a hybrid of the two), this passage is one that he renders with the pick. And another general principle to keep in mind here is the use of *alternate picking according to rhythm*, for single-note lines and some chordal rhythms—that is, the tendency to use downstrokes on downbeats and upstrokes on upbeats, as one would naturally do in simple strumming patterns, regardless of the direction in which the hand must move to get to the next string(s). This can be applied at the beginning of our excerpt as well as in the more linear parts, such that some of these initial chords will indeed be hit with an upstroke.

The figure in measures 1–4, really a pair of similar chord-melody phrases interspersed rhythmically with an open D-string pedal tone, is typical of the devices that help him sound like more than one musician as he plays alone. The right rhythmic mojo and pick attack can indeed involve alternate picking by rhythm, which means a lot of alternation between downstrokes for the triads on the top three strings and upstrokes on the open string 4. The swung rhythm gives us just a smidgen of extra time to get the pick from the end of the downstroke back up to where we can catch string 4 with an upstroke. To practice this pattern, let's try it first with this exercise in which the pedal is allowed to sustain as in measure 3 (using the same G major chord shapes that are found there):

All the Things
You Are
Example 1

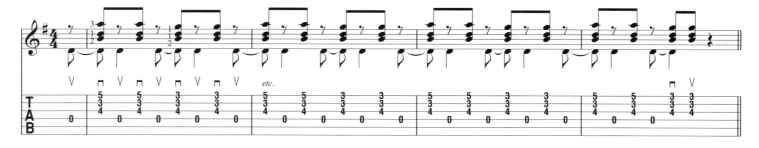

from VERY WARM FOR MAY
Lyrics by Oscar Hammerstein II
Music by Jerome Kern
Copyright © 1939 UNIVERSAL - POLYGRAM INTERNATIONAL PUBLISHING, INC.
Copyright Renewed
All Rights Reserved   Used by Permission

To achieve the rhythmic effect of the quickly muted open-string pedal as in measure 1, allow the 2nd finger to barely touch string 4 each time it frets string 3, letting go sufficiently at each "and" count to be just out of the way of string 4, and making sure the fret-hand fingers altogether don't press down on the strings too early for the next chord. We'll try this here with an exercise based on measure 1, using the C major chord shapes that are found there (the same shapes as for G major in measure 3, but five frets higher, and fitting with the Am7 harmony at this spot in the progression).

All the Things
You Are
Example 2

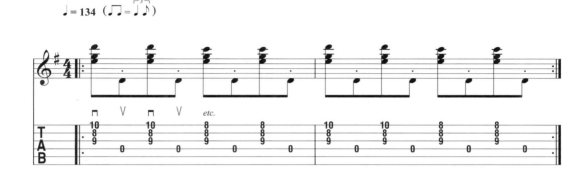

At numerous points in this excerpt, we have to make our way across the strings quickly with the pick, preferably using alternate picking. The line in measure 8 makes a great exercise for this kind of motion, as it calls for playing a single note on each of four consecutive strings in either direction and in rapid succession (notice that the index finger needs to roll between strings 2 and 3 to sound those notes individually rather than sustained together).

All the Things
You Are
Example 3

Having warmed up with the measure 8 figure, let's take a look now at measure 7, trickier in its involvement of a leap from string 4 to string 6 and the quick triplet figure at the end. Still try to use the pick strokes indicated (aiming as necessary to get to the right string) and follow the given fingering, which will indeed give the pinky a bit of a workout.

All the Things
You Are
Example 4

Note that when actually moving on from measure 7 to measure 8 in the full excerpt, you'll shift from 4th to 5th position (using the ring finger, rather than the pinky, for the E on string 5, fret 7). Fret the first note of measure 9 as well with the ring finger, but otherwise continue through that measure in the 5th position.

Measures 10–12 call for some very particular finger movement and likely a specific picking plan as well. Joe makes some quick jumps of position to play the material of measures 10–11, as you can see especially by tracing the locations of the index finger in the fingering given here (note that this finger will twice need to roll between two strings within this segment):

All the Things
   You Are
Example 5

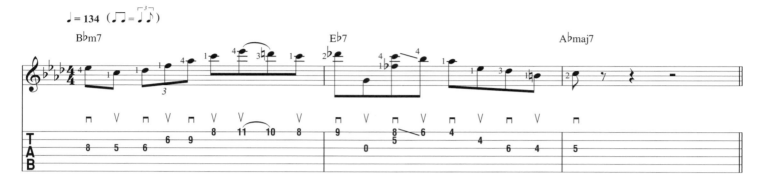

Measure 12 entails some even more detailed finger motion. As of beat 3, we have the tip of the index finger holding onto the low A♭ on string 6, fret 4, while our middle and ring fingers fret notes on strings 4 and 3 in the same area of the fretboard. But on the "and" of 3, while middle and ring fingers let go, the index needs to swivel and slightly tilt back so that its *underside*, near the base of the finger, catches string 1, fret 4 in time for the A♭ two octaves higher:

All the Things
   You Are
Example 6

*Fretted w/ underside of index finger, near base

We're in 3rd position through almost all of measure 15, but at the end, after naturally using the ring finger for the un-picked hammer-on on beat 4, we move the same finger down one fret for the next note to wind up in 2nd position for measure 16—at the end of which we do basically the same thing again (ring finger takes the hammer-on at fret 4 and then slides down one fret) to land in 1st position for most of measure 17.

At the end of measure 17 and moving into measure 18, the pinky does extra duty to keep melodically scooting up string 1 within a line that seems to get complicated in its execution. The underlying musical idea was likely something a little simpler like this:

All the Things
You Are
Example 7

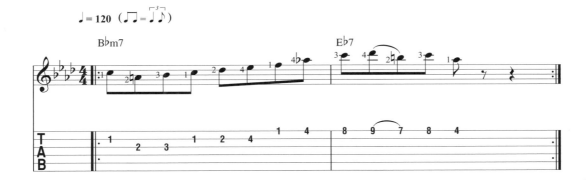

But in the heat of improvisation, Joe is going for it any way he needs to at the moment, which can lead to a little messiness along the way. To play it in the manner in which he did, follow this fingering, and keep in mind that as of the hammer-on on fret 4, he begins skating up the string somewhat evenly with the pinky leading the way, catching what he can as he goes.

All the Things
You Are
Example 8

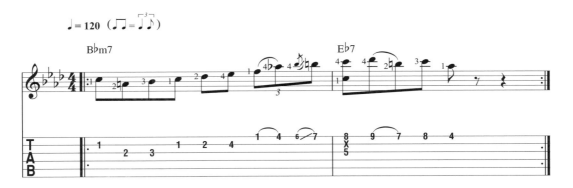

"All the Things You Are" is a staple of the jazz repertoire not just for its sheer beauty as a song, but also because of the unique harmonic challenges it offers, with chord changes that lead us into seemingly different keys along the way. Here we have it fundamentally in the standard key of A♭, but you'll notice this passage begins with the key signature for G, since that key is so strongly implied by the harmony at that point (the beginning of the bridge). By measure 5 (halfway through the bridge), the changes suggest a move to E minor (the relative minor of G major), but by surprise we land in E major—what we could call yet another *key area* within this essentially A♭ major tune. Joe outlines this cadence beautifully with what is almost a classic minor ii–V–i line, addressing the F♯m7♭5 and B7♭9, but then landing on what is mostly an E major triad arpeggio in measure 7 (making it a sort of major ii–V–I line, or deceptive minor ii–V–i). We officially return to the home key of A♭ at measure 9, though it sounds for a moment as if we're in F minor (its relative minor)—a resolution he heralds with the interesting up-and-down arpeggio of measure 8, seeming to outline a C chord with two different 5ths (between the G♯ on string 4 and the high note G on string 2), which still works just fine to evoke C7 on our way to Fm.

He continues bringing out the progression nicely whether playing actual chords or just single tones, and gives us an interesting bit of chordal variation and substitution in measures 15–16. The chords here would normally be Cm7 and B°7, on the way to the B♭m7 that follows. The use of Bm7 in place of the diminished chord, in order to have a string of parallel minor 7ths going down by half step, is fairly common among jazz musicians, at least while improvising on the progression (the melody requires the B°7 at this point). But Joe also plugs in what seems like a dominant 9sus4 shape for both Cm7 and Bm7 (the barred chord on the middle four strings, at frets 3 and then 2), adding an interesting, somewhat modern touch, even though the tones of this voicing technically fit under the heading of a minor 11 chord.

Within just this half of a chorus, we witness the sort of breathless barrage of musical ideas and devices that can make Joe sound like a one-man band while playing through a tune on his own.

All the Things
You Are
Excerpt

1:08

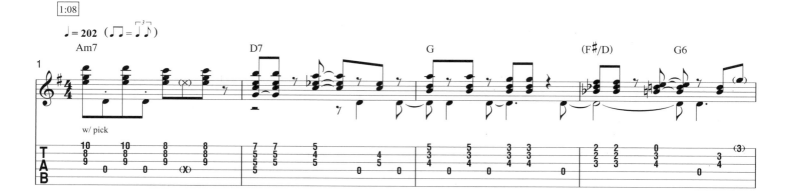

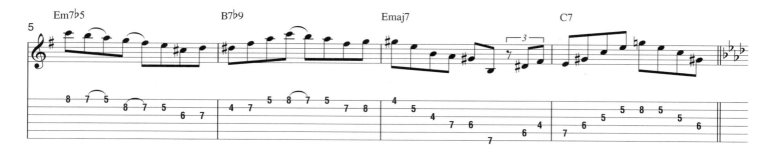

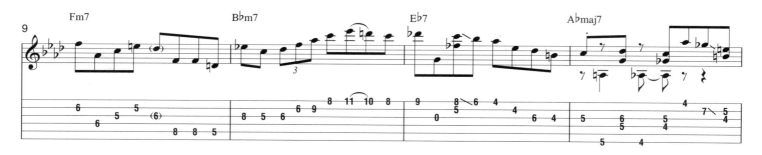

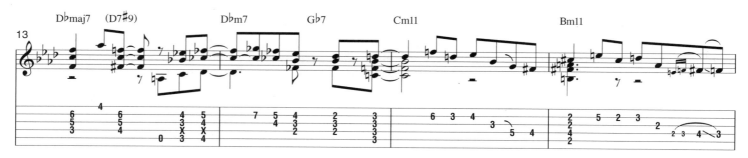

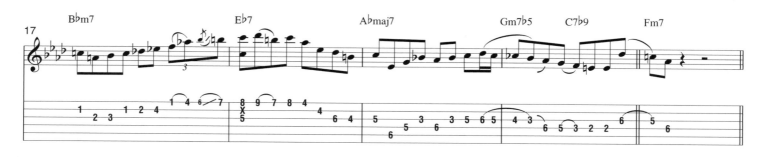

Jitterbug Waltz [excerpt]
Comping for a Horn Solo (and on a Waltz)

The 1975 album *Dizzy Gillespie's Big 4* is remarkable not only for its all-star lineup—with legendary bebop trumpeter Gillespie at the helm, our guitar hero Joe Pass, singularly revered bassist Ray Brown, and drummer par excellence Mickey Roker—but also for the chance it gives us to hear Joe in a quartet setting with a horn, and without piano. Here, all the chordal duties are his, while the presence of bass and drums precludes the need for him to rhythmically fill all the space, and we get to hear his comping behind a soloist in such a situation.

"Jitterbug Waltz," from this record, also gives us an opportunity to hear his nice feel for comping in 3/4 time, and our excerpt covers a half chorus of his work behind Dizzy's Harmon-muted trumpet solo (the second half of the form, actually from the first of two solos by Gillespie on the cut). When a pianist, guitarist, or other chordal jazz musician comps for a soloist, they need to follow the basic groove and harmonic progression of the tune, but the exact rhythms and chord voicings they use are up to them, and will generally vary along the way. The particular way in which Joe played through this passage was certainly affected by what the soloist was doing moment to moment, as well as how the group as a whole was playing, and how the flow of the tune had developed thus far on that occasion—not to mention the influence of his own musical personality. In turn, a soloist may be inspired and affected in their improvisation by the way someone comps for them.

Joe is sensing, as he goes, where to play some short rhythmic chords (as in measures 2–3 or 8–9), where to let them be more sustained (as in measures 16–22), where to play larger voicings, where to reduce them to double stops or even throw in a few single notes, and where to leave space (which he does more so towards the beginning). And in this setting that involves a swung division of the beat, a high frequency of chords played on the upbeats (the "and" counts) helps to accentuate the swinging feel of the tune altogether, as is especially clear in measures 13–14 and 23–24, as well as in the syncopated figure of measures 31–32 at the end. Notice too that through most of this passage, there's a *melodic* element to his comping, with the top notes of the chords (plus sometimes a few individual tones) forming a contour that is in itself much like a songful phrase.

It's a great lesson in chordal usage to see not only what versions of a chord he might plug in for any basic type (e.g., E♭maj7, E♭6, E♭maj9, or E♭6/9 all being used at some point where some kind of E♭ major chord is called for), but also how he employs bigger or smaller fragments of various common shapes on the fretboard, sometimes moving chromatically (by half step) between them or down into them. Each voicing he uses, whether fairly full or reduced to a couple of notes (or even just one note!), can be drawn from within one of the following mostly root-position forms, categorized here by the basic chords in the progression that they represent (note that in measures 23–24, forms of Fm7 are used to sub for B♭7, creating a B♭7sus4 kind of sound).

[The relevant chord diagrams are all on the next spread of pages, for ease of viewing.]

E♭ Major Chords

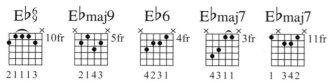

A♭7 Chords

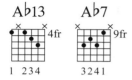

Gm7 Chords

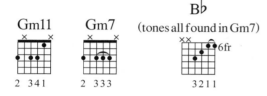

C7 Chords

F7 Chords

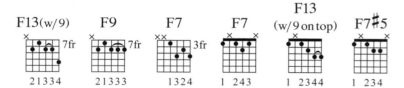

A♭m Chord

Fm7 Chords

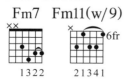

B♭7 Chords

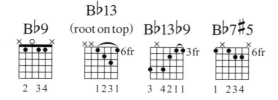

Eb7 Chords

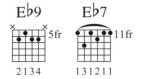

A°7 Chord

The ascending figure in measure 14 (with brief pickup) requires some quick shifting of fret-hand position and shape, as indicated in the fingerings given below. For the last isolated note, you're probably better off continuing to move up the neck and grabbing string 1, fret 8 with the underside of your 1st finger, rather than staying in position and trying to put the pinky on it. Not only is this more ergonomic, but it may have a basis in harmonic thinking as well: notice that while Gm7 is still the official chord here, Joe has really switched to C7 shapes by the middle of the measure, and could well be thinking of a C7 or C13 shape at the 8th position by the end, even if only sounding the C on top. Using fingerstyle technique for the pick hand, the thumb stays on string 4, while the next available fingers of that hand sound the other strings (the whole excerpt could also be played by pick, with pick and fingers together, or thumb-only if you'd prefer).

The quick ascent of measure 23 as well calls for some swift motion and particular fingering. The first two notes are played in 4th position before a sudden move up to 6th position to fret an Fm9 chord shape, which here involves barring with the index finger to put an 11th tone on top.

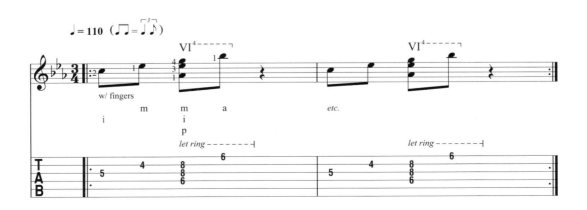

Careful plotting out of one's fingering can also help for the final chunk of the passage in measures 30–33. Here again, the pick-hand thumb can stick to string 4, while fingers *i* and *m* take care of strings 3 and 2, respectively (or, if using hybrid technique, the pick covers string 4 while *m* and *a* are used for the next strings).

Jitterbug Waltz
Example 3

And here are the 32 measures of Joe's comping in their entirety:

Jitterbug Waltz
Excerpt

2:03

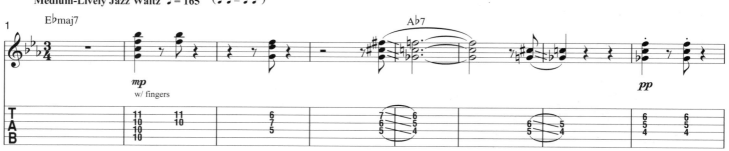

*Played by fret-hand fingers landing on strings

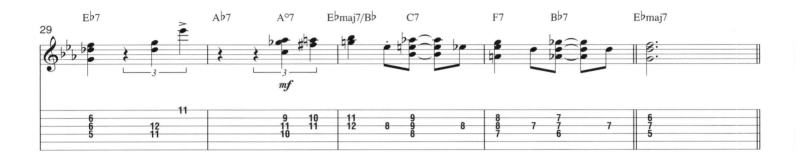

Old Folks [excerpt]
Ballad Accompaniment in a Duo Setting

Midway into Joe's performance of the old chestnut "Old Folks," from the 1979 duo album *Chops* with bassist Niels-Henning Ørsted Pedersen, we have a fine example of his work as an accompanist on a slower tune. They take the song at what could be called a "walking ballad" tempo: slow, but with the quarter-note pulse clearly emphasized and the 8th notes swung. Though "Tricrotism" (featured as a complete song in this book) is played by the same duo on the same record, the much faster tempo in that case allows Pass to be freer in how he leaves space or dances around the beat while supporting his partner's soloing. We look here at the first eight measures of the bass solo on "Old Folks" to see how he lays down the time and the chord changes under Pedersen's improvised lines at this gentle pace.

The whole excerpt is best played fingerstyle, and *pima* indications will accordingly be given throughout these preliminary exercises. If you are using a pick or the thumb alone, be aware that you'll need to mute a string anytime an unwanted one lies between those that are to be struck together, and still a couple of these chords will be altogether unplayable without modification. The muting can generally be achieved with whatever finger is fretting the lowest note, by allowing it to touch the next string with its underside.

A fundamental rhythmic feel underlying this passage is that of steady quarter-note chords, though there's much else going on as well. At times, he plays these in a quite connected (legato) fashion, as in measure 2 through to the downbeat of measure 3. We can try this segment first to be prepared for this sort of smooth motion, which we may need to maintain even while moving the fret hand quickly to a different area of the neck (like for the last chord here):

Old Folks
Example 1

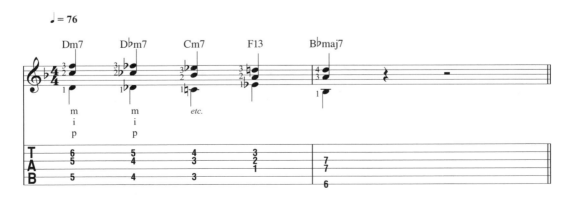

Most of the time, however, these chordal quarter notes are played a bit short, with the fret hand releasing them on the swung "and" of the beat (late in the beat as opposed to halfway through), which helps them contribute to the swinging feel even when they are placed only on downbeats. Typically, "chunky" quarter-note chords of this kind are notated simply as quarter notes, whether with individual noteheads or rhythmic notation, when it can be understood by context that they will be short (see "Integral Techniques" Example 7). But for this passage, they'll be shown as 8th-note chords each followed by an 8th rest, like we see with the last chord of measure 3, or the first chords of measures 4 and 7 (keep in mind that this rest comes in on the swung "and" count, as long as the 8ths are being swung altogether).

Let's try a distilled version of part of the "Old Folks" harmonic progression to get the feel of this chordal rhythm. Along the way, we'll also get a taste of how Joe might interject an extra chord on an upbeat in order to move by half step into the next chord, as happens in the middle of measures 5 and 8 of the passage (and which is demonstrated by the Abm7 and Db9 in our present example). For the moment, we'll stick with the 8th-note-plus-8th-rest notation:

Old Folks
Example 2

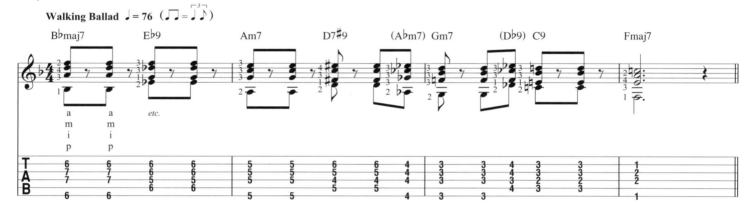

Though the texture of his accompaniment feels in part like a steady stream of pretty quarter-note chords, there is also a sense of an independent bass line underpinning everything. We hear a low A pedal tone at the very beginning, entering on an upbeat after the initial Em9 is sounded, and played under this voicing as well as the A7b9#5 that follows. After that, the low notes on strings 5 and 6 are most often chordal roots at the bottom of chord voicings placed on downbeats. But he also fills the line in with tones that lead between roots (generally approaching the next one by half step), and that appear on upbeats or in triplets, like the C# at the end of measure 1, or the C and C# in the triplet of measure 4 (on string 5). Some basics of bass-chord movement à la Joe Pass are shown in the "Integral Techniques" section of this book (with a similar chord progression, no less!), but here we can exercise the particular way it's used in "Old Folks." Note that our quarter-note chords are now just written as such, and understood to be played a little short:

Old Folks
Example 3

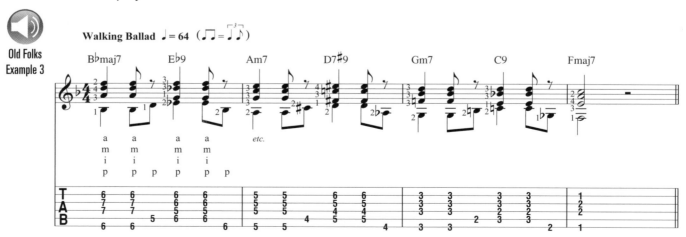

Various other chord tones are often echoed or added on the "and" counts as rhythmic accents throughout the passage, either individually—like the F♯ repeated after the D7♯9 chord on measure 4, beat 3, or the A that comes in after the Gm7 on measure 5, beat 1, to make it Gm9—or in partial chord voicings, such as the overlapping portion of B♭maj7 that comes in on the "and" of 1 in measure 3. Joe's habit of rhythmically re-plucking string 4 on the upbeats (between chords played on the downbeats) is exemplified in the middle of the passage, and touched upon in the "Stylistic DNA" section of this book. But here let's expand our bass-chord texture exercise to include chordal fragments, as well as bass notes, on upbeats:

Old Folks
Example 4

Joe uses a colorful set of variations for the basic chords in the progression, not least among them the occasional *tritone substitute*: basically, a dominant 7th chord whose root is three whole steps away from the one it replaces. These typically resolve down a half step into the next chord; the original dominant 7th would've led to that chord in a V–I motion. Looking at chord movement alone, we'll put a spotlight now on the last half of measure 5 through the end of measure 7, to more closely identify what version of each chord has been chosen, and also to map out the moves needed in both hands to get through this segment. Tritone subs are used twice here (and shown in parentheses), after the original chord is stated on the previous beat in each case. Regarding technique, the pick-hand pinky is now involved for sounding a couple of five-string chords (indicated by the *c* added to the usual *pima* instructions); the move from C9 to B♭13 requires an efficient jump and sudden barre with the fret hand; and a barre will be quickly put into place also for the G7sus4 (and held for the duration). It's in this sequence that pick- or thumb-only players will encounter voicings they are unable to play as is (the B♭13 for sure, and probably also the second form of G7sus4), and others for which they'll need to use a different fingering from what is shown (the A7♯9♯5 and the remaining forms of G7sus4 or G7).

Old Folks
Example 5

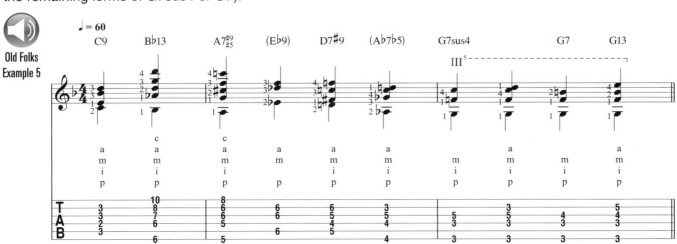

With this preparation, we're ready to follow in Joe's footsteps as he fills the space, augments the harmonic progression, and keeps the slow groove moving, all in his role as a duo partner on a walking ballad.

What's Your Story, Morning Glory [excerpt]
Tasteful Slow Blues Improvisation

Joe Pass is among those jazz musicians who have a well-known affinity for the blues, which he demonstrates here as well as anywhere else, in this rendition of a classic slow blues from the jazz repertoire. But what he shows here better than almost anywhere else is an abundant and super-tasty use of space, a contrast to the famously dense playing that often permeates the work of this "chopsy" guitarist, who from so early on was coached by his own father to fill every corner of a song with notes. On this cut from *Checkmate*, his exceptionally graceful 1981 duo album with pianist Jimmy Rowles (on which his guitar sound is purely acoustic), he moves into a textbook slow 12-bar blues solo chorus after accompanying his partner's delivery of the melody. This is the passage that we will explore here.

Repetition and variation (of the old-school blues kind) are key elements in this brief solo, and some of the variation is in the particulars of feel and timing, beyond what can be truly notated on the page. He begins with a simple, soulful five-note phrase that will occur a total of four times, each time with a twist, whether subtle or substantial. Through each of the first three times, the first four notes are basically 16ths. But in the first iteration (starting in the pickup to this chorus), he gets a little on top of the beat on the first note; the next time, he plays the 16ths (at the end of measure 1) with a more pronounced evenness and separation of the notes; and the third time, he gets a bit on top again as he enters (on measure 2, beat 4), leaving a little space between the first and second notes. The fourth time, at the end of measure 3, he stretches the phrase out into a clearly different rhythm, making it feel more swimmy or laid back than before.

This repeated gesture is also treated differently one time to the next with regard to how it ends, or how it is followed. He ends it quickly and plainly the first time; answers it with a little four-note phrase in the middle of measure 2 the second time; sustains the last note the third time; and on the fourth go-around, sustains the same note but then leads directly into a whole new, longer melodic phrase through measure 4.

We'll detail most of this longer phrase in the following exercise (but be aware: though we're looking at the material from beats 3 and 4 of measure 4, it'll be placed on beats 1 and 2 for our present purpose). Harmonically, this is a beautiful example of Joe heading up and down through changing chordal arpeggios to bring out the movement of the progression, which is in this case a blues progression of a more complex nature than what is found in many 12-bar blues songs, though still very much within the tradition. The first five notes of this segment are an ascent through the tones of Fm11 (from the chordal 3rd on up), and what follows is a descent through B♭7#5 (from the sharp 5th on down), until the resolution to E♭7 where the line lands on G, the chordal 3rd. (B♭7#5 is closely related to, and in this case largely interchangeable with, the E7 played by Rowles on the piano.) Technically, some jumping and shifting around within the lower part of the fretboard is needed to play it, so it's worth a try with the fingerings shown here, as well with the *pima* indications (though this line could well be played with a pick, if desired). A key spot to prepare for is the pinky hammer-on on string 2 followed by a jump from 1st to 3rd position, led by the index finger.

Returning to the formula of near-repetition, the simple blues tone–laden phrase starting on measure 5, beat 2 is commented on with a similar remark in measure 6, which leads again into new territory as it ends. Measures 7 and 8 are filled with more diatonically songful and flowing phrases, accented by poignantly laid-back notes like the high D at the end of measure 7 or the midrange D three notes later in measure 8. Then we're again back to statement-and-response format, with the bouncy figure of measure 9 echoed in measure 10, its tones modified to fit the new chord. Here's an exercise to get the mojo of that shape working (using the tones of measure 10), with the rhythmic alternation between strings 1 and 2 that moves without break to strings 3 and 4:

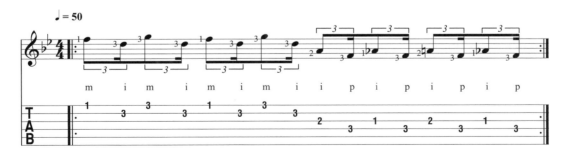

After a blues-styled repetitive insistence on the tonic tone B♭ in measure 11, Joe launches into a triplety final statement that exudes plenty of greasy flavor, between its profuse blues scale tones and the twangy double stops at the beginning of measure 12. Within the last beat of this measure, Joe makes a characteristically smooth change of textures, first letting E and C sustain together (like a partial C7 chord), and then grabbing the three-string B7 chord at the very end of the measure in preparation to resolve back to B♭7 at the top of the next 12-bar chorus (note that the C7 and B7 at this point are imposed by him as the soloist, and are not an essential part of the progression). He has slickly, and seamlessly, transitioned from single-note lines to chords while concluding his solo, preparing to once again accompany his duo-mate.

A couple of particular technical challenges are involved in the execution of this figure, and the remainder of our exercises will be dedicated to addressing them. For one thing, a more sizable jump up the fretboard needs to be handled with great efficiency following the Eb on measure 12, beat 3. We'll zone in first on the crux of that quick change with Example 3, exercising the move from string 4, fret 1 (fretted with the index finger) to string 2, fret 8 (reached with the pinky), as smoothly as we can. (Here we'll exercise also the reverse movement to be thorough, although that won't actually be needed in playing the passage.)

What's Your Story,
Morning Glory
Example 3

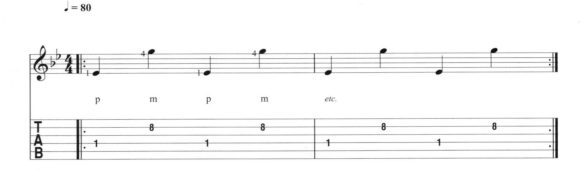

Next, we put that big upwards leap in just a little more context, involving a few notes on either side of it, so that we can try it right after moving down along string 4 with the index, and with some follow through on the other end (sliding into fret 9 with the pinky, for one thing, since the G on fret 8 was only a grace note):

What's Your Story,
Morning Glory
Example 4

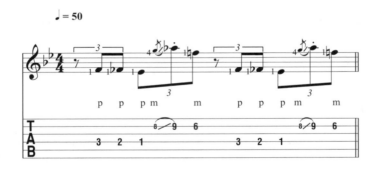

And finally, the following example walks us through all of measure 12 and into the concluding chord on the other side of the bar line. The suggested fingerings are helpful in executing the bluesy double stops and slur on beat 1, after which we have the big jump (within beat 3) that we've been drilling. Notice that two different fingerings are then used to fret the same dominant 7 chord shape on strings 6, 4, and 3: after using fingers 2, 3, and 4 at the end of the measure, the index moves in to barre fret 6, which allows not only for the same chord shape a half step lower (once the 2nd finger hammers onto string 3, fret 7), but also for the addition of the high root note Bb on top right afterwards. Incidentally, this is the spot within the passage that really does require fingerstyle technique in order to be played as is.

What's Your Story,
Morning Glory
Example 5

Let's check out Joe's whole chorus on this jazz-tinged slow blues, which he delivered with such exemplary patience, subtlety, melodiousness, and soul.

What's Your Story,
Morning Glory
Excerpt

*Played behind the beat

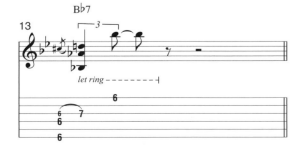

A Foxy Chick and a Cool Cat [excerpt]
Easy-Swinging Chord-Melody Composition

"A Foxy Chick and a Cool Cat," from the 1982 record *Eximious*, provides an excellent study in Joe's basic approach to combined chord and melody playing, as well as a very hip example of his writing. Tastefully simple and catchy, this AABA-structured tune swings with a relaxed, sunny, and groovy demeanor. It also has just a touch more of a modern air about it than most of his work, especially with the sus chord endings to the A sections. In what was almost a purely symmetrical 32-bar composition, there is a built-in tag at the end of the head (melody) that expands it to 34, though solos are taken on an evened-out 32-bar form. We will look at the complete head in (melody at the beginning) as it appears on this album.

He plays here in a trio setting, with bass and drums, such that both chordal and melodic duties essentially belong to him. Generally speaking, most any song can be rendered in chord-melody fashion in this situation, but this one in particular seems like it was meant to be that way from the outset! To get a better idea of how Joe actually combined these two elements for the head of the tune, and to better appreciate how integral this approach is to the composition itself in this case, let's first check out what the melody on the A section would sound like if played only in single notes (no accompaniment is provided on the audio):

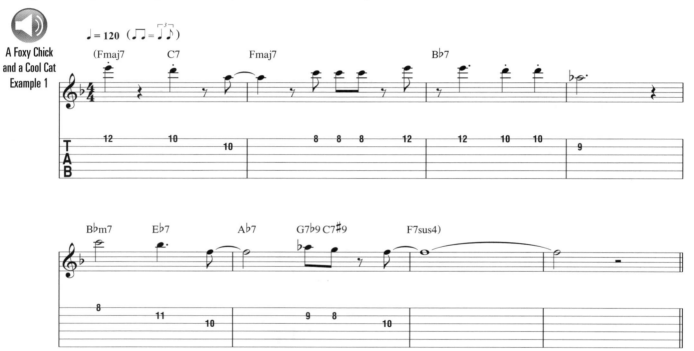

This is, in a sense, the pure melody, and it could potentially be accompanied by chords played on another instrument. But it doesn't have nearly the same impact as when Joe plays a whole chord for each note, keeping these tones on top, as heard on the original recording.

In any case, he chooses from different possible versions of each of the fundamental chords in order to support the melody in this way (such that the top note of each voicing is the note needed at that point in the tune). These are mostly played as rootless voicings, which one could look at as familiar chord shapes with the root that would ordinarily have been at the bottom (usually on string 5 or 6) left off.

F Major Chords

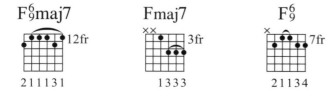

Bb7 Chords or Substitutes

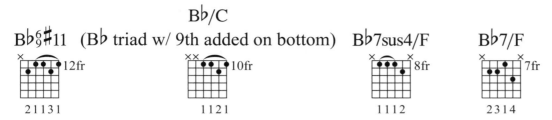

$B\flat^6_9{}^{\sharp}11$ (Bb triad w/ 9th added on bottom)   Bb7sus4/F   Bb7/F

21131   1121   1112   2314

For Bbm7 and Eb7, he uses common 9 chord voicings:

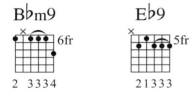

Bbm9   Eb9

2 3334   21333

But for the C7 at the end of the bridge, we have a less common C13#9 shape:

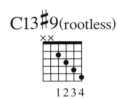

C13#9(rootless)

1234

Notice that sometimes the same moveable chord shape or fingering on the fretboard is used for different exact chord types. The G13b9 and C7#9 in measure 6, for example, have identical shapes on the fretboard (one fret apart), but differ in terms of which chord member is on which string (in the first instance, the tone on string 1 is the b9th, in the second case it's the 5th, and so forth). Still, the handy use of this same physical shape for these two chords makes for smooth chromatic chord movement within the progression. The voicings used for C9#5 in measures 1, 9, and 25, and for Db9#5 in measure 22, might seem to be the same shape for the same chord quality, but here again, the tones are stacked differently (9th on top in the first case, #5th in the other).

To play the tune as the chord-melody piece that it is, we need to be able to move quickly—and un-hesitantly—from one chord to the next on the fretboard. In preparation, we can map out our fingerings for the whole sequence of voicings involved, and practice playing through them slowly but steadily, without yet putting them in rhythm or hitting any of them twice in a row. Here are the chord shapes needed for the A sections of the song, presented as a steady stream of quarter notes, and at half the original tempo (the G13b9 and C7#9 towards the end are allowed to remain as 8ths though, like they appear in the song, so that we resolve to F13sus4 neatly on beat 1 of the next measure). Originally played with the pick-hand fingers, as suggested here by the *pima* indications given, one could use thumb or pick for these voicings as well if desired (none of them require any un-plucked strings in the middle).

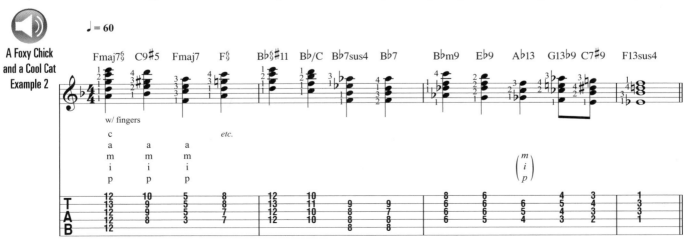

Joe sticks quite purely to the harmonized phrases of his tune during the head, with a nice touch of rhythmic variation along the way, generally allowing his bassist to play a fill when there's a break or sustained chord at the end of a melodic phrase, and throwing in just a few fills himself. One of these is the bluesy double-stop/hammer-on gesture of measure 16, another is the groovy little pickup to the last A section (in measure 24), and he also interjects a couple of single tones towards the end of measure 28. For the lick of measure 24, we can strategize and exercise our fingering as follows, in order to smoothly handle the four-fret slide, the triplet, and the octave-interval landing (if using pick or thumb instead of fingers, just be sure to let your fret-hand index finger mute string 2 when you hit that octave):

A Foxy Chick
and a Cool Cat
Example 3

Also worth exercising is the pattern of chromatically rising 13sus4 chords (each one resolving to a regular dominant 13) that occurs in the built-in tag at the end of the head, and which contributes to the modernized sound of this composition. We take this pattern a notch further here than where it goes in the actual song (from F13 up to Ab13, instead of just to G13).

A Foxy Chick
and a Cool Cat
Example 4

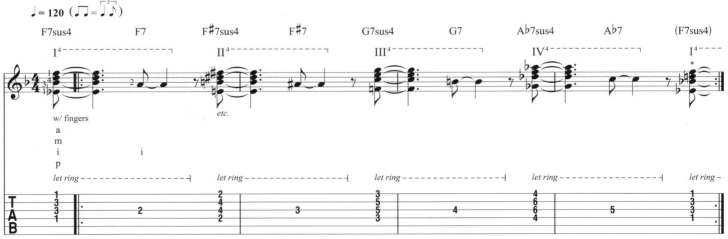

*Play 1st time only

In the tune itself, as you can see in measure 33, the G7 (G13) will lead to a sustained C7#9#5 chord at the end. When the solos take off from there a measure later (after the head in), there will again be an F major chord at the top as the form repeats. But when the whole performance concludes (after the head out), the trio leaves that C7#9#5 hanging, holding it and letting it fade without ever resolving the tension, for another slick and somewhat modern touch! This tune of Joe's may indeed be simple in its economy of notes and rhythms, but really only deceptively simple, given the sophisticated way in which all its elements are put together.

A Foxy Chick
and a Cool Cat
Excerpt

Moonlight in Vermont [excerpt]
Swinging Ballad Approach on Solo Guitar

As he'd done 13 years earlier on *I Remember Charlie Parker*, Joe played exclusively nylon-string guitar for the 1992 solo session that ultimately resulted in the albums *Song for Ellen* and *Unforgettable.* "Moonlight in Vermont," from the latter, is among the many recorded solo performances of his career in which he starts off rubato (not in fixed tempo) and eventually settles into a regular beat, before playing more freely again to conclude. And this passage, taken largely from the in-tempo portion of the track, provides a lovely example of how he might play alone on a ballad with a slow swing feel, and also gives us a taste of his dramatic and creative use of pedal tones. It is meant to be played fingerstyle, as opposed to with a pick, although much of it could potentially be executed with pick or hybrid technique.

Our excerpt begins as Joe comes out of his initial rubato presentation of this tune, which has an AABA form that includes a brief built-in tag (added onto the last A section as an ending). But right where he might've played that concluding phrase, he launches into a striking interlude of second-inversion major triads (on strings 1, 2, and 3) moving in parallel against an open A-string pedal tone. At the outset, he is actually mimicking the melodic shape of the usual tag, with the rising arpeggio in the pickup to this passage, and the more incrementally descending triads that immediately follow (in measures 1 and 2). With the constant A in the bass (the 5th, in our key of D), these triads move along the pattern of a diminished scale, that is, down or up in a pattern of alternating half and whole steps. Colorful dissonances result along the way, and the overall effect is one of mystery and mounting tension, resolving only when he briefly lands on a D major triad on measure 2, beat 3, or finally arrives at the Dmaj7 on measure 5, beat 1. (Notice that this is a somewhat different use of triads over a pedal tone than in the "All the Things You Are" passage, where they all fit within the chord changes to the song.)

The following exercise can help us get a feel for this patterned movement up and down the fretboard, and also for the alternation of fingers and thumb required to play the figure. Here the pedal tone is allowed to sustain (as it does towards the end of the figure in the excerpt), but the fret-hand fingers need to release their pressure on the "and" of each beat to keep the triads short.

Moonlight in
Vermont
Example 1

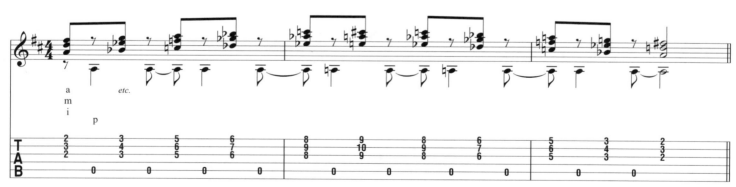

Next, we'll try it closer to how the figure actually first appears, with the A in the bass also limited to concise 8th notes. The pick hand can use a rhythmic motion in which the thumb, after each time it plucks the open string 5, lands right back on it to mute the low A just as the fingers pluck the top three strings (and we could do the same the other way around, such that the pick-hand fingers handle the muting of the triads as the bass note is sounded).

Moonlight in
Vermont
Example 2

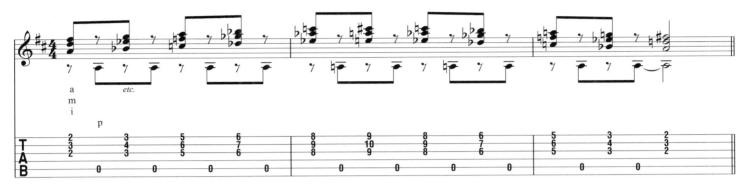

This pedal figure is largely played in tempo and at a quicker pace than the rest of the performance, but as it begins to wrap up in measure 4, Joe slows down in preparation for his restatement of the whole song, establishing a slow swing groove by measure 6 (measure 5 is the actual beginning of the new chorus, and from there through measure 10, we are looking at its first 6-bar A section). This rhythmic feel is similar to the one he employs for "Old Folks," in that the tempo is a bit faster than on a really slow ballad and there's a swung division of the beat. But here we get a little more sense of a *two feel*, which basically entails a greater emphasis on beats 1 and 3, rather than an even accent on each beat of a 4/4 measure.

He approaches the tune itself with a mixture of textural elements, including pure chord-melody (such as everything in measure 5 after the first chord), mid-range fills between phrases, and a stride piano–like alternation of bass notes with higher notes or chords. To make this all happen, some specific maneuvers may be needed, especially for the fret hand.

Let's take a closer look at how to get through measure 6, from two beats before it to one beat after, using the fingerings and *pima* indications given (the wide interval on beat 1 of this measure is the spot in this passage that would be most unplayable if using a pick alone). Be aware of a particular move to be made with the index finger: after using it to barre at least strings 3, 4, and 5 at fret 2 for the second chord here, we do not need to suddenly curl it up to be on its tip for the F♯ that follows on string 1, fret 2, even though we need to release the barre. Rather, we should just tilt the finger back slightly and use its underside, closer to its base, to catch that single note—which is easier in and of itself in this case, and will also leave the hand in a better position for the jumps or stretches that follow. The next time the same F♯ appears in this measure, fret it this way again, for similar reasons. (The same technique is used twice in "Summertime," and once in the "All the Things You Are" passage, though in a more difficult context in the latter instance.)

Moonlight in
Vermont
Example 3

*Fretted w/ underside of index finger, near base

Note that after the F♯ (plus low E) on measure 6, beat 1, the rest of the material from there through the next beat 1 is all filler between actual phrases of the song, combining a melodic and chordal fill with a bass line.

Particular fingerings are demanded by the content of measure 8 as well, especially in the move from beat 1 to beat 2. After barring with the index finger at fret 3 for the three-note C7 chord on beat 1, that finger must once again tilt back to fret F♯ with its underside on string 1, fret 2 (like it did twice in measure 6), this time quickly shifting down a fret to do it, and immediately afterwards returning to a barre position at fret 3 for the Gm7 on beat 2. Most of measure 8 is previewed in the following exercise; notice that yet two more barres will briefly be needed later in the measure:

Moonlight in
Vermont
Example 4

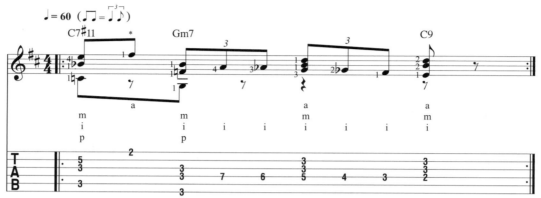

*Fretted w/ underside of index finger, near base

From measure 9, beat 2 to measure 10, beat 1, the movement from chord to chord works best if the fret-hand pinky is allowed to stay on string 2 (staying put on fret 7 for three of these four chords). We'll detail here the motions of measure 9, from its sliding pickup to its landing point on the downbeat of measure 10:

Moonlight in
Vermont
Example 5

After separately getting down the mechanics of measures 8 and then 9, it's a good idea to put these parts together and practice them as a continuous segment (before attempting the whole passage):

Moonlight in
Vermont
Example 6

Within the pretty run Joe plays at the end of this passage, descending in scalar and then chromatic motion, the index finger will naturally wind up scooting fret by fret down one string for a few notes. For some thorough practice moving in this way, we'll try it in the following exercise going both downwards and upwards, with a different finger for each direction. This could be tried on other strings as well, or with other fingers (keep in mind that a degree of squeak may be hard to avoid while we're moving this way on a wound string, especially on a classical guitar).

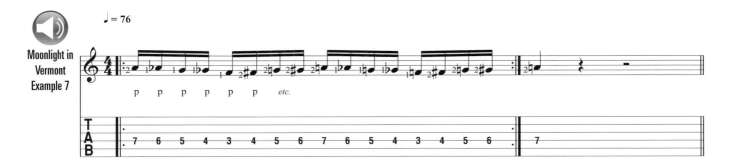

Putting all of these components together, we have the lovely passage that is Joe's interlude and subsequent entry into a slow two-feel on "Moonlight in Vermont."

INTEGRAL TECHNIQUES

A lot of what makes one able to play the music of Joe Pass, as far as physical skill, is just good conventional guitar technique. But depending on your own abilities in different technical areas, you can get started here with alternate picking, basic fingerstyle technique, hybrid picking (using both pick and fingers), and a couple of concepts for mapping out the fretboard… plus some bass-chord or bass-melody technique, along with some special strategies for fingering tricky chordal passages, that might be a little more unique to Joe!

Alternate Picking

Basic ability to use the pick with alternating downstrokes and upstrokes, on largely 8th-note lines, is important for playing much of Joe's melodic material. There are various ways that guitarists may grip a pick between thumb and forefinger, but a good starting point is with the last segments of these two digits overlapping each other (on either side of the wide end of the pick) and pointing in opposite directions (see photo). There are also many variants on the exact motion with which the pick may be brought through the strings, but in any case, we want to have a clear sound and one that is consistent enough while picking in either direction. It's best to have the pick facing the strings and nearly perpendicular to the surface of the guitar (see photo), rather than angled or twisted too much one way or the other, before it swings through.

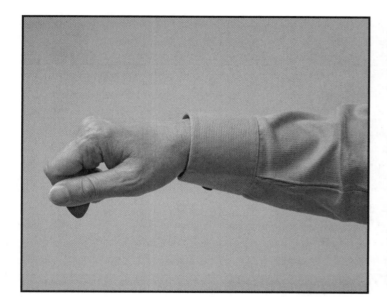

Here's a common B♭ major scale fingering (one that conveniently lies entirely in 5th position) on which to try this technique, rendered in 8th notes. Notice from the pick-stroke indications that this is strict alternate picking according to rhythm, that is, continuously alternating downstrokes on downbeats and upstrokes on upbeats, regardless of the direction in which the hand moves to get to the next string:

♩ = 90

Techniques
Example 1

There are many who espouse what is called "efficiency picking" (or "economy picking"), in which the pick-stroke direction, instead of strictly alternating, is indeed affected by the movement from string to string, as follows (the same Techniques Example 1 audio can be used for reference for the following two variations):

Joe claimed in an interview that he generally alternate-picked, but always used a downstroke when moving to another string, which would affect our picking pattern like this:

It seems unclear that this actually held true, and either way it's unlikely useful for our technique to insistently practice towards this particular approach. Alternate picking by rhythm, however (as in our initial example), can allow the hand itself to stay in a groove with a continuous motion, especially for swung 8th notes. But ultimately it's up to us to find what works well for our own proficiency, and to let the desired rhythmic feel be expressed through our hands one way or another.

Some of the fastest lines Joe might play on a reasonably up-tempo tune may involve continuous 8th-note triplets, for which strict alternate picking can be extra helpful. To get a feel for this picking style when applied to triplets, we'll try it here while moving up and down a chromatic scale, keeping in mind that now there will be a downstroke on only every other downbeat:

Techniques
Example 2

Basic Fingerstyle Technique

Joe Pass famously ventured further into fingerstyle territory than most jazz guitarists, and he did so more and more as his career went on. He always retained the use of the pick at least for faster single-note soloing, but would often put it down to play chordal passages with his pick-hand fingers… if not already exploring the musical possibilities of a whole tune played in that way. Some of the songs and excerpts in this book are very much meant to be played with fingers only (especially the nylon-string pieces "Summertime" and "Moonlight in Vermont"), and in case you are attempting these without any prior fingerstyle experience, we have here a quick primer in the basics. (This will be quite brief and rudimentary indeed, and if you'd like a more thorough introduction to this technique, the *Hal Leonard Fingerstyle Guitar Method* would be a great resource.)

First of all, where there are written directions as to which pick-hand finger or fingers to use at a given point, they are in the form of *pima* instructions—the letters *p*, *i*, *m*, and *a*, representing the thumb and the index, middle, and ring fingers, respectively (and occasionally *c* for the pinky).

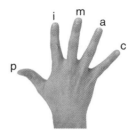

Between classical, folk, country, etc.—and even within each of these genres—there are various approaches to the exact position and motion of the fingers, but a good basic place to start is with this fairly classical hand posture (see photo below):

- Thumb straight and ready (near its tip, towards the outside edge) to pluck downwards on a bass string

- Opposing fingers lined up ready to pluck upwards on higher strings at an angle such that they face just past the thumb, curved but not too tightly, with their tips at the strings

- All this ideally while a smooth wrist is maintained

A slight degree of long fingernails, with nicely rounded and filed-smooth edges, is helpful in order to get a clear attack (classical players tend to keep them fairly long, while Joe used just a little nail). A combination of nail and flesh is often used to sound the strings (though perhaps less so with the thumb), towards one corner of their tips/nails as they angle across the strings.

A fundamental exercise for getting used to this motion is to play up and down through an arpeggiated chord, using the thumb and the next three fingers in succession, back and forth. We'll try this with a common open A minor shape:

Am

231

Notice that in the second measure here, the pick-hand fingers will shift one string higher (from strings 2, 3, and 4 to strings 1, 2, and 3) so we can start getting comfortable moving them between strings too as we play.

Techniques
Example 3

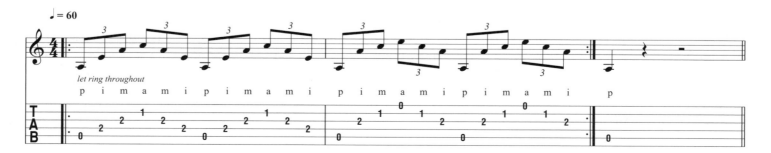

To gain better control of these pick-hand digits, the next stage is to try using them in different sequences, for other patterns within this kind of arpeggiated motion. This time we'll keep the fingers on the same three strings throughout, but the thumb will begin alternating between strings 5 and 6 as of the second repeated pattern:

Techniques
Example 4

A fingerstyle player must of course also be able to play single-note melodic material, so after our good start with sustained arpeggiated chords, we should take a look at a basic approach to playing scales without a pick. The thumb alone, or a single finger, could potentially be used repeatedly to pluck the strings. But just like efficient use of the pick can call for alternate picking, a common method of playing melodically with the fingers is to alternate between two of them, especially for faster streams of notes. We'll revisit our B♭ major scale at 5th position here to try this, first with a *p–i* combination (alternating between thumb and index finger), and then using *i–m* (the index alternating with the middle). The ring finger could be involved too, and other combinations are possible, but we'll use these pairs for starters. (A further step with this technique, not necessary at the moment but helpful for a strong attack, would be to use *rest strokes* with *i–m*, allowing the fingers to follow through and land on the next string each time they pluck.)

Techniques
Example 5

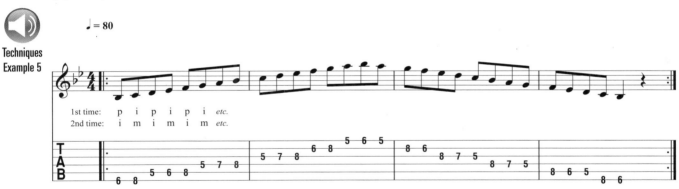

Joe Pass, in his developing years, had some experience with classical methods, and he certainly brought a grounding in fingerstyle technique with him into his jazz career. But in playing single-note material without the pick, he often took a more unorthodox approach as far as alternation or repetition of fingers. He tended to favor the thumb for the lowest two or three strings, and the index and middle fingers for the upper strings. And unless playing at a tempo that demanded an alternating approach, he might well have used one of these fingers alone for consecutive notes on a single string, until moving to another string and using the next available finger in that direction. Approaching it in this way, our same B♭ major scale might be played like so:

Techniques
Example 6

Chording with Fingers and/or Pick

When playing chords (speaking now mainly of solid chords as opposed to arpeggiated), Joe might use either a pick, his thumb (with pick-like motion), all the fingers of the pick hand, or a combination of pick and fingers. We would do well to be comfortable with all these ways of striking multiple strings, and in the exercise below we'll try the first three of them on the same chord sequence (a separate look at that last option will follow). Keep in mind that when it's thumb and fingers, with the kind of fingerstyle hand position described in the previous section, they will tend to look as though they are heading past each other as they together pluck the strings. Along with these pick-hand techniques, we'll also try a particular chordal rhythm that is important in his work, and in the art of jazz guitar altogether: that of steady quarter-note chords played with a swung feel, sounding a bit "chunky" as they are given just a little space in between (rather than being sustained one to the next in legato fashion). This release time is akin to an 8th rest on the upbeat, assuming a swung division of the beat where the "and" count comes later than halfway through.

But where it can be understood from context that this feel is appropriate, such chords are generally still written as quarter notes, as in the following exercise. We'll play four times through this progression (which is very similar to part of the "Old Folks" progression, though in the key of G), once with downstrokes of the pick, once with downstrokes of the thumb, and then twice using fingers *p*, *i*, *m*, and *a* simultaneously:

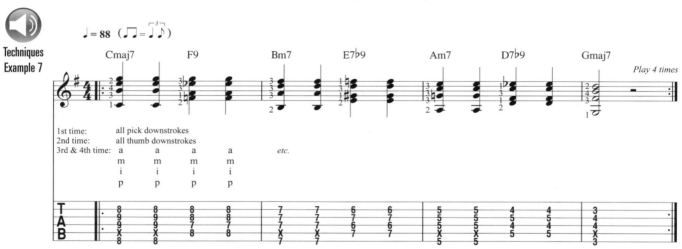

There are many occasions on which Joe needs to hang onto the pick even while wanting to play chords in a fingerstyle manner (consider the trading on "Tricrotism," for example, where every eight measures he switches between soloing and accompaniment). This is the sort of situation in which hybrid picking may come into play, with the pick held between thumb and index finger and used for lower-range notes, while the other fingers pluck the strings directly in the usual upwards motion (see photo).

To get started with this technique, we'll try it with the previous chord progression, except that we'll omit the notes on string 2 (leaving a chordal-shell type of voicing for each chord). The pick is replacing the thumb for the bottom notes, and with both *p* and *i* occupied in holding it, *m* and *a* each move down a string (towards the lower range):

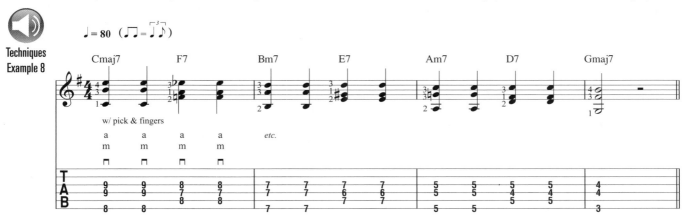

While not much use is made of the pick-hand pinky within traditional classical technique, this finger indeed can, and sometimes must, be involved when chords are handled with a fingerstyle or hybrid picking approach. Let's work it in by adding the notes on string 2 back into the chord sequence we've been playing, while still using hybrid picking, such that this extra digit is needed in order to pluck these top notes. Here we'll indeed add *c* to the usual *pima* instructions to indicate where a note should be played with the pinky:

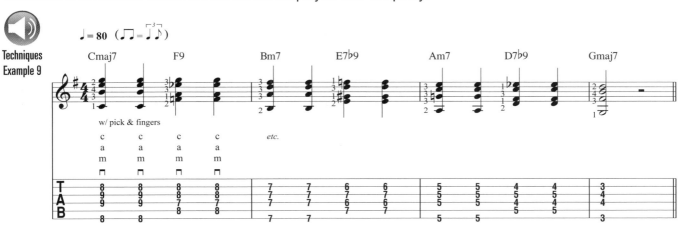

The pinky may also come into play for purely fingerstyle execution of five- or six-string chord voicings. We'll use all five fingers of the pick hand in the following exercise, in which the progression is really the same one we've been playing but with bigger (and mostly more complex) versions of the chords. Notice that for the six-string E7#9#5 voicing at the end of the second measure, the thumb will be used to pluck through *two* strings while the other fingers each play one:

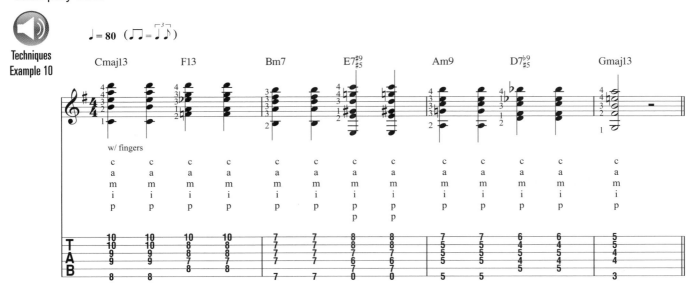

For our next chording technique, we're back into pick territory. Strumming with a continuous up-and-down motion is common among guitarists of many styles, but Joe of course does it in a particular way that is well-suited to a jazz setting. When playing as an accompanist, he might bust into this type of 8th note–based rhythm in the middle of a lively swing or Latin groove, with a steady stream of downstrokes on downbeats and upstrokes on upbeats, the chords interspersed with percussive pick strokes on stopped strings (muted by the fret hand between chords). Remember as you try it to let the hand keep moving freely down and up in rhythm, even when not hitting the strings:

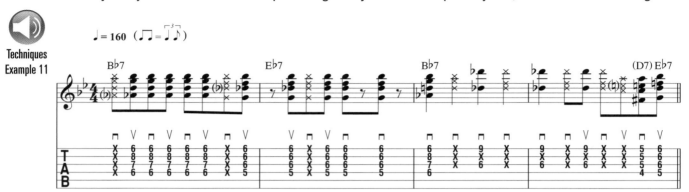

Mapping out the Fretboard with Scales and Arpeggios

An important skill for improvising in the manner of Joe Pass, one that is as mental as it is physical, is the ability to quickly see and access different positions all over the guitar for any given key, scale, or chordal arpeggio. Whether or not he's thinking directly about scales or arpeggios as he plays, such knowledge of the fretboard helps him to find pertinent musical ideas wherever he may be located along the neck, and to flow freely from place to place through the whole range of the instrument. Indeed, this ability is important for jazz guitar playing in general, but it is especially so for the lengthy and/or jumpy phrases that are the hallmark of Joe.

To get an idea what it means to navigate the fretboard in this way, and to get a start in doing it, we'll take a look here at a major scale in just one key (the key of D♭, conveniently, for any work you might be doing on "Tricrotism"), but in five different locations on the guitar. Each scale form basically relates to a common moveable major chord shape, which will be shown above the staff. In this exercise, they also each lie entirely in one position or close to it (with minimal shifting involved for the fret hand), ascending from a low tonic tone (D♭) to the highest scale tone reachable in the position and then heading back down. You may want to try each one individually, out of strict time, before playing them end to end in tempo as presented here:

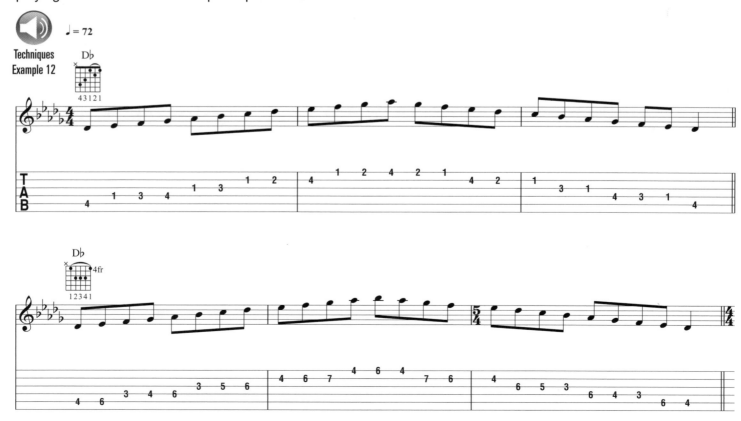

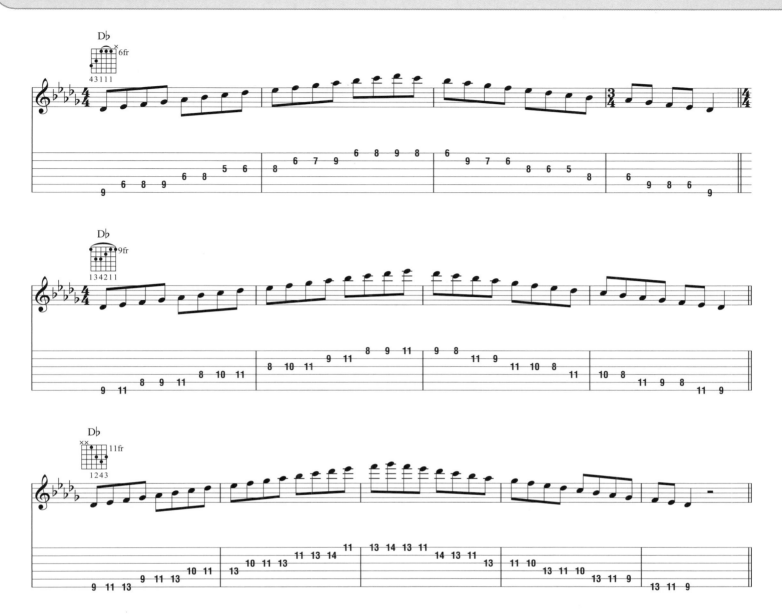

We've looked here at just one example of how the tones of a scale may be found all over the instrument, though thorough study of the fretboard of course entails playing multiple scale forms like these in all keys, and not only with major scales, but with minor, dominant, and other types as well. This is beyond the scope of this book, but a good resource for further work of this kind is the *Guitar Fretboard Atlas* from Hal Leonard.

The same thing holds true for chordal arpeggios; we need to learn them for numerous chord types and be able to play them on any root, besides knowing where to find them in different areas of the fretboard. But presently we'll use a Dbmaj7 arpeggio as a single example, located in five positions that correspond to the previous Db major scale forms (an arpeggio being all the tones that belong to a given chord, played successively in their theoretical order, and generally derived from going up the appropriate scale in 3rd intervals). For the exercise below, it'll be played in the standard root–3rd–5th–7th ascending order and then repeated in the next octave as far as possible within each position. As with the scales, every fingering here lies either in or near one exact position on the neck, though some of them will require a little stretching or sliding with the fret-hand fingers:

Techniques
Example 13   ♩ = 60

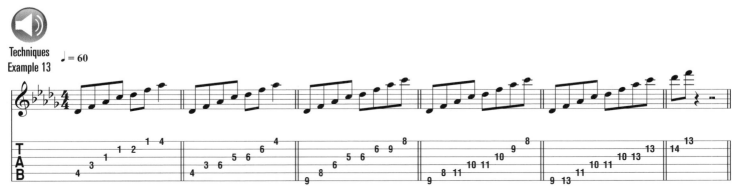

Next, rather than starting to repeat the basic 7th-chord arpeggio at the octave, let's continue going up in 3rds past the octave for the 9th, 11th, and 13th tones in each of these positions. In this way, we can see how the arpeggio of a fully extended 7th chord may be mapped out in different places, as we're now laying out the tones of D♭maj13♯11 (for all except the first form here, which reaches no further than the sharp 11th tone, yielding D♭maj9♯11). What we have with these added tones is the *upper extension* of that chord, which by itself, you may notice, constitutes an E♭ major triad (the notes E♭, G, and B♭). The 11th tone, which corresponds to the 4th degree of the scale, has been raised from G♭ to G so that it may harmonize neatly with the 3rd (F) voiced below it. With that, the tones are no longer entirely from the D♭ major scale, though one could say that they come from D♭ *Lydian*.

Techniques
Example 14

*Upper extensions of D♭maj7

The technical ability to quickly jump up or down the neck in the middle of a line, essential in much of the work of Joe Pass, may seem like a largely physical skill. But from the perspective of an improviser, who must *find* the notes they want to play (rather than just playing a rote, rehearsed melodic idea), it is also a mental skill, for which the kind of fretboard-mapping that we have done in the last few exercises can be quite pertinent. Consider the patterned key-of-D♭ phrase in our next example, which, after starting out in 1st position, requires a sudden shift up to 6th position, and then 11th. When you compare the indicated fingerings in these areas with the first, third, and fifth D♭ scale forms from earlier, the location of each note here could be seen as coming from one of these scale positions, even as the line quickly makes its way up string 1. Realize that the fret hand must indeed make a fast and clean jump at both changes of position, with the 1st finger landing at a higher fret than where the whole hand just was, in either case:

Techniques
Example 15

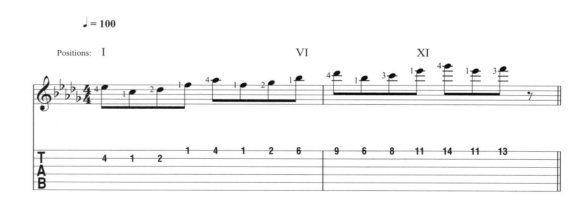

Certainly, there are other factors that can figure into an improvising guitarist's ability to find tones in this way, such as scale forms that are more vertical (meaning more up and down the neck), ear skills that allow one to hear the desired intervals and relate them to distances on the guitar, and of course the rote learning of some melodic bits and pieces that will work their way into one's soloing. But every bit of awareness of where certain tones can be found, in the context of a scale or otherwise, can help in navigating the fretboard. And from a Joe Pass angle, the position-oriented approach seems particularly useful.

Oftentimes, rather than jumping so abruptly between positions, he might shift between them in a more fluid way within a phrase, seeming almost to blend them together as he goes. Here's an example of that sort of motion, using a line that is basically a descending D♭ major scale with some ornamentation. It snakes its way down between three of the previously studied scale positions (the fourth, third, and then second forms shown in Example 12), starting at 8th position on the fretboard, reaching and sliding near the end of the first measure to get to the 6th and then 5th positions, and again near the end of the second measure to wind up at 3rd position. Note that this movement could also be achieved without the slide-slurs on strings 2 and 4, in which case the index finger would still be used to fret both notes in those pairs, but the second note would be plucked, with *m* or *p*, or with a downstroke of the pick.

Techniques
Example 16

Multiple Slurs

Slurring, whether with hammer-ons, pull-offs, slides, or all of the above, is a technique in the Joe Pass toolbox that can bear some specific practice, especially for those situations that involve multiple slurs consecutively. The exercise below runs us through a few such combinations of hammer-ons and pull-offs, working all the fingers of the fret hand through the top four strings of the guitar. Fingerings are given only once for each figure here (the same fingering can be used when the figure is repeated through the next three strings), and the last one of these could also be played using the 1st, 2nd, and 3rd fingers, to opt for a stretch instead of involving the pinky. Note that by string 4, it can get more challenging to make all the notes speak, at least when using the thicker strings typically favored by many jazz guitarists:

Techniques
Example 17

His slurring may be compounded by a combination of hammer-ons/pull-offs and slides within a line, and our next exercise provides us with a hands-on demonstration of this phenomenon. Notice that in both halves here, it is actually the same phrase that is run through the top four strings, but with a change of fingering/slurring the second time around (such that a different finger handles the one-fret slide, both up and down, in each case). Again, fingerings are only given once for each pattern:

Techniques
Example 18

Playing in Intervals

Whether soloing with single tones or comping with medium- or large-sized chords, Joe is prone to occasionally throw in a segment of *double stops*, in which two strings are played at a time. This may give the effect of either a harmonized melodic line or a series of two-note chords, but in any case, he is generally then playing in harmonic intervals of one kind or another. Sometimes this means a fixed distance between the two tones, as when playing in octaves or perfect 4ths, and sometimes it is a varying interval like 3rds or 6ths, which can be major or minor (bigger or smaller by a half step). Playing in intervals can require particular approaches to fingering, as well as to picking, fingerstyle, or hybrid picking technique, and we'll take a look here at how this might apply to some of the intervals commonly found in his work.

Let's try first with 3rd intervals, the simplest way in which a scale or melodic line can be harmonized by one other part. In the following example, we have a D♭ major scale through one octave, in a fairly concise area of the fretboard, played in 3rds. In this case, it's the note below that seems to be the added or harmonizing tone, though this could also be done such that the harmony note is on top. Notice that these intervals vary between minor and major 3rds (the notes being either one and a half or two steps apart), depending on where they sit in the scale. The top notes here make up a familiar major scale form for D♭ in the upper range of the 6th position, but clearly we won't be able to use the same fingering as if we were just playing the single-note scale. In order to play these double stops, more back-and-forth movement of the fret hand is needed, as well as some brief barring with the index finger. Try it with the fingerings given, and for the moment, with only downstrokes of the pick, or using only *i–m* for fingerstyle.

Techniques Example 19

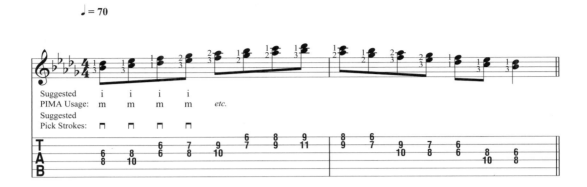

We can also use a more stretched-out approach on the fretboard for a scale in 3rds, or for a largely scalar melodic phrase in 3rds. Here is such a phrase, one that really just goes up and back down through a chunk of the D♭ major scale with a couple of chromatic passing tones thrown in, all harmonized below in 3rds, and played entirely on strings 2 and 3. Notice that with the suggested fingerings, you'll need to jump significantly up the fretboard at the fourth harmonized note, and similarly back down at the fourth-to-last one. This time try alternate picking, letting the pick hand stay in rhythm such that the upbeats are played with upstrokes, and using a light enough touch to get through it smoothly (still use *i–m* for fingerstyle technique):

Techniques Example 20

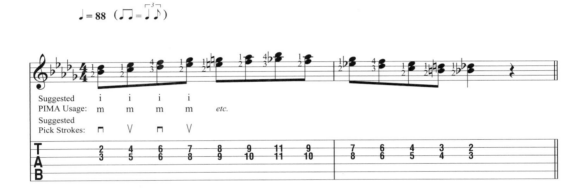

Playing in octaves, of course, amounts to playing the same note or line in two different registers at once. And so, as noted in the "Essential Licks" section of this book, using this double-stop interval has the effect of simply beefing up the texture of single-note material, rather than creating a harmonized phrase. In the case of octaves especially, the fret hand has to move a lot more than if playing the same line without the added tones, since the usual fingering for each octave involves the index finger on the lower note. We'll exercise this motion here with two different approaches to a one-octave F major scale in octaves: first in a more compact position, and then with more continuous movement up and down the fretboard. If using a pick, use all downstrokes, and you'll need to mute the in-between string with the underside of the fret-hand index finger. Otherwise, *pima* indications are given for fingerstyle, and the pick plus *m* or *a* could be used for hybrid picking:

Techniques Example 21

The inversion of a 3rd interval (the interval that results if flipping one of the notes above or below the other one) is a 6th, and this is another favorite of Joe's for use in the middle of either melodic statements or comping passages. As with 3rds, the exact width of the interval varies by a half step (between major and minor 6ths) depending on what is needed harmonically. To get a start with the technique of playing these, let's try this one-octave F major scale, harmonized below in 6ths, and laid out very vertically on the fretboard on just one pair of strings, with an unplayed or muted string in between. Notice that with the suggested fingering, there are places such as the fourth double stop where the fret hand will have to jump substantially along the neck, and also that the given fingerings for some note pairs are different on the way down than on the way up, according to what lies more naturally in either direction. Fingerstyle technique will likely sound best for the scale as presented here, probably using *i–a* throughout (or it could be hybrid-picked with the pick + *m*). If you do use the pick alone, go with all downstrokes and mute the in-between string with the fret hand—for this you'll actually need to use the *same* fingerings on both the way up and the way down for each note pair (that is, always using the 3rd and 4th fingers where an index-finger barre is shown here):

Techniques
Example 22

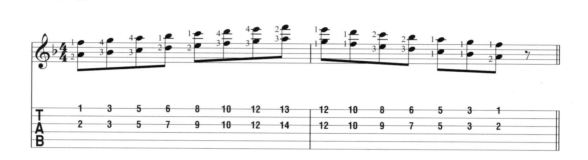

This harmonized scale could also be positioned in a more compact area, and harmonic 6ths in general could also be played on two neighboring strings if "stretchier" fingerings are used.

Tenth intervals, which are the equivalent of 3rd intervals expanded by an octave (and can therefore also be either major or minor), figure into Joe's playing as well. This wide interval needs a wider span of strings, with two silent strings in between the two that are sounded together, making it pretty unwieldy for being played with pick only. Try using *p–m* for fingerstyle (or pick + *a* for hybrid picking) for the exercise below, which is an F major scale in 10ths, ascending and descending through one octave on string 6 and harmonized on string 3. Here again, the fret hand is moving a lot in general, but will need to make a bigger jump between the third and fourth double stops (and at the same place on the way down):

Techniques
Example 23

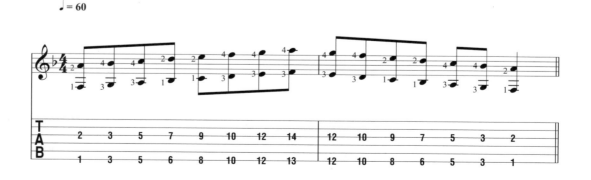

Bass-Chord Technique

The ability to combine chords with a walking bass line is a staple of Joe's "one-man band" kind of guitar playing, and we'll get an introduction here to the basic technique involved, in three stages. Note that for each of these exercises, fingerstyle is the most preferred method of execution, and *pima* indications are given, though one could also use hybrid picking (with the pick used in place of the thumb, and the rest of the pick-hand fingers shifting from *i*, *m*, or *a* to *m*, *a*, or *c*, respectively). The use of pick or thumb alone is possible too, if desired, though this would require muting string 5 when it sits between simultaneously played chord tones.

First, for a harmonic progression in which the changes come every half measure in 4/4 time, let's try simply adding single bass notes between root-position chords, so that the chordal roots together with the notes in between form a quarter-note bass line. The added tones in this pattern each lead into the next root from a half step above or below. Be ready to move quickly between fingerings, particularly where either the index or middle finger needs to hop between two or more notes in a row.

Techniques
Example 24

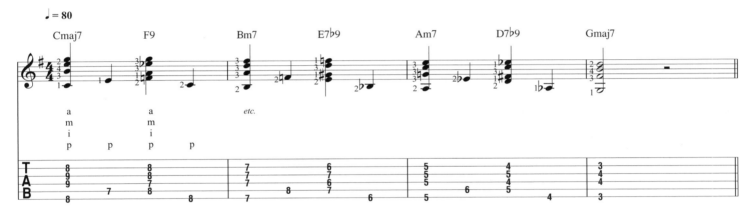

Having gotten a start with both some bass-line logic and the type of hand movements needed, we can begin to emulate Joe's actual rhythmic approach to such a texture by placing the chords on upbeats, for a swingin', syncopated feel. This really just means waiting until the "and" of 1 or the "and" of 3 (in swung time) to play the remainder of each chord after laying down its root as a bass note on beat 1 or 3. If you're playing this with a pick only, you could add in upstrokes for the chords on the upbeats, particularly if you eliminate the notes on string 2 to create smaller voicings (which is a musical choice you could make even if using fingerstyle or hybrid technique).

Techniques
Example 25

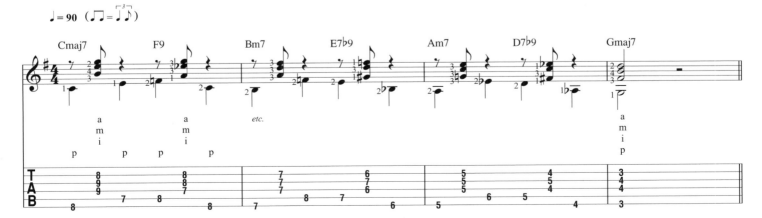

In the following example, we take a hands-on look at some ways of further developing the bass-chord texture. We'll try a different progression (still in the key of G), in which some chords are officially there for a whole measure before the next change. Our bass line will move in a more scalar fashion to connect the chordal roots through those parts, with a couple of chromatic passing tones thrown in. There will also be more of a sudden jump up the neck (at beat 2 of the fourth measure), and some 8th-note embellishment of the walking bass line (in beat 4 of the fourth measure) that creates a chromatic enclosure of the following A in the bass (circling around that targeted note by half step). Here too, you could use upstrokes for the chords on upbeats if playing with a pick (again, possibly skipping the notes on string 2). Be particularly prepared this time to scoot along the fretboard with one finger, especially as the bass line ascends towards the concluding G major chord.

Techniques
Example 26

Bass-Melody Counterpoint

In the course of his solo guitar work, Joe Pass also uses the combination of bass line and melodic line (written or improvised), and for this too, we'll have a three-stage introduction to the required technique. Fingerstyle or hybrid picking can work here (*pima* indications are again given, with some adjustment needed for hybrid technique), but for this texture, pick playing by itself will become impracticable.

Let's get started by trying a pattern of combined bass and melody tones on a circle of 5ths–oriented progression (mostly a series of dominant 7th chords moving along that cycle), with quarter notes only. You'll indeed need to hop around a fair amount with the fret-hand index finger for bass notes, and make a sizable stretch between index and pinky for each beat 2 double stop. For hybrid picking, the pick of course replaces the thumb, but the use of *m* and *a* can remain the same.

Techniques
Example 27

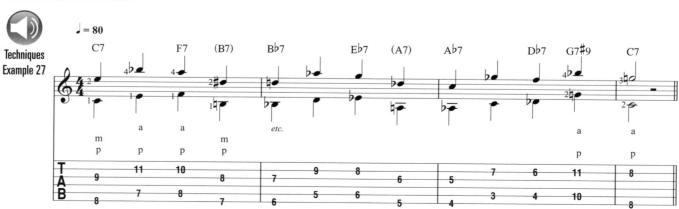

Next, we'll flesh out the bass-melody texture by using 8th notes in the melody part of this pattern. Notice that we're just filling in with extra tones between the ones we were already playing above the bass line on the downbeats, but also that the required fret-hand fingering does get more involved. Three times within this exercise, an index-finger barre needs to be put in place ahead of time for tones that will ring together at the same fret a moment later. Again in this case, for hybrid picking, the use of *m* and *a* remains the same while the pick replaces *p*.

Techniques
Example 28

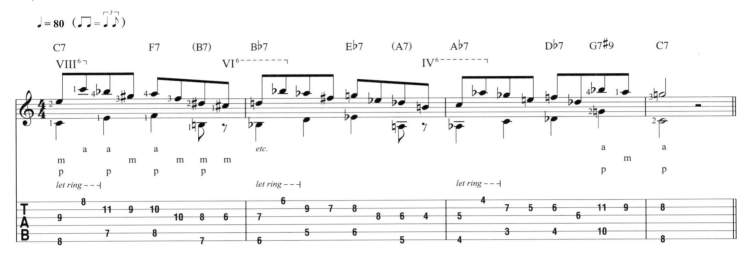

And finally, we can make our pattern a little more organic (closer to the varied way in which such a passage might actually be played) by staggering some of the bass and melody notes in a triplet rhythm and adding in small chords to harmonize a couple of tones in the melody. Notice that the fret-hand stretch we've had on beat 2 of the pattern (between index finger and pinky) eases up in this version, since the bass note is played alone and allowed to be short, while the corresponding melody tone is played right afterwards as the second note of an 8th-note triplet, giving us just a moment to shift up the fretboard. By the end, a couple of larger chords are thrown in (G7#9 and C9) for the V–I resolution in C, with the thumb required to pluck two strings on the bottom for the five-string final chord. Hybrid pickers: pick replaces thumb, *m–a* replaces *i–m* where those two fingers are used together, *a* replaces *m* for the last note in each of the first three measures, and *m–a–c* replaces *i–m–a* for the final chords.

Techniques
Example 29

Special Fingering Strategy for Chordal Movement

In the execution of intricate Joe Pass–style chordal or chord-melody passages, there can frequently be a need to use alternative fingerings for familiar chord voicings, depending on what other shapes they are coming from or leading to on the fretboard. In practice, this could mean either trying different finger configurations when working out a specific sequence, or using an unusual fingering (if necessary) to grab the next chord when coming up with a new combination of voicings on the fly.

As an example, the following exercise first has us try three different fingerings for the same common dominant 13 voicing, and then shows how one or the other might be preferred in a mixed chord/single-note context, according to what comes immediately before or after. Note that only the first of these fingerings, where there is no barre across the unplayed string 5, is playable with the pick or thumb alone (since it allows for fret-hand muting of that string)—the others are essentially meant for fingerstyle or hybrid picking. The material in the second measure here, through the Cmaj7 on beat 1 of the next measure, is actually from measures 97–99 of the "Summertime" performance included in this book (although quarter notes are used in the full transcription where we see 8th notes below). The movements at the end of this chunk are especially particular. When Db7#9 is played, string 6 should be muted by either the fret-hand middle finger or the pick-hand thumb, and going into Cmaj7, the index finger must shift slightly across the neck in its barring position to catch strings 5 and 1, releasing string 4 in the process.

Techniques
Example 30

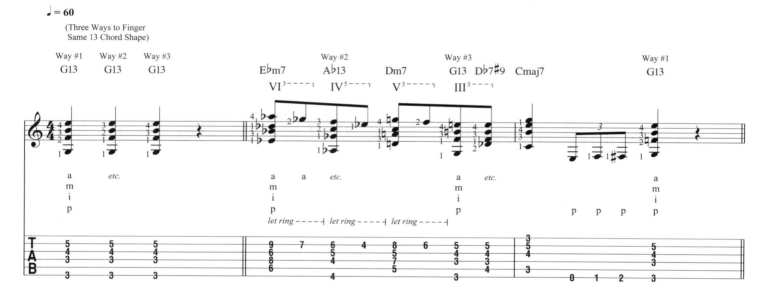

STYLISTIC DNA

In this section, we zero in on the micro-elements and specific ways of thinking that help Joe Pass sound like Joe Pass. Keep in mind that a few of the fundamental aspects of his style, like a sense of swing, the language of bebop, and the feeling of the blues—not to mention an unabashed spontaneity—are bigger than what can be put on paper (and may be best demonstrated through his music itself). Still, we can certainly examine some of his idiosyncratic musical traits and get a better idea of what makes him tick!

Characteristic Melodic Shapes

Amid the plethora of melodic ideas put forth in his linear improvisation, certain shapes and devices are especially prevalent, ones that may be common enough in the jazz lexicon but used with a particular flair by Joe. We will sample these here in isolated form.

Simple melodic patterns within a scale are a frequent component of his lines, often with a kind of circular or rolling quality to them, as in the B♭ major example below:

DNA
Example 1

A common feature both of his playing and of the bebop language altogether is the shape of an enclosure, in which a targeted note is approached from tones that lie just above and below it (whether in the key or chromatically). The following phrase over C major contains a few enclosure shapes, the first of which starts with the very first note here and lands on C two beats later (this particular figure is very much part of the vocabulary of fellow jazz guitar greats such as Grant Green or Pat Martino). The next enclosure is a special favorite of Joe's, in which he uses the brief inflection of a sharp 5th tone, relative to a major chord (the G♯ on beat 4), in targeting the 6th (the A on the next beat 1). Finally, the last enclosure here targets a lower C (on beat 3 of the second measure), from the D above it and the B below it in the scale.

DNA
Example 2

Note that this line could actually work in an A minor setting as well, in which case that G♯ becomes a leading tone, more like the 3rd of a momentary V chord (E7). The line also sounds nice on a D9♯11 chord, where the G♯ becomes the sharp 11th!

There are a couple of melodic devices favored by Joe that involve a chordal arpeggio and its neighbor tones: that of proceeding through the arpeggio while encircling each note with an enclosure (either chromatically or with tones from the pertinent scale), and that of leading up into each chord tone from a half step below. In this next example, we combine these two motifs, heading up for most of two measures through tones of an F major triad with an enclosure on each one, before descending through two octaves of an F7 arpeggio, with most of its tones preceded by a chromatic lower neighbor. Notice that the initial pattern here creates a rhythmic hemiola, a syncopation that results from the continuous groups of three 8th notes against the 4/4 meter. Some shifting around of the fret hand is needed to execute the line. Be particularly prepared to jump from the 7th/6th position area to 9th position on beat 4 of the first measure, and back down to 6th position for the last three notes of the whole figure.

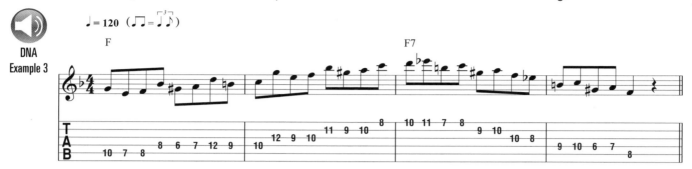

Arpeggios, in their pure form, figure hugely into Joe's linear improvisation, whether they are simple triadic or 7th chord arpeggios, or those of more extended chords. They may appear briefly within a line, with only one iteration of each chord tone, but often a single arpeggio will cover more ground (and a larger range) by being fully or partly repeated at the octave. Here we have an example of this approach using both a simpler and a more extended chord, with an ascending Fmaj7 arpeggio (actually coming from its 7th tone, in the pickup) repeated at the octave, and an ascending Dm11 arpeggio repeated in the higher register without its root.

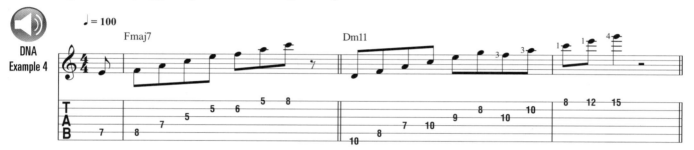

A frequent arpeggio-related contour in his soloing is that of going through the chord tones both upwards and downwards in succession. This could mean the same chord tones in either direction, or a partial or complete change of chord when heading the other way. In the following line, we have an example of both possibilities. First, we ascend and descend through tones of an unchanging D13#11, and next through those of G7, but differently on the way up and on the way down: with G13 tones on the ascent, but then with an alteration on the descent that gives us a G augmented triad (suggestive of G7#5), for a more pointed resolve to C9. Note that these in particular are not pure arpeggios in the strict theoretical sense, where the chord tones always appear in order. Rather, they are based more on certain chord voicings, especially as found on the guitar (pertinent chord diagrams will be shown here to help visualize).

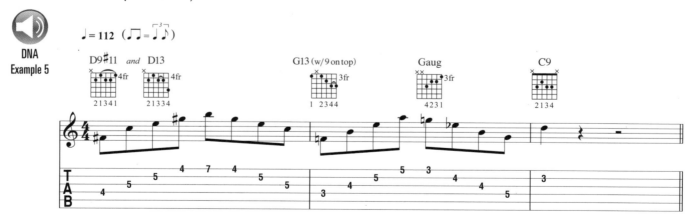

Another typical way in which Joe uses arpeggios is in sequence (with changing chords), and played in the same direction. Following is an example of how this may play out for a quick ii–V–I in C major, allowing some complex chord tones to be involved along the way. By using a three-note figure for the first arpeggio, as opposed to the four-note groupings that follow, a momentary sense of syncopated rhythm is created within this continuous 8th-note line. Be aware that these arpeggios are not complete (at least one chord tone is missing from each) and not all moving entirely in 3rds (they are not all in theoretical order). Also, be prepared to quickly shift from 5th position to 3rd and then 2nd position, as we move from chord to chord.

DNA
Example 6

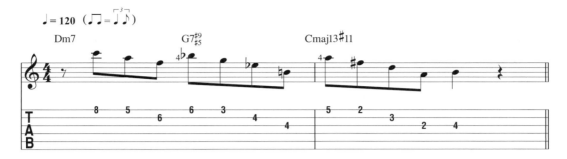

Sometimes a very symmetrical musical pattern can coincide with a uniformly patterned movement along the fretboard, and such devices are a signature ingredient of Joe's playing. This next example demonstrates two such patterns, the first of them being a rising motif through a whole tone scale (a scale made entirely of whole steps), for which the pertinent chord could be considered A9♭5 just as well as A9♯5, or potentially a similar kind of B7, C♯7, etc. The second figure, moving down in half steps as it does, can't exactly be said to belong to any one scale (other than the chromatic), but due to where it starts and ends, it is suggestive of a diminished scale or chord that relates well to the A7♭9 chord at hand. Try the suggested fingerings and picking patterns to see how each of these may be played with a consistent repetitive motion.

DNA
Example 7

Blues and Bop Flavor

Through our "Essential Licks," as well as some of the melodic shape observations outlined in this "Stylistic DNA" section, we've already detailed numerous ways in which the sounds of bebop and the blues permeate the music of Joe Pass. Here though, we'll check out a select few additional elements of these major influences, and how they figure into his personal style.

The phrase below exemplifies Joe's use of the kind of groovy blues material that sounds at once both major and minor (it is one that could indeed fit over Fm as well as the indicated F major), in this case with tones that all technically belong to what could be called an F major pentatonic scale with a flatted 3rd. Another common blues-tinged feature of his playing demonstrated here is his frequent habit of quickly sliding up into a note from a half step below. Notice that the snaky 16th-note figure pans out a little differently in its slurring when repeated in the lower octave, on two strings instead of one, but that its basic feel remains the same.

DNA
Example 8

He could hardly evoke a blues feeling any more than when he throws in a couple of his characteristic down-and-dirty double stops, as heard in this next example. Also involved here is the mixing of blues and diatonic scale material so often heard in the playing of jazz improvisers, not least among them Joe. Notice that after the flatted 3rd and 5th tones, relative to the key of C, that are heard in the first measure (the Eb and Gb found on the first three "and" counts), the line winds up leading to the major 3rd (E) on the next beat 3 (via an enclosure), such that it more directly relates to a C major or dominant 7 chord.

His often copious use of ornamentation is a particular stylistic trait that calls to mind the great horn players and pianists of the bebop movement. Within a largely 8th-note line, this usually involves hammered-on and pulled-off 16th notes or 8th- or 16th-note triplets. The following example shows three different versions of such a line (on a I–iii–VI–ii progression in Eb major) as Joe might play it: first unadorned, then with a couple of slurred embellishments that lie neatly enough under the fingers in one position, and finally with slightly different ornamentation that requires a quick jump in position (in this case, down to 6th position at the second measure) in order to play two of these slurred figures in a row.

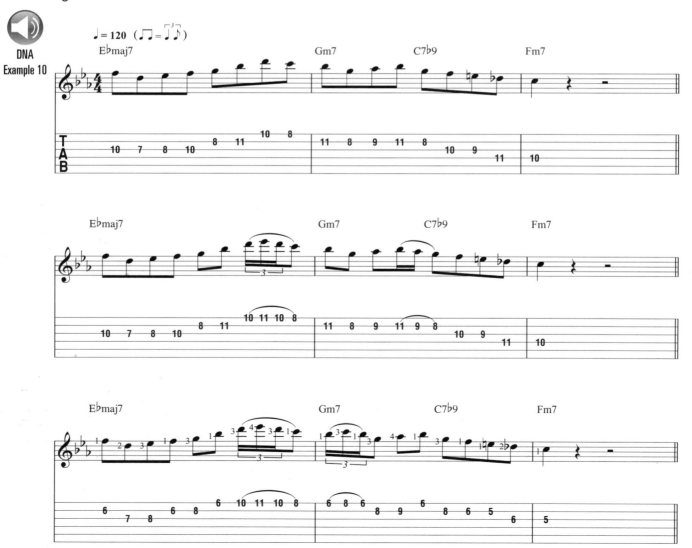

Next, we'll take a quick, close-in look at a key aspect of playing bop (or many other styles of jazz, for that matter), and that is the ability to improvise melodically through chord changes. This is of course a huge part of the art of jazz improvisation—indeed it is effectively demonstrated in several of our previous DNA examples and most of our "Essential Licks," let alone all of the guitar solos in the songs and excerpts—and below we have just one tip-of-the-iceberg example of how it may figure into Joe's soloing. This little phrase is in large part a shortened version of Lick 3 from the "Essential Licks" chapter, showing how the same basic idea might be adapted to work on a shorter-scale I–VI–ii–V–I progression in C. The line moves down through what seems to be C major scale material before a couple of tones are altered to become the 3rd and flatted 9th of A7 (the C♯ and B♭, respectively). The arrival of Dm7, too, is heralded by its chordal 3rd (the F on the downbeat of the second measure), this time coming from the 7th of the previous chord, a typical melodic movement with this kind of chordal motion. The line then proceeds upwards in 3rds through tones of a Dm9 arpeggio until an altered form of G7 is prettily suggested on beat 3 by the note E♭ (the enharmonic equivalent of D♯, the raised 5th of the chord), which then, after bouncing off the chordal 3rd (B), resolves down a half step to D, a color tone of the Cmaj7 chord (its 9th).

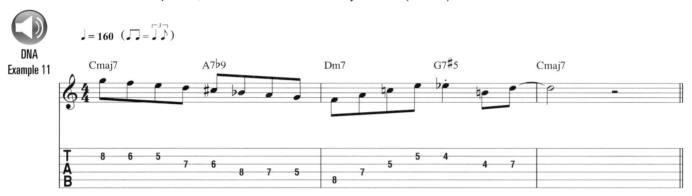

It's worth noting that Joe himself said he viewed the ii–V part of a progression, for purposes of improvisation, as just one chord, and would thus treat both chords together as simply the V7. This is logical enough, given the strong relationship between the two and the way they often function as a unit to lead home to the tonic. Some of the natural flow from one to the next, however, may still come out in his lines, in the manner shown in Example 11 (and if he substitutes a dominant II7 for the usual minor ii7 chord, this becomes a different harmonic situation, with a greater distinction between II and V).

Characteristic Chordal Devices

A certain essential vocabulary of chords, along with a basic underlying feel for playing them in rhythm, is within the domain of jazz guitarists in general. But Joe has his own trademark ways of creating variety and motion in their use, which we'll explore in the following examples.

Whether comping (providing chordal accompaniment) or interjecting some chords into his own guitar solo, he often moves up or down through a series of different voicings or variations of a single chord, giving a sense of movement where the chord in the progression doesn't technically change. This tends to create the effect of a brief chord-melody segment, with the tones on top forming an ascending or descending melodic phrase. Here we have a couple of such chordal phrases, in typical fashion made up of mostly rootless voicings, with hardly any voicings at all in root position. Several of these shapes are even more incomplete as versions of the given chord, and are really more like formations of tones that harmonize with it. For Gm7 we have, in order: Gm9, Gm7, Gm9 (another voicing), Gm11 (no 3rd), and Gm9 (same as the earlier voicing but an octave higher). And over C7, it's C/D (C major triad with 9th on the bottom but no 7th), C13, C13 (no 3rd or 7th), C9sus4, C13 (another voicing), and C9. Notice that these two basic chords are very related; the C9sus4 shape is really the same as Gm7, and the C9 shape could also be considered Gm6. The Gm7 series in particular could also work for B♭maj7.

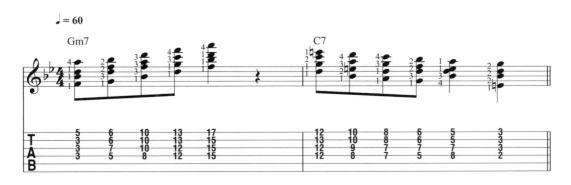

A favorite swinging rhythmic texture for Joe, heard during the renditions of "Blues for Basie" and "Summertime" included in this book (and somewhat also in "Old Folks"), is that of chords played on the downbeats with a quick percussive midrange note on each upbeat in between. With the longer and shorter halves of the beat commonly used in swung timing, these essentially feel like quarter-note chords with a little gap between them for the brief "and"-count notes, which in this situation wind up especially short, probably not fully sustained into each following chord. Played with a light touch, these in-between notes may even be ghosted (barely sounded) in such a way that they could be parenthesized when written on the page. It is typical for these rhythmic tones to be on string 4— sometimes as the open D, as seen in the early part of the sample below (where D largely works as a pedal tone with the given chords), and sometimes as an echo of the chord tone that was just played on that string, like we see in the rest of this sequence. It should be noted that this is fundamentally a fingerstyle texture.

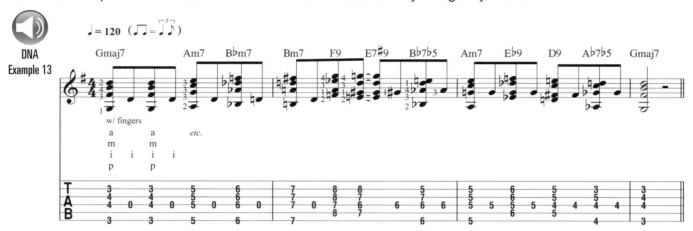

Comping, in jazz, usually refers to a way of playing chords with varying rhythms, at the discretion of the individual musician as long as it fits the music at hand. But like many other chordal players, Joe will occasionally set a groove by comping through a passage with a regular, repeating rhythm, and his particular manner of doing so is heard in the following segment. This is the first five bars of a 12-bar blues in B♭, with essentially only two chords present (B♭13 and E♭9)—though his tendency to so often move into a chord from a quick half step above or below, whether striking the strings for both chords or sliding from one to the next, is another element of his comping style typified here.

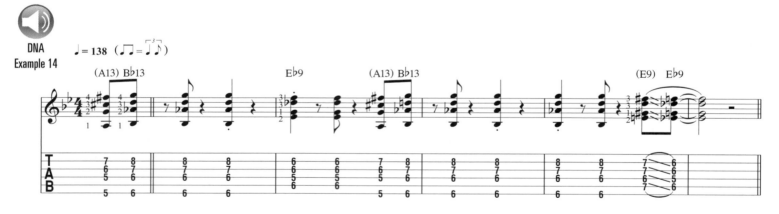

Beyond a single half-step movement into a targeted chord, he may extrapolate with more extensive chromatic motion of this kind, as in this smaller chunk from the beginning of a B♭ blues. Here too, the principal chords are just B♭13 and E♭9 (aside from a brief visit to E°7), but a sense of departure and return is created by approaching them from multiple half steps above or below.

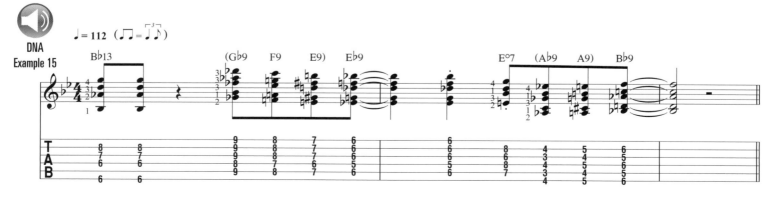

A couple of fundamental ways in which he may vary the texture or density of his comping are by reducing the chords down to double stops, or by using extra-widely spaced voicings. An example of each is found in the segment below, yet again from the beginning of a B♭ blues progression, where the basic chords are just B♭7 and E♭7. The first measure here contains a short, harmonized melodic figure of the sort that he might throw into his accompaniment, and the second measure begins with a brief groove on a two-string shell of E♭7. After that, the larger voicings used for B7 and B♭7 are spread out by including not one, but two wider intervals that each involve a silent string between chord tones. Note that these chord shapes really require fingerstyle or hybrid picking technique to accommodate the suggested barre fingerings (so that strings 2 and 5 can be unplucked, versus muted).

DNA
Example 16

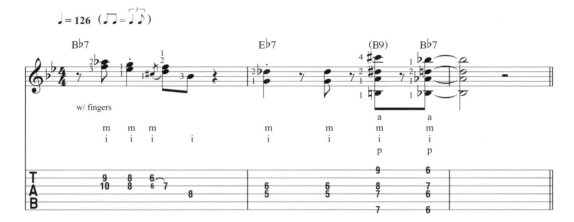

A more specific and complex chordal trick in Joe's bag is that of moving a souped-up diminished 7th shape around by increments of a minor 3rd, yielding different versions of an altered dominant chord along the way. To understand what this means, let's first take a look at one way we might add a tone to a simple diminished 7th chord on the guitar (sacrificing one of the basic chord tones in the process):

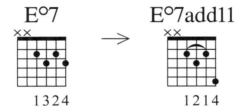

The added tone, on top, is from the same whole-half diminished scale that would relate to the original chord. This new shape, as we have it here, could also be considered a rootless voicing of C13♭9 or F♯7♯9. When a plain diminished 7th chord is moved up or down by minor 3rds, the result is simply different inversions of the same four notes, making it a conveniently mobile unit in this regard. The particular chordal device we're looking at here could be considered an extrapolation of that concept, with the realization that if we move the added-tone version around by the same increment, the resulting chords will bear some relation to each other, though their exact note content won't be the same. Here's how that pans out if we take the new shape from where we found it, and move it up in minor 3rds through its four possible permutations along that track, against an A in the bass (we'll name each one according to what kind of A7 chord it represents):

DNA
Example 17

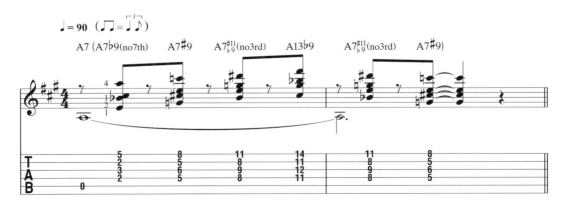

Chordal Abundance

Though the work of Joe Pass is marked by a tremendously varied chordal vocabulary, he claimed to view chords as belonging to only three basic types: major, minor, and dominant. Certainly he had awareness of other basic chord qualities as well, such as diminished and half-diminished (even while these two could also be seen as related to one of the main three). But the key to his complex harmonic usage within such a simple framework—and a large part of what defines his sound as a chordal player—is his knowledge of so many variations of each of these main types, along with his way of choosing which ones to use from moment to moment while playing a tune.

As an example of how he might approach a single basic chord, we'll consider the possibilities for a dominant 7th alone, by taking a look at no fewer than 50 different ways he might conceive of D7 on the guitar. Only in a couple of instances here is the same exact voicing shown in a different place on the fretboard, with a different fingering; otherwise, they are all distinct. These represent larger and smaller voicings, extended chords (with odd-numbered tones beyond the 7th), and altered chords (with raised or flatted tones). Most of them are shown in root position (with D on the bottom), which is helpful for hearing how they relate to the root, but Joe would often leave that tone out to play them as rootless voicings. Accordingly, these roots on the bottom have been parenthesized to indicate that they may be omitted, yielding almost twice as many distinct versions of the chord as we originally had! Alternative fingerings have been provided to show how each of these would be played without the root in the bass, which is handy not only for chordal variety but also because the full voicing is sometimes especially difficult to play, or may require fingerstyle technique in the pick hand. You don't necessarily need to play all these D7 chords in this order or in tempo, though the audio is provided that way as a resource for hearing each one.

DNA

Example 18

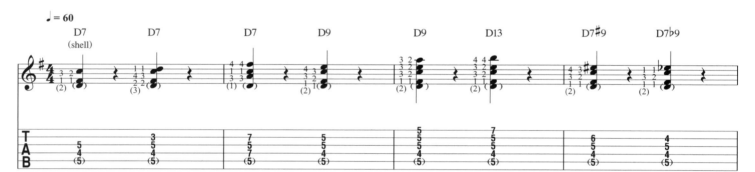

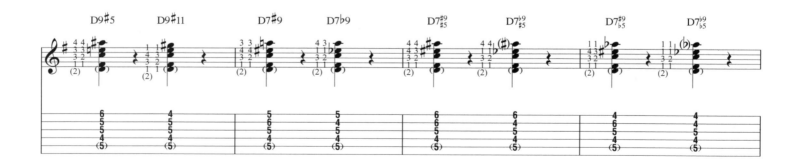

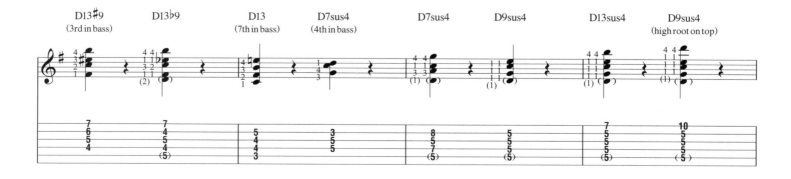

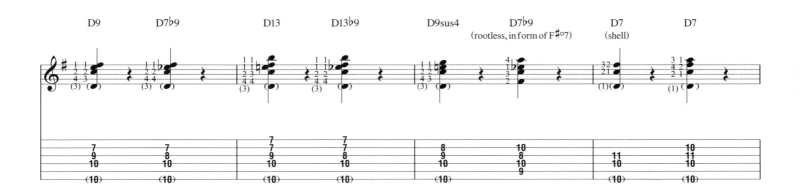

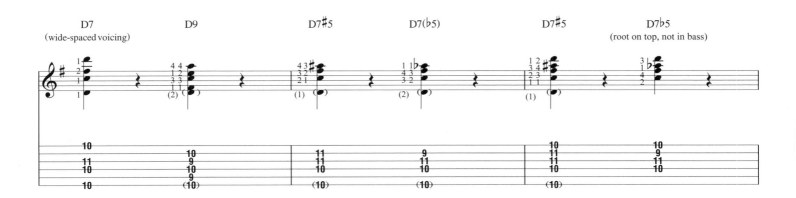

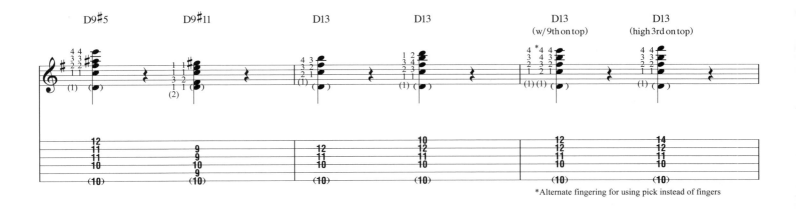

*Alternate fingering for using pick instead of fingers

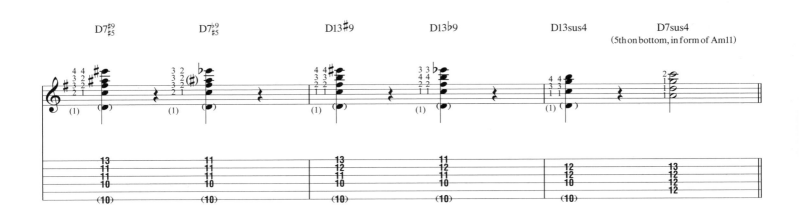

Of course not every single one of these options is appropriate any time D7 comes along in a progression. Joe, like other chordal jazz players, must use his harmonic understanding and aesthetic judgment when deciding which version to plug in, case by case.

In order to see how some of these may actually appear in context—and how he may expand his variety of harmonic movement by involving different versions of major and minor chords as well—here are 10 chord-choice possibilities for just a ii–V–I sequence in G major. Further variation yet comes from the occasional substitution of a dominant chord for the major I (which lends a blues sound to the progression) or for the usual minor ii (a special favorite device of Joe's). On top of that, he may use a tritone substitute for the V (Ab7 in place of D7), effectively creating still another variant of the original chord. Here again, the root found on the bottom of most of these voicings could be left off for easier fingering and a lighter comping texture.

DNA
Example 19

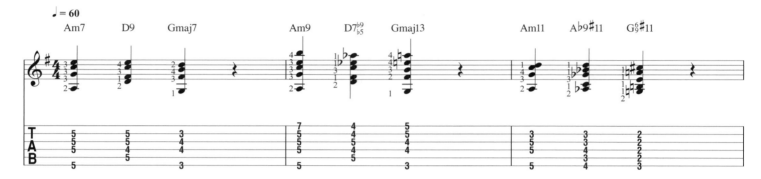

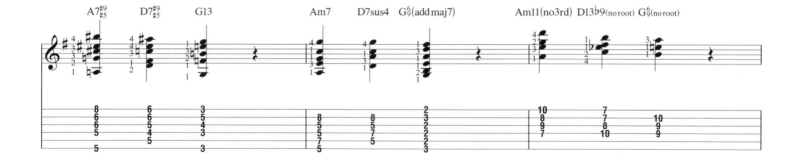

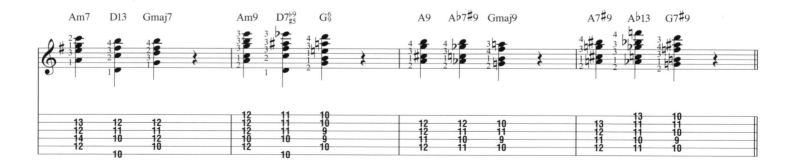

Chording with Pedal Tones

Joe occasionally creates a particular harmonic effect with the use of a *pedal tone*, or constant note in the bass under changing chords. To do this, he often avails himself of one of the lower open strings of the guitar, perhaps even choosing to transpose a song to a key in which E, A, or D is the tonic or the 5th. Within the realm of standard chordal movement, it's pretty common that a series of chords will seem to fit with one of these tones of the key (especially the 5th) sustained below, as in our next example. We're looking in this case at a I–VI–ii–V–I progression in A major, with the 5th (E) in the bass, and rootless chord voicings above (though the low E is of course the root of E7b9).

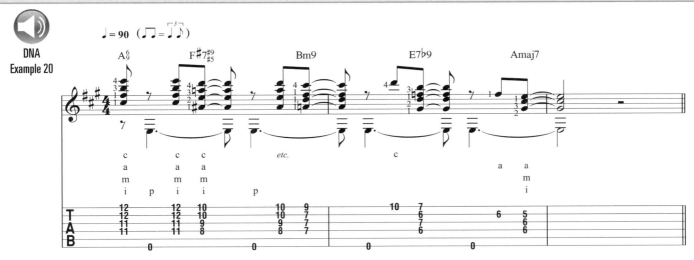

He will also use pedal tones for a "further out" kind of sound, with a simple chord moving in parallel motion along a pattern or scale over one note in the bass (you may notice that the more complex chord moving around in Example 17 is also shown with a pedal tone, but in that case it's there more for reference, and the figure could very well have been played without it). As an example, here's a first-inversion major triad on the upper strings that starts out as A major, moves up and down by half steps, and then traces part of a blues scale before coming back to A major, all with the tonic A ringing underneath. This results in some colorful dissonances along the way, even though we start and end at home on the I chord in the key of A.

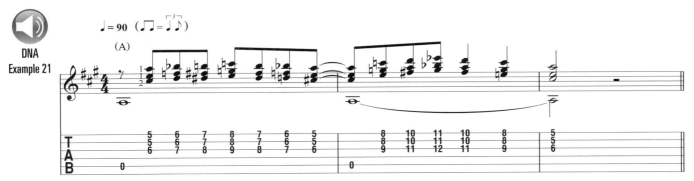

Band-Like Texture in Solo Guitar

Part of what strikes the listener in Joe's solo work on albums like *Virtuoso* is the feeling that this is too much music to be made by one guitarist alone. With the density and completeness of these performances, he seems to make of himself a one-man band. Although some of this has to do with the simultaneous playing of melody, chords, and bass lines (or at least two of these at a time), another factor is his readiness to jump between these elements, moving from one to another so rapidly and seamlessly as to give the impression of playing them all at once. The following segment features such a mix of parts (occasionally overlapping), with chords, short melodic phrases, and bass notes or fills all combined in a busy solo guitar texture (a fingerstyle approach is recommended, though it's possible to use pick or hybrid technique):

MUST HEAR

Joe Pass had an amazingly prolific recording career, not only through his own studio albums, but also in his joint or sideman appearances with many a fellow jazz great, let alone the innumerable live recordings that have been issued. Here are, relatively speaking, just a few choice tracks with which to start exploring his work:

Studio and Live Albums

Sounds of Synanon (with fellow Synanon resident musicians), 1962

Joe's recorded introduction to the jazz world was made while he was still an inmate at the California rehab center, in the good musical company of a septet from the institution. Among these cuts, on which he spun out his fluent improvisation from a Fender Jazzmaster solidbody guitar owned by the residence, is the lively, impressive original "C.E.D." (co-written with pianist Arnold Ross).

Catch Me!, 1963

From a few of the numerous sessions he did for the Pacific Jazz label in the early '60s came his debut album as a leader, in a quartet setting with keyboardist Clare Fischer alternately on piano or organ. One rendition of his aggressively swingin' tune known as "Catch Me" appeared on the original LP (this was initially the only version bearing that title), while re-releases of the album also include "Catch Me (Forward Pass)" and "Days of Wine and Roses" (previously heard only on opposite sides of a 45 rpm single). Joe plays a Fender solidbody on most of these tracks and acoustic guitar on some others. "Just Friends" is another high-tempo highlight.

Joy Spring, 1964

Another strong quartet effort from the Pacific Jazz catalog, this one recorded live (and by now on his Gibson ES-175). Particularly striking are his super-sensitive delivery of the wistful waltz "Sometime Ago" and his seemingly unending flow of linear ideas on "The Night Has a Thousand Eyes."

For Django, 1964

His true breakout album, it is remarkable not only for its exceptional performances and special theme (an homage to iconic guitarist Django Reinhardt), but also as his first collaboration with fellow guitarist and longtime associate John Pisano. The latter sticks strictly to a chordal support role within the quartet, humbly never taking either the melody or a solo. Standout cuts include Django's own "Nuages" (among other selections from the Gypsy genius' repertoire), the lovely title track (a Pass original), and the absolutely burnin' "Night and Day."

Intercontinental, 1970

An excellent example of Joe in a guitar/bass/drums trio context, stretching out to make good use of the melodic and harmonic space it affords him, while achieving an especially nice tone. German bassist Eberhard Weber, better known for a more modern or experimental brand of jazz, fits the bill just right for this relaxed session of swingin' standards and bossa novas, as does English drummer Kenny Clare (who plays almost exclusively with brushes here). Recorded in Germany, some of its highlights are the swift-paced "I Love You," the classic bossa "Meditation," and the easy-going "Li'l Darlin'."

The Trio
(with Oscar Peterson and Niels-Henning Ørsted Pedersen), 1973

This revered, high-energy live recording marked the rebirth of a piano/guitar/bass trio built around the singularly dazzling pianist Oscar Peterson, with Joe and Danish bass phenomenon Niels-Henning Ørsted Pedersen filling the old shoes of Herb Ellis and Ray Brown, respectively. It also marked the beginning of Joe's fruitful relationship with impresario Norman Granz and his new Pablo record label. The breathtakingly fast "Blues Etude" and bright swinging "Secret Love" are complimented by two classic slow blues numbers, and a lovely rubato ballad presentation of "Come Sunday" by Joe alone.

Virtuoso, 1973

With this landmark album, a unique place was established for Joe in the jazz guitar world as a superlative master of solo performance on the instrument. It was the insistence of producer Norman Granz that he try doing a whole record in this format, and the rest, as they say, is history—despite a technical glitch that left all but one of the tracks with only the miked sound of his jazz box and no amplified tone. Intricately intertwining the elements of melody, chords, and bass, he manages to sound like three guitarists at once, while still playing with the utmost taste, and often taking a free approach to time as only a solo performer can. The set is made up of almost all standards, with must-hear renditions of "All the Things You Are," "Night and Day," "'Round Midnight," "Stella by Starlight"… and everything!

Jazz/Concord (with Herb Ellis), 1973

Another first, around this time, was the matter-of-factly titled inaugural album from the Concord jazz record label, involving both Joe and fellow guitarist Herb Ellis. Across a span of decades, these two would run in some of the same circles, both of them working extensively with Oscar Peterson, Ella Fitzgerald, and producer/impresario Norman Granz—besides having an affinity for playing with each other. Swingin' jazz mainstays Ray Brown on bass and Jake Hanna on drums round out the band, and highlights include "Georgia on my Mind," "Look for the Silver Lining," and Ellis' "Bad News Blues."

Two for the Road (with Herb Ellis), 1974

The compatible guitarists were paired this time for a duo recording, also on Concord, resulting in marvelous renderings of tunes such as "Gee Baby, Ain't I Good to You" and "Carnival (Manha de Carnival)" (a song also widely known as "Black Orpheus").

Live at Donte's, 1974

These performances from two nights at an L.A. club, originally issued on a double LP, find Joe once more in a standard trio lineup, though with Jim Hughart playing electric bass (somewhat of a fad of the era, for the jazz scene) while Frank Severino holds down the drumming duties. The high energy of "You Stepped out of a Dream" is typical of these tracks, but his beautiful rendition of the ballad "Darn that Dream" (one of a few solo numbers interspersed along the way) is a particular treat.

Dizzy's Big 4 (Dizzy Gillespie), 1974

It's a meeting of giants as Joe joins on for a session led by the revolutionary bebop trumpeter, in a quartet anchored by all-time great bassist Ray Brown and drummer Mickey Roker. Besides his prodigious soloing here, this context gives him ample room to display his comping (chordal accompaniment) abilities, with a horn soloist out front, and no pianist in the lineup. Essential listening here includes the blistering (and appropriately titled) "Be Bop (Dizzy's Fingers)," the groovy minor blues "Birks' Works," the swingin' "Jitterbug Waltz," and the serene "September Song."

Joe Pass at the Montreux Jazz Festival 1975, 1975

While numerous live solo albums were recorded by the guitar master, this one is particularly revered for the masterful playing it documents. Within the magnificent set, his own "Blues for Nina" morphs between sensitive, slick, and steamin', and he gives perhaps his best presentation ever of a transformed pop tune with this version of the Stevie Wonder hit "You Are the Sunshine of My Life" (the same actual performance is viewable on YouTube, as described in the "Must See" section).

The Big 3 (with Milt Jackson and Ray Brown), 1975

Another conclave of legends, this time in partnership with vibraphone great Milt Jackson, and once more Ray Brown, for a refreshing timbral combination. "Blue Bossa" is an especially fine cut.

Fitzgerald and Pass... Again (with Ella Fitzgerald), 1976

Joe and the First Lady of Song reached a new height with this, their second album as a voice-and-guitar duo (and the perfect context for the display of his accompaniment skills). "I Ain't Got Nothin' but the Blues" and "One Note Samba" are among the numerous excellent examples of their work here.

Virtuoso No. 2, 1976

With this follow-up solo album in the *Virtuoso* series, he ventured into new and different areas of repertoire, playing modern jazz compositions such as John Coltrane's "Giant Steps" and Chick Corea's "Windows," and the contemporary popular tunes "Feelings" and "If," along with a few standards, and a couple of originals like "Blues for Basie."

Quadrant (with Milt Jackson, Ray Brown, Mickey Roker), 1977

Technically the self-titled album of a distinct group with a band name, it finds Joe together with three of his heavy-hitting associates from other Pablo recordings of the previous few years (Milt on vibes, Ray on bass, and Mickey Roker on drums). They stretch their bounds a bit with a few originals that each involve a more contemporary rhythm and/or an interesting twist, one of these being "Ray's Tune"—which is, quite literally, Ray's tune—a slick number that is played with an actual funk groove throughout, as opposed to the swing, Latin, or ballad rhythms typically expected of this bunch.

Tudo Bem! (with Paulinho da Costa), 1978

Joe's joint venture with the great Brazilian percussionist represented a more full-fledged foray into authentic bossa nova, as well as Brazilian-tinged funk, to the point of bringing fellow guitarist (and bossa master) Oscar Castro-Neves into the session for his spot-on chordal rhythms. Within the small group is also Don Grusin, playing both piano and, interestingly for a Joe Pass record, electric keyboard. "Corcovado," "Wave," and "Gentle Rain" stand out among these refreshingly different tracks.

Chops (with Niels-Henning Ørsted Pedersen), 1978

The aptly titled duo album from these Oscar Peterson bandmates is replete with strong performances on a nicely varied set of bop, blues, bossa, and ballad repertoire. Joe and monster bassist N.H.Ø.P. take turns playing stunning solos and providing rock-solid accompaniment, sometimes taking off in flights of contrapuntal improvisation, or blending their tones in new and unexpected ways. Among its high points are the cookin' "Oleo" and "Tricrotism," and Joe's sublime work on the slower-paced "Old Folks" and "Lover Man" (the latter being converted from a ballad to a medium-tempo swing waltz).

I Remember Charlie Parker, 1979

A rare solo outing played entirely on a classical (nylon-string) guitar, his tribute to Bird consists entirely of standard songs on which the bebop saxophone giant famously put his stamp, rather than on the busier bop melodies that he penned. Highlights include "Easy to Love" and especially "Summertime."

Checkmate (with Jimmy Rowles), 1981

This musically mature duo effort, with pianist and kindred spirit Jimmy Rowles, is a both underrated and beautifully understated gem in the Joe Pass catalog. The pair seem to represent the antithesis of Joe's work with Oscar Peterson, letting the music breathe and showing no compulsion to get busy or fill all the space. From this album, on which he uses strictly the acoustic sound of his archtop, some especially nice cuts are "As Long as I Live," "What's Your Story, Morning Glory," and "'Tis Autumn."

Eximious, 1982

Heading a trio with powerhouse bassist and close colleague Niels-Henning Ørsted Pedersen and English drummer Martin Drew, Joe's playing is alternately mellow, bluesy, or blazingly busy as he delivers a set of all standard tunes, aside from his tasty and relaxedly swingin' original, "A Foxy Chick and a Cool Cat."

Meditation, 2002 (recorded 1992)

These posthumously released tracks are from the solo portion of his last live recordings, made in early 1992 at the famed jazz club Yoshi's in Oakland, California. His creativity never ceased as he rendered and re-rendered many of the same standard tunes through the years, always adding a new twist to keep them fresh. "All the Things You Are" and "How Deep Is the Ocean" are a couple of notable selections.

Unforgettable, 1998 (recorded 1992)

Joe's last solo session, in the summer of 1992, was only the second such project for which he played exclusively nylon-string guitar. Material from the session was released on *Song for Ellen* in 1994 as well as on 1998's *Unforgettable*. On this latter volume, one can hear graceful renditions of "April in Paris," "Moonlight in Vermont," and more.

Collection

The Complete Pacific Jazz Joe Pass Sessions, Mosaic, 2001 (recorded 1962–64)

Many essential tracks are contained within this beautiful set, which includes the single "Catch Me (Forward Pass)," the Les McCann date with "Yours Is My Heart Alone," the albums *Catch Me!*, *Joy Spring*, and *For Django*, and numerous previously unreleased cuts. The enclosed booklet is a treasure trove of studio photos and session history.

MUST SEE

It is fortunate that many of Joe's performances, as well as much of his direct insight about the music, have been captured on film and video. Between instructional videos, interviews, and concert footage, here are some essentials for viewing the virtuoso at his finest:

On DVD

The Genius of Joe Pass, Vestapol

A wonderful variety of both concert and interview material, allowing us to see him playing at different phases of his career, in both solo and group settings, in addition to hearing him share his own story and his thoughts on music.

Joe Pass—Solo Jazz Guitar (instructional video), Hot Licks

Direct instruction and demonstration from the master on harmony and chord-melody playing.

Joe Pass—The Blue Side of Jazz (instructional video), Hot Licks

Further instructional material in this series from Hot Licks, this time with more focus on how to approach the blues as it manifests in jazz.

On YouTube

"C.E.D." - Sounds of Synanon featuring Joe Pass 1964

This footage shows the band from his early 1960s Synanon rehab center days in full action, playing an extra-cookin' version of the original he penned with pianist Arnold Ross, featuring a great view of Joe tearing it up on the Fender Jaguar.

Joe Pass - Jazz Master

An early 1960s trio appearance on the Los Angeles TV show *Frankly Jazz* provided this invaluable look at a young Joe Pass, here again on the Jaguar solidbody, burnin' through "The Song Is You."

Joe Pass You Are the Sunshine of My Life

The very same performance heard on the live album from the Montreux Jazz Festival, but complete with close-up visuals, from various angles.

Joe Pass & Ella Fitzgerald - Duets in Hannover 1975

About 25 minutes of solo Joe and close to 45 minutes with Ella, on an intimate, small studio stage—a golden opportunity for listening and viewing.

Oscar Peterson and Joe Pass: Unbridled excellence!

Cookin' on "Stella by Starlight" as this segment begins, the virtuosic piano-guitar duo spin through a few tunes with a great view of their playing.

Oscar Peterson & Joe Pass - Just Friends

In this quartet with N.H.Ø.P. and drummer Martin Drew, in addition to Oscar and Joe, the cookin' continues, along with the viewer's ease of lookin'.

Joe Pass & Niels-Henning Ørsted Pedersen — Tricotism

The dynamic duo in performance at a Copenhagen jazz club (in N.H.Ø.P.'s homeland of Denmark), offering a close-up live version of the tune from *Chops* featured in this book, from the same era.

Joe Pass - All the Things You Are

This performance shows Joe in a completely relaxed, familiar setting, in a trio with fellow West Coast jazzer Bob Magnusson on bass, stretching out and nicely displaying the contrast between his fingerstyle and pick technique within one tune.

Joe Pass Trio - Club Date 1989

Plenty of time with Joe in a very at-home situation, with bassist Bob Magnusson and drummer Jim Plank, playing through numerous choice selections and talking to the audience.

Joe Pass All the Things You Are Brecon Jazz Festival

Part of the material found on the DVD *The Genius of Joe Pass*, this solo performance from 1991 provides a beautiful contrast to his 1973 recording on *Virtuoso*. You can see the earnestness in his face as he begins presenting the tune!

Joe Pass - JazzBaltica 1992

Great later footage of the master in concert, heard with the lovely sound of his newly acquired custom Gibson ES-175, both alone and partnered with longtime associate Niels-Henning Ørsted Pedersen on bass. For an excellent demonstration of either the recurrent devices or the tremendous variation with which he might approach the same song, from one occasion to the next, compare his solo rendition of "Summertime" here with the version featured in this book. Joe and N.H.Ø.P. also revisit "Old Folks," and stretch their boundaries in the area of fast bop with "Oleo."

Rare clip of Joe Pass playing "Blues"

A very informal glimpse into Joe just doing his thing in the studio.

Joe Pass in Alex music store

A wonderfully candid moment, ca. 1980, of Joe stopping in at a New York music store and treating a small crowd of young fans to some guitar playing and musical banter.

 **play like**

The Ultimate Lesson

Study the trademark songs, tones, and techniques of your heroes with this book/audio series. The comprehensive books provide detailed analysis of legendary artists' styles, songs, licks, riffs, and much more. Audio examples available online for download or streaming provide valuable demonstration assistance. And each book includes actual music examples and full song transcriptions to solidify your lessons!

GUITAR

PLAY LIKE CHET ATKINS
00121952 Book/Online Audio $22.99

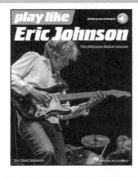

PLAY LIKE ERIC JOHNSON
00139185 Book/Online Audio $19.99

PLAY LIKE METALLICA
00248911 Book/Online Audio $24.99

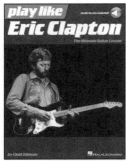

PLAY LIKE ERIC CLAPTON
00121953 Book/Online Audio $22.99

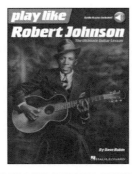

PLAY LIKE ROBERT JOHNSON
00198552 Book/Online Audio $19.99

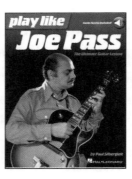

PLAY LIKE JOE PASS
00141819 Book/Online Audio $29.99

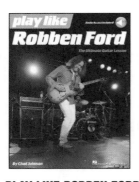

PLAY LIKE ROBBEN FORD
00124985 Book/Online Audio $22.99

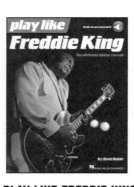

PLAY LIKE FREDDIE KING
00122432 Book/Online Audio $24.99

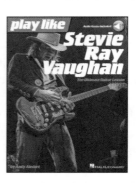

PLAY LIKE STEVIE RAY VAUGHAN
00127587 Book/Online Audio $19.99

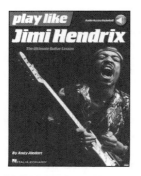

PLAY LIKE JIMI HENDRIX
00127586 Book/Online Audio $24.99

PLAY LIKE JOHN MAYER
00144296 Book/Online Audio $19.99

PLAY LIKE T-BONE WALKER
00255175 Book/Online Audio $19.99

BASS

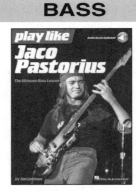

PLAY LIKE JACO PASTORIUS
00128409 Book/Online Audio $19.99

DRUMS

PLAY LIKE KEITH MOON
00148086 Book/Online Audio $19.99

PIANO

PLAY LIKE ELTON JOHN
00128279 Book/Online Audio $19.99

HAL•LEONARD®
www.halleonard.com
Visit our website to see full song lists.

Prices, content, and availability subject to change without notice.